Ultimate Penetration Testing with Nmap

Master Cybersecurity Assessments for Network Security, Monitoring, and Scanning Using Nmap

Travis DeForge

AF516841

www.orangeava.com

Copyright © 2024, Orange Education Pvt Ltd, AVA™

All rights reserved. No part of this book may be reproduced, stored in a retrieval system, or transmitted in any form or by any means, without the prior written permission of the publisher, except in the case of brief quotations embedded in critical articles or reviews.

Every effort has been made in the preparation of this book to ensure the accuracy of the information presented. However, the information contained in this book is sold without warranty, either express or implied. Neither the author nor **Orange Education Pvt Ltd** or its dealers and distributors, will be held liable for any damages caused or alleged to have been caused directly or indirectly by this book.

Orange Education Pvt Ltd has endeavored to provide trademark information about all of the companies and products mentioned in this book by the appropriate use of capital. However, **Orange Education Pvt Ltd** cannot guarantee the accuracy of this information. The use of general descriptive names, registered names, trademarks, service marks, etc. in this publication does not imply, even in the absence of a specific statement, that such names are exempt from the relevant protective laws and regulations and therefore free for general use.

First published: March 2024

Published by: Orange Education Pvt Ltd, AVA™

Address: 9, Daryaganj, Delhi, 110002, India

275 New North Road Islington Suite 1314 London,

N1 7AA, United Kingdom

ISBN: 978-81-97081-86-6

www.orangeava.com

Dedicated To

My beloved wife, Mercee
and my beautiful daughter, Ava

Without your support, this book would have never happened. thank you for always being there for me

About the Author

Travis DeForge is the Manager of Cybersecurity Engineering at Gotham Security, a US-based boutique cybersecurity firm that provides high-quality penetration testing, malicious adversary simulation, threat intelligence, and cybersecurity strategy services. In this role, Travis routinely conducts network and web application penetration tests, social engineering engagements, and cloud security assessments for multibillion-dollar global organizations.

Travis holds a Bachelor of Arts from the University of Vermont in Mandarin Chinese and a Master of Science from Western Governors University in Information Technology Management as well as numerous certifications in networking, project management, cyber security, cloud computing, and information technology including CompTIA Security+, Network+, Pentest+ and Lean Six Sigma Blackbelt.

Before joining Gotham Security, Travis served as a Military Intelligence Officer in the United States Army for several years. During this tenure, he held several positions related to signals intelligence (SIGINT), open-source intelligence (OSINT), electronic warfare (EW), and information operations at both the tactical and operational levels. Travis brings his experience working in the Department of Defense and the intelligence community together with penetration testing expertise to provide high-quality insight to clients.

Travis routinely creates open-source content for the cyber security community through a recurring video series he cohosts called Cyber Judo; as well as by engaging in numerous speaking engagements for local chapters of the Open Web Application Security Project (OWASP) as well as the Federal Reserve Bank. While professionally, Travis is an engineer, he is a teacher at heart and loves to help mentor and educate those interested in cybersecurity.

About the Technical Reviewer

Michael Hallmen is an Associate Security Engineer at Gotham Security, where he conducts day-to-day activities such as penetration testing applications and APIs. He also performs social engineering engagements and risk assessments.

Michael is an AWS Cloud Practitioner and a dual-degreed cybersecurity professional. He has participated in numerous CTF competitions, including USCC, Hack a Sat, Defcon, and NCL. He is highly experienced in vulnerability assessment, enumeration, and digital forensics, utilizing multiple tools in penetration testing for network and application security.

He is proficient in various operating systems, including Windows, Server, Linux, and MacOS.

He is skilled in using a wide range of tools such as NMAP, Nessus, Nikto, Burpsuite, Zap, Dirbuster, Gobuster, Feroxbuster, Wireshark, Netcat, John, Hydra, Hashcat, Exiftool, SQL Map, FTK Imager, Autopsy, Foremost, Zeek (formerly Bro), Snort, and Kibana.

Michael's skills include enumeration, social engineering, SQL injection, cross-site scripting (XSS), network penetration testing, and web application OWASP 10.

Acknowledgements

Having the opportunity to give back to the amazing cyber security community by writing *Ultimate Penetration Testing with Nmap* has been a true honor. I am eternally grateful to all those individuals who have supported me throughout this process.

To my family - Thank you for your unwavering support. In particular, I want to express my deepest appreciation for my wife, Mercee DeForge, whose encouragement and patience over the last year has been crucial in making this book a reality. Mercee, there were so many days spent researching late into the night to make sure this book was on track and even with a rambunctious toddler, moving across the country, and countless other challenges, you always supported me. For that, I will be forever grateful.

I would also like to acknowledge and thank Christian Scott, my mentor and longtime friend who originally brought me into the world of cyber security and has invested countless hours training, coaching, and empowering me to be in a position to write such a book. Christian, thank you for being such a champion of putting good into the world by sacrificing your time to contribute so much to the open-source community through https://cyber-judo.com/ and https://enclave-regenerous.com. Your unwavering passion has always been contagious, and I am eternally grateful for the opportunity to continue learning from you.

To all those at Orange AVA who helped make this project a reality, I would like to express my sincere thanks. Every single interaction from the first introduction through the final project was incredibly smooth, organized, and professional. It has been truly a collaborative and enriching experience.

Finally, to the readers, I sincerely thank you for choosing this book as a tool in your toolkit to enhance your skills. I know there is information overload with endless content available for you to study, and the fact that you have chosen this book is extremely meaningful to me.

Preface

Penetration testing is an extremely fast-paced career field, where it seems like every time you learn something new, there is immediately something else to master. For many, Nmap was the first tool that they learned to use when embarking on the journey of offensive security; yet very few know how to use it to its fullest capacity. That is the opportunity that this book provides.

Over the course of 9 meticulously curated chapters, you will refresh (or learn for the first time!) the basics of Nmap. You'll learn what it is, how it works, and, most importantly, *why* it is used so often. You'll learn how to craft nuanced and complex scan profiles; and what techniques make sense for penetration tests, purple teaming, and even red teaming engagements. You'll learn how to bypass intrusion detection systems and how to map the attack surface of an extremely large network in a short period of time.

This book builds on itself progressively, with each chapter reinforcing what you learned in the previous and challenging you to elevate your skills to new heights. With each new tactic and technique that is introduced, your confidence as a network penetration tester will increase. By the end, you'll be among a small percentage of pen testers who can run circles around the competition by truly comprehending what Nmap is capable of.

Chapter 1. Introduction to Nmap and Security Assessments: The book starts by exploring what Nmap is, why it is used, and why it is essential for a cybersecurity professional to understand how to leverage it. The versatility and power of Nmap are explored through the perspective of Penetration Testing, Red Teaming, and Purple Teaming, and mapped to both the MITRE ATT&CK framework as well as the Lockheed Martin Cyber Kill chain.

Chapter 2. Setting Up a Lab Environment for Nmap: Throughout chapters 3 through 8 there are a series of step-by-step walkthroughs and challenges for the reader to complete to solidify their understanding of Nmap, this chapter will discuss options for building a home lab environment to complete these challenges. This lab will provide not only the typical vulnerable virtual machines but also a functional security incident and event management system to use when testing evasion tactics in Chapter 7.

Chapter 3. Introduction to Attack Surface Mapping: This chapter begins to dive into Nmap from a fundamental level by discussing the essential technology models that are critical to understand. Once a grasp of how ports and services work is established, the reader will be introduced to basic scan techniques and the concept of mapping an attack surface. This will also be the first introduction to both case studies, which are real-world stories of leveraging Nmap in a variety of situations, as well as challenges designed to help solidify the readers' expertise.

Chapter 4. Identifying Vulnerabilities Through Reconnaissance and Enumeration: Building off of Chapter 3, this chapter goes deeper into the capabilities of Nmap to include fingerprinting systems to determine a common platform enumeration and use that information to identify potential vulnerabilities. Through additional case studies and challenges, the reader will begin to understand the depth and versatility of Nmap during this chapter.

Chapter 5. Mapping a Large Environment: One significant challenge that is very rarely covered in instructional books or videos is the unique difficulty of penetration testing in a very large environment. Scanning a single /24 subnet is one thing, but mapping a /8 is another thing entirely. This chapter will explore this complexity and introduce strategies to fully leverage Nmap in large corporate environments.

Chapter 6. Leveraging Zenmap and Legion: This chapter explores two main options for adding a graphical user interface (GUI) on top of Nmap to provide additional context and ease of use. By exploring both Zenmap as well as Legion, readers will be exposed to options that work well on both Windows and Linux operating systems and demonstrate how each can be used to improve productivity and streamline analysis.

Chapter 7. Advanced Obfuscation and Firewall Evasion: This chapter covers the advanced techniques that can be employed to avoid detection and evade network defenses using Nmap. By first understanding how default Nmap scans operate, the reader will learn how to manipulate and obfuscate the network traffic to avoid detection.

Chapter 8. Leveraging the Nmap Scripting Engine: This chapter explores the use of NSE scripts and how to leverage them to significantly increase the capacity of the tool itself. By exploring the structure and function of several individual scripts and script categories, the reader will further broaden their understanding of Nmap's versatility.

Chapter 9. Best Practices and Considerations: This chapter concludes the direct content of the book by exploring industry best practices related to port and vulnerability scanning, verification of findings to reduce the rate of false positive and false negative results, communicating results to clients, as well as common mistakes made by inexperienced practitioners.

Appendix A. Nmap Practice Questions: While this book does not aim to be a certification study guide by any means, questions on Nmap do frequently appear on many well-known certification exams such as CompTIA Security+, CompTIA Pentest+, Certified Ethical Hacker, and many others. This additional resource will provide a key check on learning for the reader as they may challenge themselves to answer numerous port scanning, enumeration, and Nmap-based questions stylized in a way very similar to those certification exams.

Appendix B. Nmap Command Quick Reference Guide: This section will provide a neat and organized breakdown of the key flags and scripts mentioned throughout the book in one place to serve as an easy reference guide for the reader.

Get a Free eBook

We hope you are enjoying your recently purchased book! Your feedback is incredibly valuable to us, and to all other readers looking for great books.

If you found this book helpful or enjoyable, we would truly appreciate it, if you could take a moment to leave a short review with a 5 star rating on Amazon. It helps us grow, and lets other readers discover our books.

As a thank you, we would love to send you a free digital copy of this book, and a **30%** discount code on your next cart value on our official websites:

www.orangeava.com

www.orangeava.in (For Indian Subcontinent)

☑ **Here's how:**

Leave a review for the book on Amazon.

Take a screenshot of your review, and send an email to **info@orangeava.com** (it can be just the confirmation screen).

Once, we receive your screenshot, we will send you the digital file, within 24 hours.

Thank you so much for your support – it means a lot to us!

Downloading the code bundles and colored images

Please follow the links or scan the QR codes to download the ***Code Bundles and Images*** of the book:

https://github.com/ava-orange-education/Ultimate-Penetration-Testing-with-Nmap

The code bundles and images of the book are also hosted on ***https://rebrand.ly/cd9c04***

In case there's an update to the code, it will be updated on the existing GitHub repository.

Errata

We take immense pride in our work at **Orange Education Pvt Ltd,** and follow best practices to ensure the accuracy of our content to provide an indulging reading experience to our subscribers. Our readers are our mirrors, and we use their inputs to reflect and improve upon human errors, if any, that may have occurred during the publishing processes involved. To let us maintain the quality and help us reach out to any readers who might be having difficulties due to any unforeseen errors, please write to us at :

errata@orangeava.com

Your support, suggestions, and feedback are highly appreciated.

DID YOU KNOW

Did you know that Orange Education Pvt Ltd offers eBook versions of every book published, with PDF and ePub files available? You can upgrade to the eBook version at **www.orangeava.com** and as a print book customer, you are entitled to a discount on the eBook copy. Get in touch with us at: **info@orangeava.com** for more details.

At **www.orangeava.com**, you can also read a collection of free technical articles, sign up for a range of free newsletters, and receive exclusive discounts and offers on AVA™ Books and eBooks.

PIRACY

If you come across any illegal copies of our works in any form on the internet, we would be grateful if you would provide us with the location address or website name. Please contact us at **info@orangeava.com** with a link to the material.

ARE YOU INTERESTED IN AUTHORING WITH US?

If there is a topic that you have expertise in, and you are interested in either writing or contributing to a book, please write to us at **business@orangeava.com**. We are on a journey to help developers and tech professionals to gain insights on the present technological advancements and innovations happening across the globe and build a community that believes Knowledge is best acquired by sharing and learning with others. Please reach out to us to learn what our audience demands and how you can be part of this educational reform. We also welcome ideas from tech experts and help them build learning and development content for their domains.

REVIEWS

Please leave a review. Once you have read and used this book, why not leave a review on the site that you purchased it from? Potential readers can then see and use your unbiased opinion to make purchase decisions. We at Orange Education would love to know what you think about our products, and our authors can learn from your feedback. Thank you!

For more information about Orange Education, please visit **www.orangeava.com**.

Table of Contents

1. **Introduction to Nmap and Security Assessments 1**
    - Introduction 1
    - Structure 2
    - Introduction to Nmap 2
    - Using Nmap to Boost Your Career 9
    - Using Nmap Legally and Ethically 12
    - Vulnerability Scans Versus Penetration Tests 13
    - Applying Nmap to Red and Purple Teaming 16
    - Conclusion 17
    - Points to Remember 18
    - Multiple Choice Questions 18
    - Answers 20
2. **Setting Up a Lab Environment For Nmap 23**
    - Introduction 23
    - Structure 24
    - Components of a Good Lab Environment 24
    - Installing Nmap, Virtual Box, Kali, and Additional Tools 25
    - Setting Up the Target Servers 30
    - Securing the Lab Environment 34
    - Conclusion 36
    - Points to Remember 37
    - Challenge 1 – Customize Your Lab 37
    - Multiple Choice Questions 38
    - Answers 38
3. **Introduction to Attack Surface Mapping 39**
    - Introduction 39
    - Structure 41
    - Understanding Attack Surfaces 42
    - Stages of Penetration Tests 43

Fundamental Nmap Flags 44

Leveraging Nmap to Map the Attack Surface 49

Case Study - Continuous Attack Surface Monitoring of a Small Business 55

Challenge 1 - Getting Hands-on with Basic Scans 56

Challenge 2 - Map the Attack Surface of Your Home Network 57

Conclusion 57

Points to Remember 58

Multiple Choice Questions 59

Answers 60

4. Identifying Vulnerabilities Through Reconnaissance and Enumeration 61

Introduction 61

Structure 63

Common Platform Enumeration (CPE) and Common Vulnerabilities and Exposures (CVE) 63

Introduction to Nmap Scripting Engine 66

Intermediate Nmap Flags 67

Exploring the Nmap Scripting Engine 71

System, Service, and Operating System Enumeration 75

Misconfigurations 75

Inherently Flawed Protocols 77

Technical Debt 78

Vulnerability Scanning with Nmap 79

Case Study - Real-World Internal and External Penetration Test 83

Challenge 1: Fingerprinting Vulnerable Systems 84

Challenge 2: Home Network Vulnerability Scanning 84

Conclusion 85

Points to Remember 85

Multiple Choice Questions 86

Answers 87

5. **Mapping a Large Environment** **89**
Introduction 89
Structure 90
Working with Large Networks 90
Black Box Subnet Discovery Techniques and Mass Scanning 92
Optimizing Scans for Speed 95
Case Study: Real-World Account of Pentesting a Very Large Environment 98
Challenge: Optimizing a Custom Scan for Speed 99
Conclusion 100
Points to Remember 101
Multiple Choice Questions 101
Answers 102
6. **Leveraging Zenmap and Legion** **103**
Introduction 103
Structure 104
Leveraging Zenmap for Analysis and Scanning 104
Leveraging Legion for Analysis and Scanning 107
Modifying the Legion Configuration File 110
Challenge: Creating a Custom Legion Configuration and Zenmap Profile 114
Conclusion 115
Points to Remember 116
Multiple Choice Questions 116
Answers 117
7. **Advanced Obfuscation and Firewall Evasion Techniques** **119**
Introduction 119
Structure 120
Understanding and Manipulating Default Nmap Scan Parameters 120
Advanced Flags for Obfuscation 121
Intrusion Detection System (IDS) and Firewall Evasion 124

Avoiding Blue Team Detection 125
Case Study: Purple Teaming with Nmap.... 126
Case Study: Red Teaming a Bank.... 129
Challenge: Evading Detection in Your Lab Environment 132
Challenge: Breaking Down Complex Scans.... 133
Conclusion.... 133
Points to Remember 134
Multiple Choice Questions....134
Answers....135

8. Leveraging the Nmap Scripting Engine 137

Introduction....137
Structure.... 138
Introduction to Nmap Scripting Engine (NSE).... 138
Script Syntax and Usage 141
Locating, Modifying, and Adding NSE Scripts....143
Introduction to NSE Scripting.... 146
Challenge: Create a Custom NSE Script and Post it to GitHub 148
Challenge: Test and Refine a Custom Script in the Lab environment 148
Challenge: Scanning with Multiple Concurrent Scripts 148
Conclusion.... 149
Points to Remember 149
Multiple Choice Questions.... 150
Answers....152

9. Best Practices and Considerations 153

Introduction....153
Structure....154
Identifying the Right Scan at the Right Time 154
Key Considerations to Avoid a Negative Impact on Client Systems....157
Effective Communication of Results....160
Conclusion.... 161
Points to Remember 162

APPENDIX A. Additional Questions **163**

Multiple Choice Questions 163

Answers 174

APPENDIX B. Nmap Quick Reference Guide **175**

Port States 175

Flags for Basic Scanning 176

Mapping the Attack Surface 176

Timing and Performance 179

Scanning Large Scopes 179

Obfuscation 180

Stealth Scanning 180

Nmap Scripting Engine 182

Top 10 Handy NSE Scripts 183

Index **184**

Chapter 1
Introduction to Nmap and Security Assessments

Introduction

Nearly anyone currently working in cyber security, or any student learning the fundamentals will inevitably come across Nmap. At its core, it is a port scanner that can empower the security analyst to gain additional insight into systems by looking at what ports and services are open. But to say that Nmap is *just a port scanner* would be akin to saying that paint is simply for walls. Sure, you can use Nmap as a simple port scanner just as you can simply paint the walls of your home eggshell white and call it a day. But in the right hands, just as a paintbrush can elevate a canvas into a work of art, Nmap can elevate the insight you provide to clients into something truly remarkable.

Throughout this book, we will be taking a deep dive into how you can leverage Nmap to its fullest extent to conduct world-class security assessments, demonstrate tremendous value to clients and employers, and provide real insight to help make the world a more secure place. We will be looking at each function of Nmap, starting from the very basics and progressing to advanced techniques. These methods are used to maintain stealth in an engagement, bypass firewalls, and help fine-tune blue-team detection capabilities.

This book is structured specifically to answer the common questions often asked when speaking to cyber security students, training junior penetration testers, and even when presenting security assessments to executives at multi-billion-dollar corporations. One of the phrases I hear the most in my professional life is "Wow, I didn't know Nmap could do that", and by the end of this book, you will start hearing that phrase too.

Each section of this book will build upon the last by introducing and explaining new skills, explaining with real-world stories of security assessments why those skills are so critical, and helping you solidify your understanding with hands-on practical exercises. Every penetration tester can run a Nmap scan; however, by the end of this book, you will be doing things with Nmap that most people assume requires an extremely expensive commercial product to do. You will be able to provide tremendous value and insight to any organization through a well-thought-out and systematic analysis of systems with a 100% free and open-source tool.

Structure

In this chapter, we will explore and answer the following questions:

- Introduction to Nmap
- Using Nmap to boost your career
- Using Nmap legally and ethically
- Vulnerability scans versus penetration tests
- Applying Nmap to red and purple teaming

Introduction to Nmap

It is mentioned in the introduction that Nmap is at its core a port scanner, and that is fundamentally correct. Nmap is probably the most widely used port scanner ever created and has been used extensively by security professionals since Gordon Lyon first published it in 1997. That's right, this wonder tool, claimed to elevate your penetration testing skillset to new heights, was released before Google. However, despite its age, just as technology has advanced over the last couple of decades, Nmap has kept pace with regular updates, new features, improvements, and community contributions, which add to its incredible versatility.

To understand what Nmap is, we first need to understand its most basic function, port scanning. Fundamentally, a port is a virtual anchor point that is used to associate particular services and enable computer systems to sort and effectively process the network traffic that is being received. In total, over 65 thousand ports utilize the **Transmission Control Protocol (TCP)** or the **User Datagram Protocol (UDP)**. Both TCP and UDP are standards that define how a connection between two systems is established and dictate the method by which data can be transmitted between them. However, the distinction between these two protocols is critical to understand if you want to truly become an expert-level user of Nmap.

TCP is used for protocols that require secure transmission of data between the sender and receiver. This is accomplished by establishing what is known as a three-way handshake. During this exchange, the originating system will first send a synchronize (`SYN`) packet to the receiving system, once received that system will reply with an acknowledgment (`SYN-ACK`), and the originating system will then reply to that reply with an acknowledgment of the acknowledgment (`ACK`) before sending any additional data.

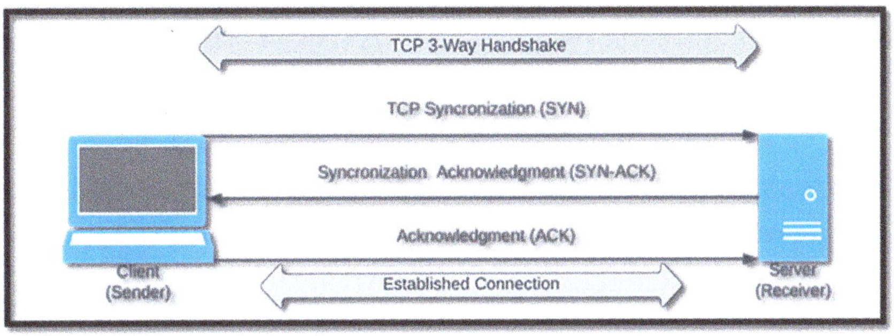

Figure 1.1: *TCP Three-Way Handshake Diagram*

Does this seem slightly redundant? It is, but it is redundant to ensure that a full connection is made with the system. If at any point the three-way handshake is interrupted, such as by an **Intrusion Prevention System** (**IPS**) or firewall, a full connection will not be established, and thus the data will not be sent from the sender to the receiver; in these instances, instead of an ACK packet, a reset (RST) will typically be sent.

Most of the common services you will be searching for during security engagements will be served over common TCP ports such as `80` (Hypertext Transfer Protocol, or HTTP) and `443` (Hypertext Transfer Protocol Secure). Don't worry, we will discuss all the common ports to be aware of and how to fingerprint them later. The key takeaway from TCP is that it is a secure connection, requiring an acknowledgment from the receiver to be established, and that process is known as the three-way handshake.

In contrast to the three-way handshake verification between the sender and receiver that is utilized in TCP, UDP takes a far more haphazard approach. UDP speeds up the process by neglecting to establish a formal connection in the first place. So rather than wait for an acknowledgment from the receiver, a computer utilizing UDP will just send the packet immediately. This certainly increases the speed of the data transmission, but that increase in speed comes with a decrease in reliability as packets can become lost in the process. In introduction to Networking courses, most of the examples surrounding UDP relate to video transmission where it is paramount to the consumer to avoid the dreaded buffering lag. While you will occasionally see UDP being used for video transmissions in penetration tests (security camera feeds come to mind), several other protocols tend to be far riper for exploitation such as the **Intelligence Platform Management Interface (IPMI)**, which is often seen on UDP port 623.

No coverage of networking concepts would be complete without touching on the **Open Systems Interconnection Model (OSI model)**. This model is a framework to describe how computer systems can communicate with one another. From the physical layer, which involves cables and electrical signals, all the way to the application layer that the user directly interacts with. It is worth contextually mentioning that transport protocols like TCP and UDP operate at layer 4 (Transport Layer) of the OSI model. While a deep dive into networking concepts is beyond the scope of this book, additional details surrounding Nmap's interaction with the OSI model will be covered in *Chapter 3: Introduction to Attack Surface Mapping*:

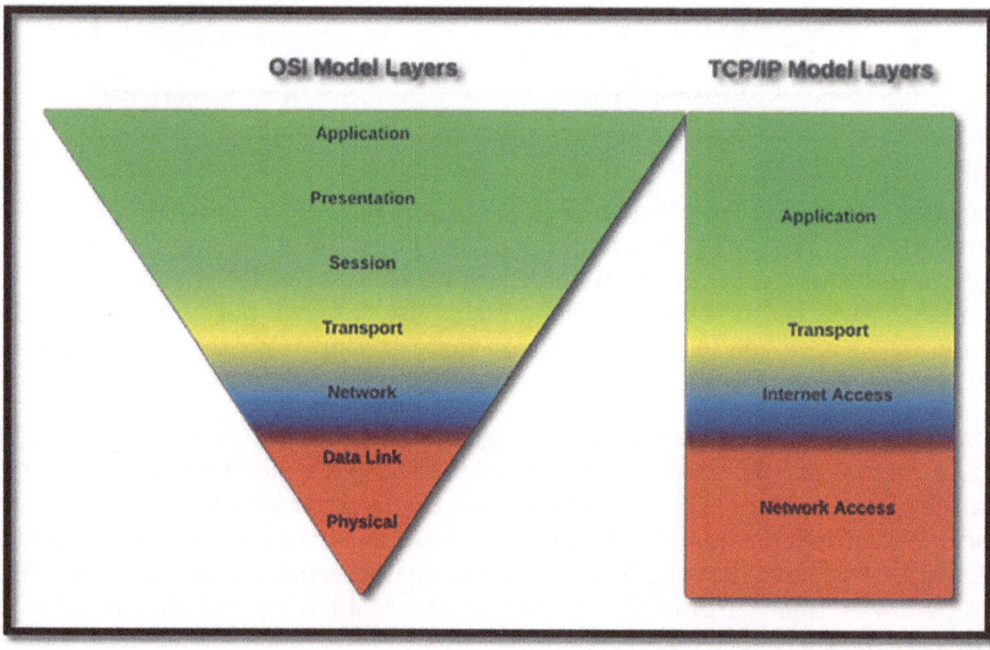

Figure 1.2: *OSI and TCP/IP Model Comparison*

As you begin your journey into penetration testing in general, but especially Nmap, you will naturally begin to memorize a lot of ports and services, which are the most interesting from an attacker's perspective. We will get into that a lot in later chapters, but for now, just take note of the major differences between TCP and UDP, and make sure you understand the three-way handshake.

Now that we have touched on the very basics of prerequisite networking knowledge, let's get down to brass tax and take a look at how Nmap actually functions. Most commonly as a penetration tester, you will be using Nmap on a Linux machine, typically Kali Linux, but there are several other distributions such as Ubuntu, Parrot, and Black Arch, which you may see from time to time. While Kali Linux is likely the most common platform you will see Nmap used on it is worth noting that Nmap can be easily installed and works well on, both Windows and MacOS too. We will go into installing Nmap in the next chapter when we walk through setting up a lab environment to practice the scans and techniques you will learn throughout this book. But for now, let's look at and discuss some real Nmap scans.

NOTE: Understanding the three-way handshake is the minimum prerequisite knowledge required for the next several sections. However, understanding additional network fundamentals such as the OSI Model would be beneficial to anyone studying Nmap.

We will start with a default Nmap scan against http://scanme.nmap.org. This is a website designed specifically to allow people to practice using Nmap and can be freely used as a target for scans that are not overly aggressive. A default scan simply requires the command nmap followed by the target scanme.nmap.org, like so:

```
> nmap scanme.nmap.org
```

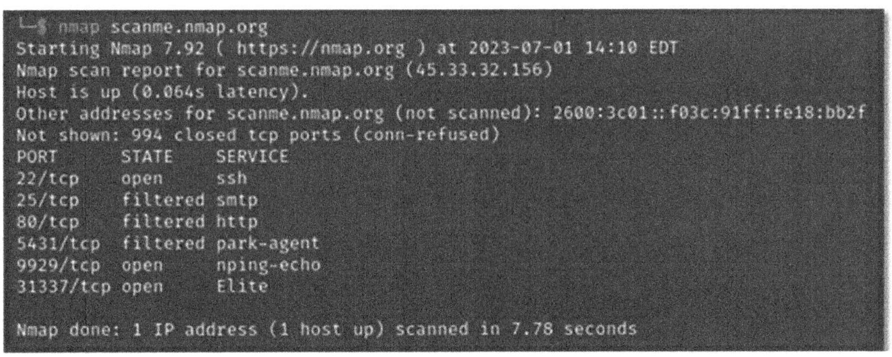

Figure 1.3: *Default Nmap Scan Enumerating Ports*

We can see a lot of interesting things in this result. Starting from the top, we can tell that this version of Nmap is version 7.92 as well as the date and time that the scan started. In the next line, we can see that Nmap was able to resolve the hostname to an IP address (45.33.32.156). Next, we can see the results of the scan, which says that `994` TCP ports were closed, with Ports `22`, `9929`, and `31337` listed as open, with `25`, `80`, and `5431` listed as filtered. There are a couple of important things to take note of here, the first is that in total 1000 ports were scanned, the default setting of Nmap, if you do not otherwise specify, is to scan the top 1000 most common ports.

The next thing to clarify is the state of the ports. Nmap has the capability of classifying six distinct states of ports which are important to understand:

Open	The port is actively accepting connections
Closed	The port is accessible, but there is no application listening on it
Filtered	Nmap cannot tell if it is opened or close, often due to a firewall
Unfiltered	The port is accessible, but Nmap cannot tell if it is open or closed. This status is rarely seen unless you are doing a very specific type of scanning to map firewall rulesets
Open|Filtered	Nmap cannot tell if it is Open or Filtered, possibly because of a lack of response
Closed|Filtered	Nmap cannot tell if it is Closed or Filtered

Table 1.1: *Overview of Port States*

Finally, we can see the services that Nmap believes to be running on each port. In *Figure* 1.3, they are **secure shell (SSH)**, **simple mail transfer protocol (SMTP)**, **hypertext transfer protocol (HTTP)**, park-agent, nping-echo, and Elite.

While understanding which ports and services are open and potentially open is helpful, we can elicit much more information by adding what are called flags. Flags are additional commands which can be added to the Nmap scan to add, remove, or modify the default functioning. Let's use a few of these flags to try to enumerate the operating system of the host, as well as the version of each service. To do this, we will use the following syntax:

```
> nmap -A scanme.nmap.org
```

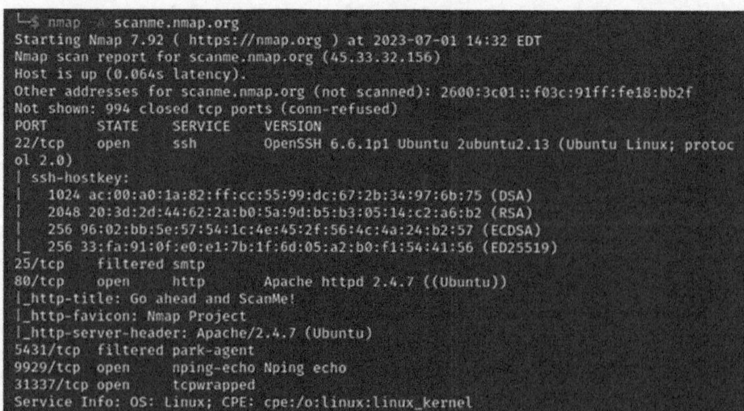

```
└─$ nmap -A scanme.nmap.org
Starting Nmap 7.92 ( https://nmap.org ) at 2023-07-01 14:32 EDT
Nmap scan report for scanme.nmap.org (45.33.32.156)
Host is up (0.064s latency).
Other addresses for scanme.nmap.org (not scanned): 2600:3c01::f03c:91ff:fe18:bb2f
Not shown: 994 closed tcp ports (conn-refused)
PORT      STATE    SERVICE    VERSION
22/tcp    open     ssh        OpenSSH 6.6.1p1 Ubuntu 2ubuntu2.13 (Ubuntu Linux; protoc
ol 2.0)
| ssh-hostkey:
|   1024 ac:00:a0:1a:82:ff:cc:55:99:dc:67:2b:34:97:6b:75 (DSA)
|   2048 20:3d:2d:44:62:2a:b0:5a:9d:b5:b3:05:14:c2:a6:b2 (RSA)
|   256 96:02:bb:5e:57:54:1c:4e:45:2f:56:4c:4a:24:b2:57 (ECDSA)
|_  256 33:fa:91:0f:e0:e1:7b:1f:6d:05:a2:b0:f1:54:41:56 (ED25519)
25/tcp    filtered smtp
80/tcp    open     http       Apache httpd 2.4.7 ((Ubuntu))
|_http-title: Go ahead and ScanMe!
|_http-favicon: Nmap Project
|_http-server-header: Apache/2.4.7 (Ubuntu)
5431/tcp  filtered park-agent
9929/tcp  open     nping-echo Nping echo
31337/tcp open     tcpwrapped
Service Info: OS: Linux; CPE: cpe:/o:linux:linux_kernel
```

Figure 1.4: *Nmap Scan Enumerating Ports, Services, and Operating System*

As you can see, this time we have a lot more information. We can tell that `scanme.nmap.org` is utilizing OpenSSH 6.6.1 and Apache version 2.4.7 on an Ubuntu Linux system. You may also notice that this time, the status of port 80 changed from filtered to open as additional information was queried, and Nmap was able to confirm the port was opened. Adding the single "-A" flag provides substantially more information than the default scan. This flag is very useful as it tells Nmap to expand the scope of its scan to include information on the services and the operating system of the endpoint.

Let's see if we can get even more detailed information about port 80 on this host. This time we will use three different flags: `-sV -v` and `-p`:

```
>nmap -sV -v -p 22 scanme.nmap.org
```

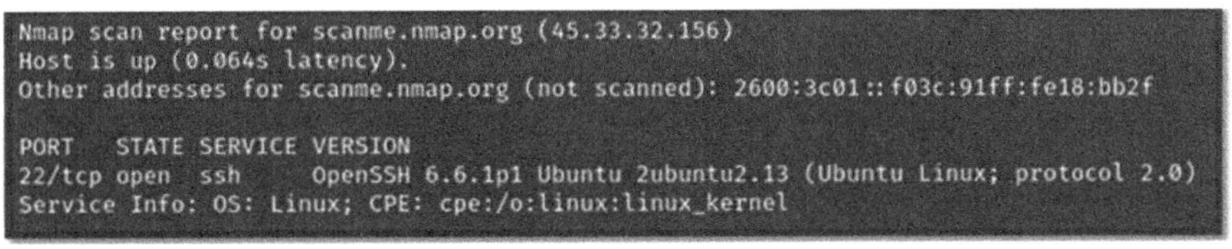

Figure 1.5: *Adding Verbosity and Demonstrating Single Port Scanning*

This scan works a little bit differently; instead of using `-A`, we have replaced that flag with `-sV`, which will only enumerate the service versions. Since we already established the system is Ubuntu Linux, we can omit redundantly scanning for the operating system to save time. Next, the `-v` flag stands for verbosity, it will provide a more verbose output, which in turn may provide additional details on the service. Finally, `-p` indicates which port(s) to scan. Since the default of Nmap is to scan 1,000 ports, but we are just interested in port 22, we set `-p` 22 to only target that port.

In this case, there wasn't a lot more information on the OpenSSH instance than we had previously gathered, beyond the additional service info. But we have another trick up our sleeve; this time we will include a script called `vulners.nse`, which will search the `vulners.org` database and determine if there are any vulnerabilities associated with that version of OpenSSH:

```
>nmap -sV -v -p 22 --script vulners.nse scanme.nmap.org
```

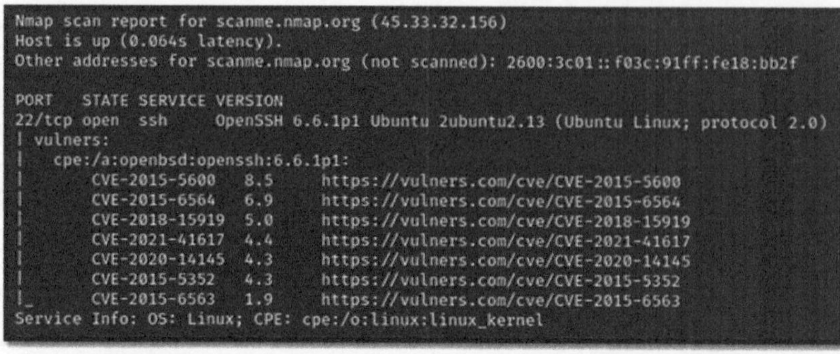

```
Nmap scan report for scanme.nmap.org (45.33.32.156)
Host is up (0.064s latency).
Other addresses for scanme.nmap.org (not scanned): 2600:3c01::f03c:91ff:fe18:bb2f

PORT   STATE SERVICE VERSION
22/tcp open  ssh     OpenSSH 6.6.1p1 Ubuntu 2ubuntu2.13 (Ubuntu Linux; protocol 2.0)
| vulners:
|   cpe:/a:openbsd:openssh:6.6.1p1:
|       CVE-2015-5600   8.5     https://vulners.com/cve/CVE-2015-5600
|       CVE-2015-6564   6.9     https://vulners.com/cve/CVE-2015-6564
|       CVE-2018-15919  5.0     https://vulners.com/cve/CVE-2018-15919
|       CVE-2021-41617  4.4     https://vulners.com/cve/CVE-2021-41617
|       CVE-2020-14145  4.3     https://vulners.com/cve/CVE-2020-14145
|       CVE-2015-5352   4.3     https://vulners.com/cve/CVE-2015-5352
|_      CVE-2015-6563   1.9     https://vulners.com/cve/CVE-2015-6563
Service Info: OS: Linux; CPE: cpe:/o:linux:linux_kernel
```

Figure 1.6: *Demonstrating vulnerability scanning with Nmap*

Now we have really got something to work with, a list of known vulnerabilities associated with OpenSSH version 6.6.1p1! The major takeaway here is that by adding different arguments, or flags, to your Nmap scan you can transform the functionality from a simple port scanner into much more. In this brief example, we used Nmap to fingerprint a system, enumerate the open ports and services, and perform vulnerability scanning to identify several vulnerabilities associated with one of the services, which may be exploitable very quickly.

If this seemed a bit overwhelming, don't worry. One of the questions I get asked all the time is "*How do I remember all of those different flags?*"; the good news is that you don't have to memorize them (although in time you certainly will remember your favorites). Instead, you have a few options, the first is to simply remember the `-h` flag. As in many scripts, this opens the Nmap help menu right in your command line, which will give you the spark notes version of the options available to you:

```
> nmap -h
```

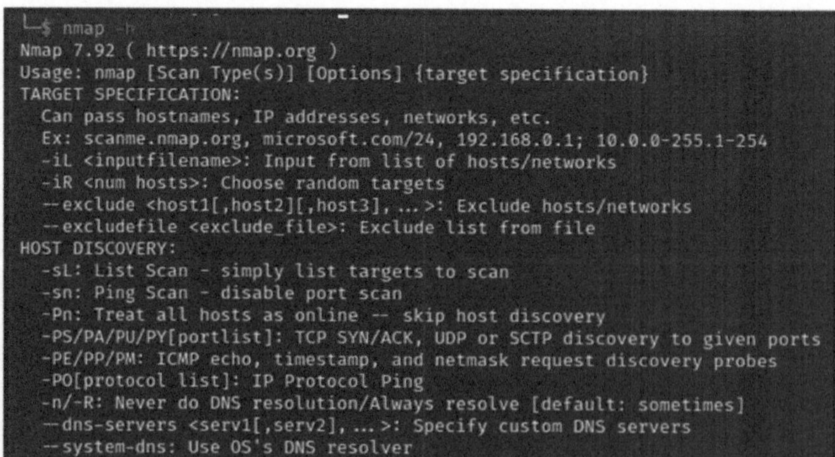

```
└─$ nmap -h
Nmap 7.92 ( https://nmap.org )
Usage: nmap [Scan Type(s)] [Options] {target specification}
TARGET SPECIFICATION:
  Can pass hostnames, IP addresses, networks, etc.
  Ex: scanme.nmap.org, microsoft.com/24, 192.168.0.1; 10.0.0-255.1-254
  -iL <inputfilename>: Input from list of hosts/networks
  -iR <num hosts>: Choose random targets
  --exclude <host1[,host2][,host3],...>: Exclude hosts/networks
  --excludefile <exclude_file>: Exclude list from file
HOST DISCOVERY:
  -sL: List Scan - simply list targets to scan
  -sn: Ping Scan - disable port scan
  -Pn: Treat all hosts as online -- skip host discovery
  -PS/PA/PU/PY[portlist]: TCP SYN/ACK, UDP or SCTP discovery to given ports
  -PE/PP/PM: ICMP echo, timestamp, and netmask request discovery probes
  -PO[protocol list]: IP Protocol Ping
  -n/-R: Never do DNS resolution/Always resolve [default: sometimes]
  --dns-servers <serv1[,serv2],...>: Specify custom DNS servers
  --system-dns: Use OS's DNS resolver
```

Figure 1.7: *Demonstrating the Nmap help menu*

Another option is to use the Linux utility **'man'** to open the Nmap reference guide in your terminal. Compared to the **Help** menu, this is far completer and more detailed, plus using **'man'** lets you go page by page through all the Nmap documentation:

```
>man nmap
```

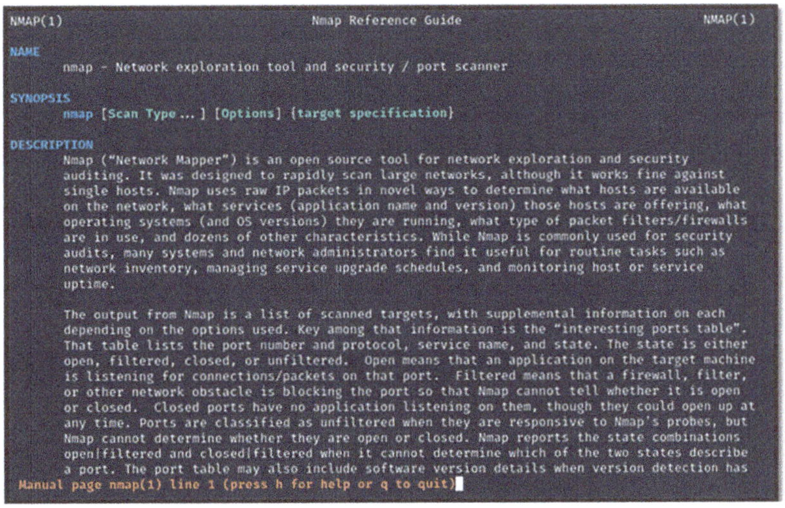

```
NMAP(1)                          Nmap Reference Guide                          NMAP(1)

NAME
       nmap - Network exploration tool and security / port scanner

SYNOPSIS
       nmap [Scan Type ... ] [Options] {target specification}

DESCRIPTION
       Nmap ("Network Mapper") is an open source tool for network exploration and security
       auditing. It was designed to rapidly scan large networks, although it works fine against
       single hosts. Nmap uses raw IP packets in novel ways to determine what hosts are available
       on the network, what services (application name and version) those hosts are offering, what
       operating systems (and OS versions) they are running, what type of packet filters/firewalls
       are in use, and dozens of other characteristics. While Nmap is commonly used for security
       audits, many systems and network administrators find it useful for routine tasks such as
       network inventory, managing service upgrade schedules, and monitoring host or service
       uptime.

       The output from Nmap is a list of scanned targets, with supplemental information on each
       depending on the options used. Key among that information is the "interesting ports table".
       That table lists the port number and protocol, service name, and state. The state is either
       open, filtered, closed, or unfiltered.  Open means that an application on the target machine
       is listening for connections/packets on that port.  Filtered means that a firewall, filter,
       or other network obstacle is blocking the port so that Nmap cannot tell whether it is open
       or closed.  Closed ports have no application listening on them, though they could open up at
       any time. Ports are classified as unfiltered when they are responsive to Nmap's probes, but
       Nmap cannot determine whether they are open or closed. Nmap reports the state combinations
       open|filtered and closed|filtered when it cannot determine which of the two states describe
       a port. The port table may also include software version details when version detection has
 Manual page nmap(1) line 1 (press h for help or q to quit)
```

Figure 1.8: *Demonstrating the Nmap manual in Linux CLI*

Yet another option is to visit https://nmap.org where you can find the complete documentation on Nmap, detailing what every single flag does.

While each of these options is extremely helpful in remembering individual flags or understanding one command in particular, the aim of this book is to expand upon the utility of the official documentation. Where, in my opinion, the documentation falls short is that the majority of examples and descriptions focus on using individual features for individual purposes. Throughout this book, you will see numerous flags, all being used together to complement and amplify the capabilities of Nmap, leading to an extremely powerful tool. These combinations are going to be covered throughout the following chapters as we progressively delve into more and more advanced techniques. However, all of the flags used during real-world penetration tests of some of the world's largest companies will be included in the Appendix of the book in a handy quick-reference guide.

Using Nmap to Boost Your Career

The field of cyber security is extremely vast, there are seemingly endless different aspects that one can specialize in. From cryptography to forensics, cloud to threat hunting, and red team to blue team, there are many potential career paths. Every week there will be at least one aspiring cyber professional reaching out on LinkedIn for advice on how to break into the industry, and the conversation usually starts very predictably. They will say they are trying to get a cyber security role but are not having any luck getting interviews. I always reply by asking what area of cyber security they are specifically targeting and studying for. To which nine out of ten times there will be a reply like this: "*I'm open to anything! I am focusing on SOC analyst, GRC, threat intelligence, and penetration testing roles.*"

Let's dig into that sentiment, because at first glance it may make a lot of sense. The person is just trying to get their foot in the door with any cyber security job they can and then figure out what they want to do from there. It makes logical sense, but in practice, it is a very inefficient approach. The skill set you need, both from a technical and soft skills perspective, is very different between all of those roles. For example, a GRC analyst would benefit certainly from a degree of technical acumen; but certainly, would not be expected to poison insecure network traffic, collect hashed credentials of enterprise users, crack those credentials, and take over an Active Directory domain. Whereas if you were applying for a junior penetration testing role, there would almost definitely be a line of questioning surrounding that concept.

Trying to study everything at once to remain "open to anything" inadvertently results in your knowledge base being a mile wide but only an inch deep. What is far more effective in this field is having a good baseline knowledge of security as a whole, then deep diving into a particular area and really building up your expertise.

The first certification I did when I got into security was the CompTIA Security+. Talk about a mile wide and an inch deep, there are questions and concepts of all kinds of things within the cyber security domain. It is designed to help people establish that baseline understanding, to be able to speak in the lexicon of cybersecurity, and to help pinpoint what areas to focus on further. There are only a couple of specific tools that tend to get regularly brought up in that exam, and Nmap is one of them.

If Nmap comes up as a topic in one of the industry's most prevalent baseline certification exams, where can it help you once you pass? Well, the title of this book should be a dead giveaway. Nmap and network penetration testing go together hand in hand. Because of this, you will see questions about Nmap on exams such as CompTIA Pentest+ and **Certified Ethical Hacker** (**CEH**), and you would be likely to rely on Nmap for critical reconnaissance during hands-on exams such as the eJPT or OSCP.

It is important to note that Nmap is by far the most applicable to network penetration tests. There are many different types of pentests, all of which require a different skill set, different tooling, and different degrees of technical knowledge. There are web application pentests, API pentests, mobile applications pentests, cloud pentests, **Internet of Things (IoT)** pentests, and so on, Remember that this field is vast, and trying to specialize in everything doesn't work well.

This book is going to focus on building your skills in three types of security engagements: network penetration tests, purple teaming, and red teaming. By learning how Nmap can apply to and be used expertly for each of these major types of security tests, you will be able to stand out from the crowd both in technical performance, but also in technical interviews.

First, consider someone who has been taking the "I'm open to anything" approach and is being interviewed for a network penetration testing role at a security company. They are asked the following question:

"What are the first steps of active reconnaissance you would take during an internal network pentest?"

Most people that I have personally posed this question to say something along these lines:

"I would scan ports and analyze the services that are on those ports with Nmap."

While that answer is not technically wrong, it is unremarkable. By the end of this book, you will confidently be able to provide an answer with far more nuance and demonstrate immediately a higher degree of knowledge within that area. After completing this book and the suggested labs that go along with it, you will easily be able to answer the same question with something more along the lines of:

"The first thing I would do in the active reconnaissance phase would be to begin mapping the attack surface. I would do this by enumerating the ports and services with a custom Nmap scan designed to minimize the noise on the network to avoid immediate detection. In addition to utilizing techniques such as packet fragmentation and reducing the speed of the scan, I would also be sure to scan only the local subnet first. This will allow me to gather information within the subnet I am scanning from without risking detection by going through an intrusion detection system to reach other subnets. I would also customize the targets to avoid scanning the gateway, again to reduce the risk of immediate detection. I would output that scan to an xml file and import it into Legion to get a graphical view of the local subnet, then determine the next steps based on that attack surface."

If only bits and pieces of that response really make sense to you at this point, don't worry. We will be exploring those concepts, and many more, in great detail.

Using Nmap Legally and Ethically

It is extremely important to understand the responsibility that comes with utilizing a tool such as Nmap, both inside and outside of a professional setting. Nmap makes connections with the target endpoints and gathers information from those endpoints through a direct connection, which makes it a tool for active reconnaissance. The distinction between active and passive reconnaissance is crucial not only from a knowledge base perspective but also from a legal perspective.

The main difference between the two is in the connection to the endpoint. Any tool or technique that is 'actively' connecting to another system that you do not own introduces legal risk to you. This is why things like **rules of engagement (RoE)** are so important during professional penetration tests. The RoE is an agreement between the client who owns the systems and the penetration tester regarding what is allowed and what is not allowed to be done to their systems. Without a RoE or another form of written permission to scan the systems, you may (depending on jurisdiction) be breaking the law by utilizing something like Nmap.

Contrary to gathering information with active means, there are a plethora of passive methods of gathering information available to penetration testers. Many of these would be classified as **open-source intelligence (OSINT)**. Using information that is already publicly available, there are often many ways to conduct reconnaissance without transitioning into active means:

For example, say we wanted to see what ports are open on a web server, in this case, at 45.33.32.156. We can gather the same information actively with Nmap, as we can passively with Shodan.io. The difference is that using Nmap would establish a direct connection and thus require explicit permission to do so. Whereas Shodan.io already has that information archived, and by searching for the server on Shodan, there is no direct connection made with 45.33.32.156, thus classifying it as passive:

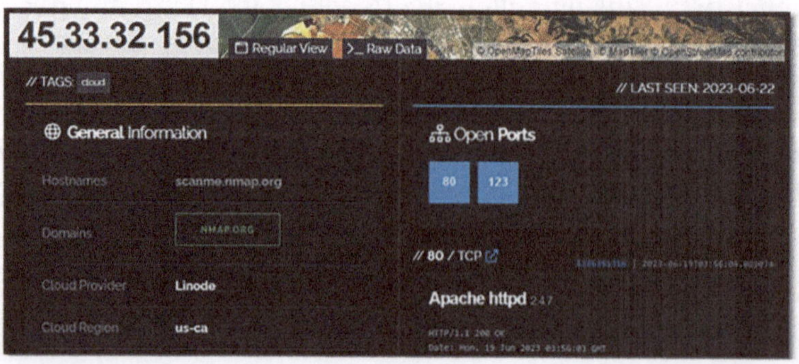

Figure 1.9: *Utilizing Shodan.io to passively gather information on open ports*

Beyond the legal ramifications, one must also consider the potential impact on systems that could occur when leveraging Nmap in a production environment. While quite uncommon for Nmap to cause a major service disruption or to restart a system on its own, there are hundreds of custom Nmap scripts (more on these later) that can be used to amplify the base capabilities of Nmap. Some of these scripts are completely safe to use without concern, but others do have a very real chance to cause system impact.

As a penetration tester one of the cardinal rules is to always avoid doing anything that will impact the CIA triad. The CIA triad is an acronym that stands for confidentiality, integrity, and availability. This is a very common, and very important concept in information security as it relates to data. In the case of Nmap, the part of the triad to be most concerned with is the availability of systems. By running unsafe arguments, untested scripts, or scanning legacy systems too aggressively, it is possible to take down production systems, leading to a bad day for your client (and a very bad day for you too):

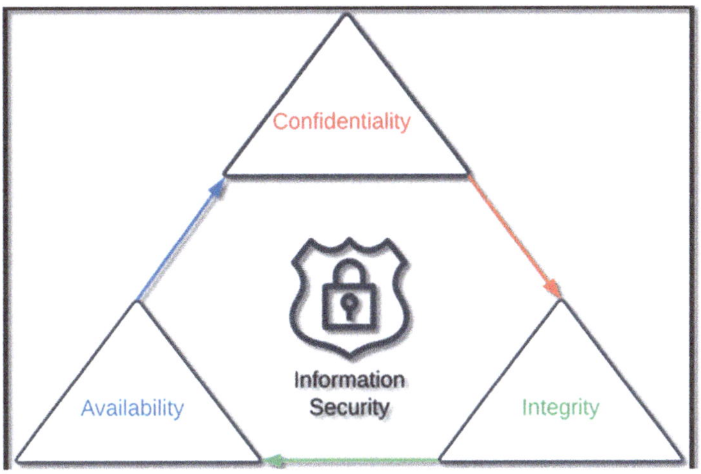

Figure 1.10: *CIA Triad*

As such, it is your legal responsibility to ensure you have permission to scan each and every target within your scope of work, and it is your ethical responsibility to ensure you understand what those scans are doing to avoid impacting the CIA triad.

Vulnerability Scans Versus Penetration Tests

Within the cyber security community, different companies will classify different actions differently. To some company standards, a penetration test is a largely automated process using commercial tools like Nessus and Sn3per. To others, it is a highly involved and intricate process focusing on the use of both automated and manual techniques. To ensure that there is a mutual understanding of the terminology used throughout the book, we will take a moment to lay out how this book defines vulnerability scans and penetration tests.

A vulnerability scanner is a tool that is used by security teams to enumerate a particular system by analyzing the operating system, open ports, services, and versions of those services to first establish a **common platform enumeration (CPE)**. Once a CPE is known, then the scanner will automate the process of sorting through tens of thousands of **common vulnerabilities and exposures (CVEs)** to identify if the system is vulnerable to any particular vulnerabilities. Many vulnerability scanners will go beyond just CPE information and also attempt proof-of-concept exploitation of things like default credentials, public SNMP communities, cross-site scripting (XSS), various forms of injection, and so on.

Vulnerability scanning is a widely used practice that is often done across particular systems or networks on a reoccurring basis to identify any new critical vulnerabilities, or determine major changes in the environment. An inherent flaw in vulnerability scans that must be understood is that they are all prone to both false positive and false negative findings.

While many vulnerability scanners are commercial products that can be extremely costly, most are fundamentally very similar to one another in functioning. To get some hands-on experience with vulnerability scanners, consider installing the community edition of OpenVas from https://greenbone.github.io/docs/latest/background.html#architecture:

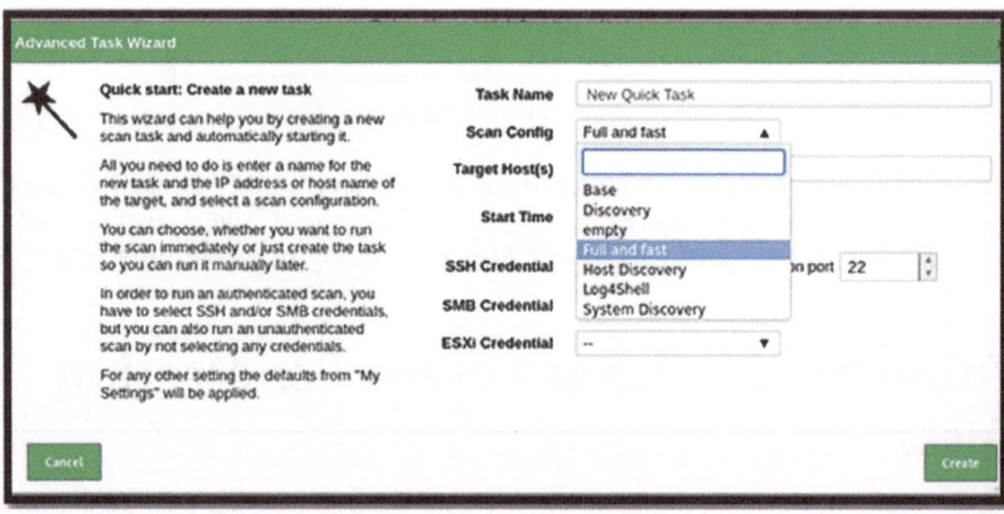

Figure 1.11: *Greenbone (OpenVas) Community Edition Running in Virtual Box*

Penetration testing on the other hand is a significantly more involved process. Fundamentally, a penetration test seeks to enumerate a real-world malicious actor using known malicious actor **tactics, techniques, and procedures (TTPs)** to actively exploit the target systems or network. Conducting a high-quality penetration test involves highly detailed reconnaissance and attack surface mapping, identifying vulnerabilities, and exploiting those vulnerabilities to cause a cascading compromise within the environment, ultimately demonstrating the potential impact of a malicious actor targeting those systems.

NOTE: Many vulnerability scanners, both open source and commercial, actually leverage Nmap under the hood to establish the CPE information. In fact, Nmap can actually be used on its own for vulnerability scanning with some custom NSE scripts.

For the purposes of this book, there are two specific types of penetration tests we will be discussing, external network pentests and internal network pentests. Both of which we will discuss from a black box perspective, meaning that we, as the testers, do not have any knowledge of the client organization beyond the scope provided in the RoE. We have neither been whitelisted by any security systems, nor have any accounts been provisioned. Additionally, we will be actively trying to avoid detection by the client's blue team to truly simulate a sophisticated malicious actor.

To accomplish this, a penetration tester will almost always follow an industry-recognized framework to ensure the test is completed to an acceptable standard. Several guidelines and frameworks exist such as the Penetration Testing Execution Standard[1] (PTES) or NIST SP 800-115[2] (Technical Guide to Information Security Testing and Assessment).

Additionally, it is becoming more and more common within the industry to also map penetration testing activities and resulting security findings to additional industry frameworks such as MITRE ATT&CK[3] or the Lockheed Martin Cyber Kill Chain. The ATT&CK framework by MITRE is a fantastic knowledge base of real-world malicious actors TTPs organized into fourteen different 'tactics' (Reconnaissance, Resource Development, Initial Access, Execution, Persistence, Privilege Escalation, Defense Evasion, Credential Access, Discovery, Lateral Movement, Collection, Command and Control, Exfiltration, and Impact). Lockheed Martin's Cyber Kill Chain is slightly different in that it illustrates the logical progression of an **advanced persistent threat (APT)** from reconnaissance to actions on objectives. Throughout this book, we will be leveraging both frameworks as a way to categorize the Nmap techniques that are employed.

---

[1] http://www.pentest-standard.org/index.php/Main_Page
[2] https://www.nist.gov/privacy-framework/nist-sp-800-115
[3] https://attack.mitre.org/

Applying Nmap to Red and Purple Teaming

Red teaming is considered as an advanced form of penetration testing where the concept of emulating a real malicious actor is taken to a higher level by reducing restrictions. For example, most penetration tests are focused entirely on technical vulnerabilities and (unless deliberately included in scope) do not include social engineering. This is one area where true red teaming differs, as the options available to the red team are generally more robust.

Another key difference is that during red teaming engagements, the blue team (defenders) are actively threat hunting trying to detect, block, and contain the red team (attackers). While this may sound similar to the way avoiding detection is described in penetration testing, there is an important distinction to be made. Typically, during a penetration test, the blue team would not block the pentester's IP, evict them from systems upon discovery, or change firewall rules mid-engagement. That would inherently minimize the potential insight into what vulnerabilities exist within the environment. When I conduct penetration tests, I encourage clients to send me evidence of when their blue team detects my actions so that I can feature that detection capability in the report. That is very different from the blue team actively trying to thwart my efforts.

The goal of a red teaming engagement isn't only to illustrate the most significant vulnerabilities within the environment as it is with a penetration test. While that is part of it, the real value of red teaming comes from the client being able to truly assess the holistic maturity of their security program from end-user security awareness to their incident response capability to their ability to contain threats within the network.

We will discuss numerous methods of modifying Nmap scans to enumerate systems and identify vulnerabilities while using stealth tactics to avoid detection from the blue team. While this is believed to be an important best practice within a penetration test, it is essential in a red teaming engagement.

Purple teaming is another advanced form of security assessment that very often contains elements akin to penetration testing within it. During a purple team engagement, the red team and the blue team will collaborate closely together, often in real-time, to identify what actions or activities the blue team can detect the red team doing. Doing this collaboratively not only provides the opportunity for both sides to learn from each other but also allows the blue team to understand their thresholds for detection.

Nmap has proven to be an immensely helpful tool during purple team engagements because the scans themselves can do so many different things, in so many different ways. For example, I may begin with an extremely obvious port scan with all default settings to make sure the blue team can detect that activity. Then progressively add more and more obfuscation techniques until a scan that bypasses detection is reached. Once that point is established, then I can collaborate with the blue team on how to adjust their IDS, EDR, or firewall settings to set more insight into that particular tactic.

Considering that Nmap can accomplish far more than just port scanning, that means it can generate more **indicators of compromise (IoCs)** within the client's network. This allows savvy purple teamers to craft numerous scenarios which align to different TTPs all while using Nmap.

Conclusion

So far, we have discussed the core of what Nmap is and a very high-level overview of what it is capable of. With a baseline understanding of networking concepts, we will begin by understanding the fundamentals before expanding into progressively more nuanced and advanced skills.

We also considered the legal and ethical implications of employing such a tool, and how, when used properly, it can provide tremendous insight to clients. The potential for unintended consequences negatively impacting a client's environment necessitates an ethical penetration tester to take the time to understand what the scans are doing and how they are doing it. Without understanding the fundamentals of networking and how different scan types may work on different layers of the OSI model, or modify the traditional three-way handshake, it will be impossible to truly build the expertise. In other words, without understanding the 'why' and the 'how' of what the tool is doing, the potential for unintended consequences will always be present.

By considering different types of security assessments such as vulnerability scanning, penetration testing, red teaming, and purple teaming, we established a common lexicon that will allow you to begin to understand what types of scans would be beneficial in certain engagements and hazardous in others. This concept will be continuously reinforced through numerous case studies of real-world security assessments as well as with hands-on challenges.

All of the information within this chapter can be considered the foundation on which we will progressively build your Nmap expertise on top of. In the next chapter, we will build a simple but highly functional home lab environment that will provide countless opportunities to gain hands-on experience with penetration testing tools, concepts, and techniques. This lab is made to be a miniature replica of enterprise environments that are often seen during real-world penetration tests, and by leveraging and learning in a realistic lab environment your skills will be reinforced.

Points to Remember

- Nmap is an extremely powerful open-source tool that can be used for port scanning, vulnerability scanning, exploitation, penetration testing, red teaming, purple teaming, and more.
- By utilizing different flags, options, and scripts the way that Nmap functions can be highly customized to suit the needs of the penetration tester.
- Port scanning is a form of active reconnaissance that requires explicit permission from the system owner to be performed legally.
- Vulnerability scanning, penetration testing, red teaming, and purple teaming are all very different types of security assessments with different techniques, purposes, and outcomes. While Nmap can be utilized in each one of these assessments, how it is used would be vastly different.
- The way to get the most out of this book is to read the chapters, thoughtfully consider the case studies, and then practice the techniques by completing the challenges in a lab environment.

Multiple Choice Questions

1. **This type of engagement involves a close collaboration between the offensive and defensive security teams:**
    a. Penetration Test
    b. Purple Teaming
    c. Vulnerability Scan
    d. Red Teaming
2. **The objective of a penetration test is to identify every possible vulnerability in a system or environment.**
    a. True
    b. False
3. **An organization wants to get a holistic view of its entire security program including detection, incident response, and containment protocols. Which would be the best security assessment to provide this insight?**
    a. Vulnerability Scan
    b. Purple Teaming

   c. Penetration Test
   d. Red Teaming

4. **An Nmap scan is an example of:**
   a. Passive Reconnaissance
   b. Active Reconnaissance

5. **Which component of the CIA Triad is most likely to be impacted by Nmap scanning?**
   a. Confidentiality
   b. Integrity
   c. Availability

6. **Which document defines the scope of an engagement and provides permission for conducting active testing?**
   a. RoE
   b. IDS
   c. EDR
   d. IoC

7. **Which framework is designed to illustrate the phases of attack by an APT from reconnaissance to actions on objective?**
   a. ATT&CK
   b. Cyber Kill Chain
   c. OSI Model
   d. TCP/IP

8. **Which port status most commonly indicates possible interference from an IPS or firewall?**
   a. Open
   b. Closed
   c. Filtered
   d. Unfiltered
   e. Open | Filtered
   f. Closed | Filtered

9. **Which layer of the OSI model is associated with TCP?**
    a. Application Layer
    b. Data Link Layer
    c. Transport Layer
    d. Session Layer
10. **This type of penetration test takes the perspective of a malicious actor with no inside knowledge of the client's infrastructure or attack surface:**
    a. White Box
    b. Black Box
    c. Red Box
    d. Purple Box

Answers

1. **b**

   Purple team engagements provide insight through the coordinated and collaborative actions of both the red team (offense) and the blue team (defense). While the actions of both sides are inputs to a red teaming engagement as well, the distinction is that in red teaming both sides are operating independently rather than collaboratively.

2. **b**

   A penetration test is meant to simulate a real-world malicious actor with the intent of breaking into an application or network for specific purposes, likely monetization. This involves identifying and exploiting the highest severity vulnerabilities to demonstrate the ability of a malicious actor to impact the organization. No penetration test will identify every possible vulnerability in an environment, rather the aim is to find and demonstrate exploitation of the most severe.

3. **d**

   The correct answer is red teaming, as this type of engagement will rapidly identify gaps in the blue team's detection and response process and demonstrate the exploitation of those gaps. While similar components could be analyzed through tailored purple team scenarios, there would be an inherent bias in that the blue team would be aware of what indicators of compromise to be on the lookout for. Assessing a red team helps minimize confirmation bias.

4. **b**

   Nmap is a form of active reconnaissance, as a complete connection is made with the target system.

5. **c**

   The most common impact caused by Nmap would be overly aggressive scanning impacting the performance of a system or network, thus the availability component of the CIA triad.

6. **a**
7. **b**
8. **c**
9. **c**
10. **b**

CHAPTER 2

Setting Up a Lab Environment For Nmap

Introduction

As discussed in the previous chapter, Nmap is an active scanner, which means that it is imperative to have permission to scan any systems with it. During each subsequent chapter of this book, we will be exploring numerous different scanning techniques and practicing them through several guided challenges. In order to be able to get hands-on with Nmap (or any other ethical hacking tool), having a lab environment is essential.

While there isn't a single correct way to build a home lab environment, this chapter will guide you through the process of setting up the same lab resources for practicing Nmap that were used to capture all the screenshots within this book. To accomplish this, we will first install Nmap on both a native Windows system and import a Kali Linux virtual machine into Virtual Box. Next, we will set up some additional tools called Legion and Zenmap, which we will explore in *Chapter 6: Leveraging Zenmap and Legion.* With these two systems, we will do the entirety of the scanning within each challenge.

However, the targets of the scans are also important to set up. Continuing to use Virtual Box, we will download several different images that can be turned on and off to provide more diversity in the results of our scans. We will include at least one Windows server and a couple of pre-built virtual machine images commonly used for penetration testing practice.

To take things to the next level, we will also install some open-source security products, such as Wazuh and Snort, which will help us visualize the difference between levels of obfuscation discussed in *Chapter 7: Advanced Obfuscation and Firewall Evasion Techniques.*

NOTE: If you already have a penetration testing lab set up that you are comfortable utilizing, feel free to skip this section and utilize your environment for the subsequent challenges.

Structure

In this chapter, we will explore and answer the following questions:

- What are the Components of a Good Lab Environment?
- How do you Install Nmap, Virtual Box, and Kali Linux?
- How do you Configure Windows and Linux Servers in a Lab Environment?
- How do you Configure an IDS for the Lab?
- How do you Make the Most Out of The Lab?

Components of a Good Lab Environment

Any good lab environment has a couple of things in common. First, it should be versatile, meaning that you can spin up or spin down different devices to simulate different environments and test different techniques. To this end, it is important to have an environment that has both Windows and Linux server infrastructure, along with one or two workstation examples. By far, the most common enterprise environments seen in penetration tests are primarily Windows workstations in an active directory environment, with some Linux servers sprinkled about.

NOTE: You want the lab you set up to be as much as possible a simulacrum of the environments you will target during penetration tests.

In order to accomplish this, we are going to set up a modular environment of **virtual machines (VM)** using Virtual Box. Virtual Box was selected for this walk-through partially because it is free, but mostly because it seems to be the easiest virtualization platform, especially for those new to the technology to set up. That being said, if you are more comfortable using Hyper-V, VMware, or any other form of virtualization, feel free to replicate in the way you find suitable.

However, all referenced hyperlinks within this chapter will direct you to a VM download for Virtual Box specifically.

We will also set up two separate hosts for conducting the Nmap scans: the first being a Windows native environment, and the second being a Kali Linux virtual machine, also hosted within Virtual Box. During penetration testing, most engineers utilize Kali Linux as the go-to operating system for all red-team activities. However, it may come as a surprise for many that a Windows 10 device is typically used, with Kali available as a virtual machine. It has been found that for the vast majority of reconnaissance and enumeration, it is easier to use a Windows device than pivot to Kali for the niche times you need it exclusively.

Recognizing that habit as an exception rather than the rule, the vast majority of scans demonstrated in this book will be conducted from the Kali Linux VM.

To begin setting up your environment, please take note of the following resources, which we will download, install, and configure over the next several pages:

Nmap (Windows)	https://nmap.org/download.html#windows
Virtual Box	https://www.virtualbox.org/wiki/Downloads
Kali Linux	https://www.kali.org/get-kali/#kali-virtual-machines
Wazuh	https://documentation.wazuh.com/current/deployment-options/virtual-machine/virtual-machine.html
Windows Server 2022	https://www.microsoft.com/en-us/evalcenter/evaluate-windows-server-2022

Table 2.1: *Summary of Lab Components*

Installing Nmap, Virtual Box, Kali, and Additional Tools

The foundations of this lab environment are Nmap installed on both Windows and Kali Linux, Virtual Box to facilitate the importing of virtual machines, and the setup up of Kali itself for additional functionality. We will break this down into a series of steps to ensure that there is no confusion in establishing the environment.

1. Navigate to the following link and download the current version of Nmap for Windows under `Microsoft Windows Binaries`: **https://nmap.org/download.html#windows.**

2. Navigate to your downloads folder and run the Nmap setup executable, follow the installation instructions, and confirm success by opening a command prompt and printing the installed version with **`nmap -v`**:

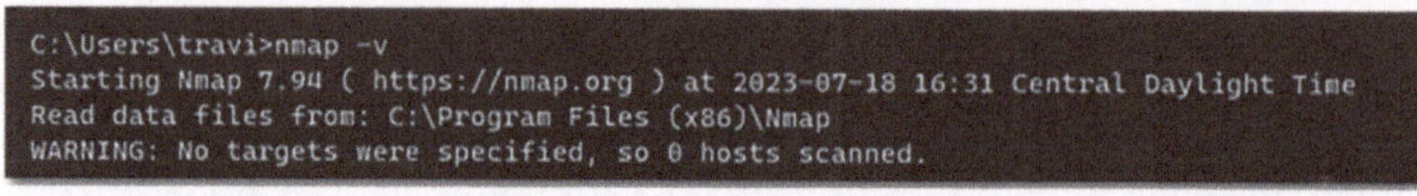

Figure 2.1: *Nmap Versioning*

3. Typically, this download on Windows will also come with Zenmap, which you can confirm by searching **"`zenmap`"** in the Windows Explorer search bar. Zenmap is a very handy **Graphical User Interface (GUI)** that works in tandem with Nmap, which we will explore in later chapters. For now, confirming that it is installed is sufficient:

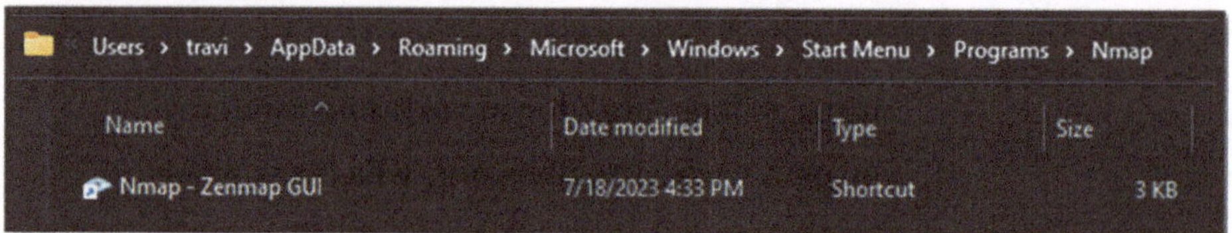

Figure 2.2: *Zenmap Download*

Next, we will import the latest version of Kali into Virtual Box. The team at Offensive Security frequently updates Kali Linux, so if your version is slightly different from the one provided in these examples, there's no need to worry. The steps are as follows:

1. Navigate to **https://www.kali.org/get-kali/#kali-virtual-machines** and download the VirtualBox option. It should be around 2.7 GB in size and will download as a .7z file.
2. Download and install 7zip at the following: **https://www.7-zip.org/download.html.**
3. Next, download and install Virtual Box for free at **https://www.virtualbox.org/wiki/Downloads.**

4. Extract the Kali Linux download using 7zip and double-click the `Virtual Box Machine Definition` file to import it into Virtual Box:

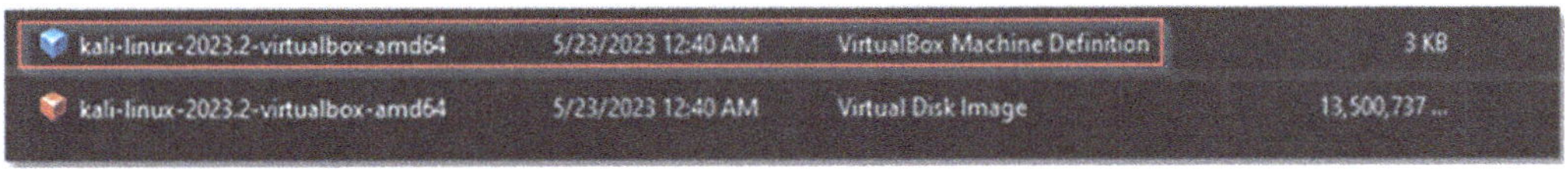

Figure 2.3: *Demonstrating Kali Linux VM Configuration (1 of 4)*

5. Right-click on the Kali machine in Virtual Box and select **`Settings`**. Go to **`System`** and adjust the Base Memory from the default of 2048 to at least 4096MB. If you have additional resources available, it is beneficial to allocate additional memory, but as a minimum, we recommend 4Gb:

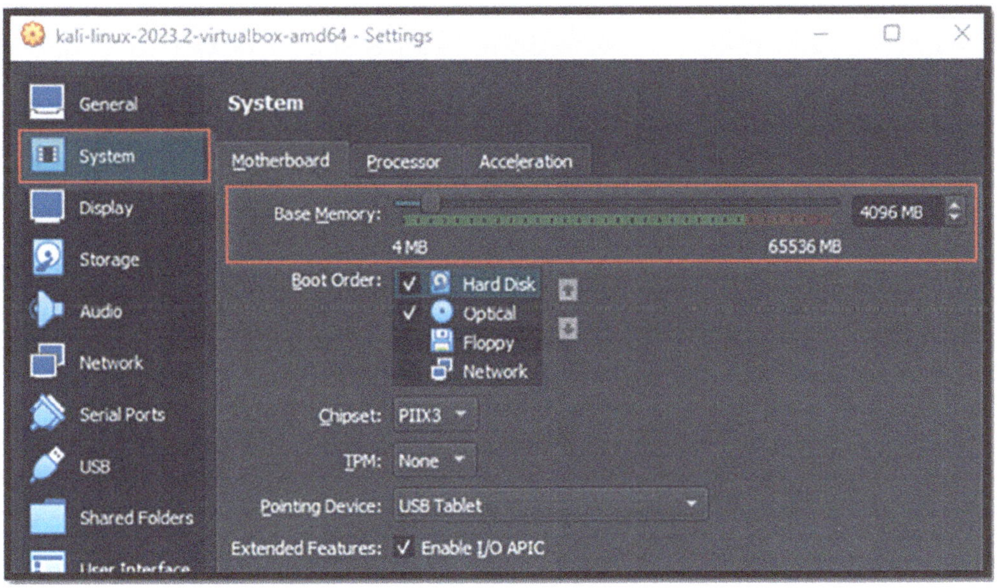

Figure 2.4: *Demonstrating Kali Linux VM Configuration (2 of 4)*

6. Now, we need to create the virtual network where we will put all of our lab machines. To do this, navigate within the Virtual Box console to **`File`** > **`Tools`** > **`Network Manager`**. From here, select the **`NAT Networks`** tab, create a new network, name it `Nmap Lab,` and enable **`DHCP`**:

Figure 2.5: *Demonstrating Kali Linux VM Configuration (3 of 4)*

7. Return to the Kali VM's settings in Virtual Box, select Network, and under **`Adapter 1`**, select **`NAT Network`** (Not the option that just says NAT); then select the drop-down for **`Advanced`** options and allow **`Promiscuous Mode`**:

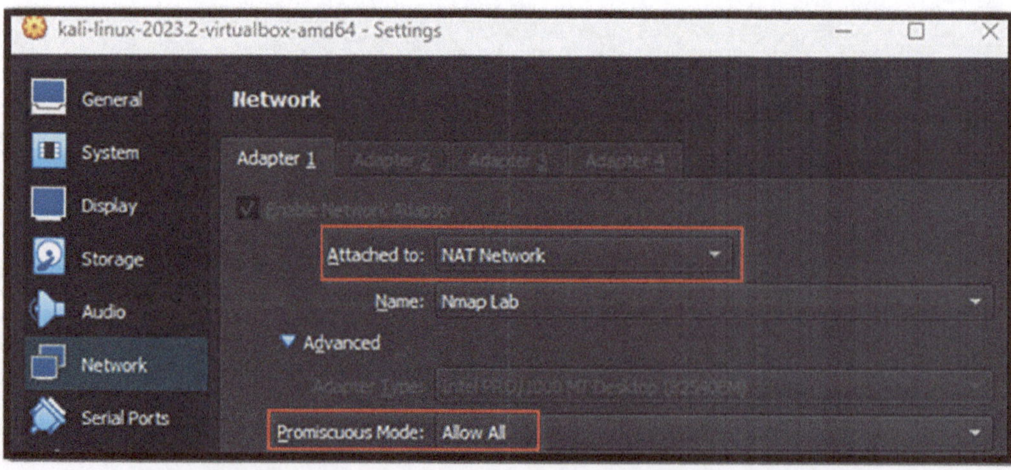

Figure 2.6: *Demonstrating Kali Linux VM Configuration (4 of 4)*

8. Boot the Kali machine by selecting start (the default credentials are kali : kali) and confirm connectivity with your local network with the `ifconfig` command. You are looking to confirm that the Kali VM has gotten an IP address on the same local subnet as your host computer:

9. Verify that you can access the host machine by running Ipconfig on the Windows Host and taking note of the IP address. Next, in the command line on the Kali machine enter:

```
> ping [host IP]
```

10. You should receive a response similar to as follows:

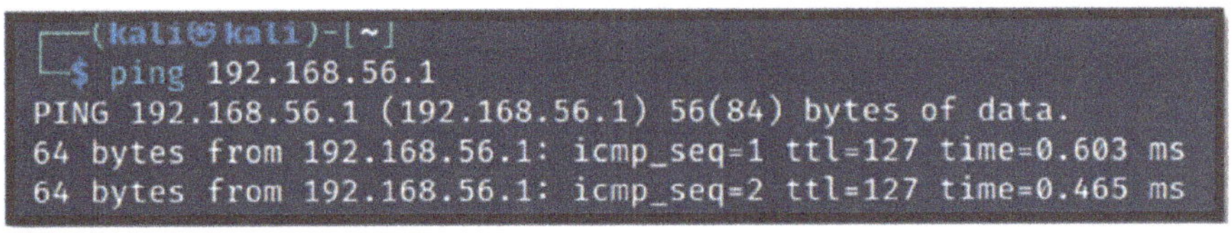

Figure 2.7: *Confirming Network Connectivity via ICMP*

11. You may further confirm connectivity to the host with a very simple **Nmap** command:

```
> nmap -Pn [host IP]
```

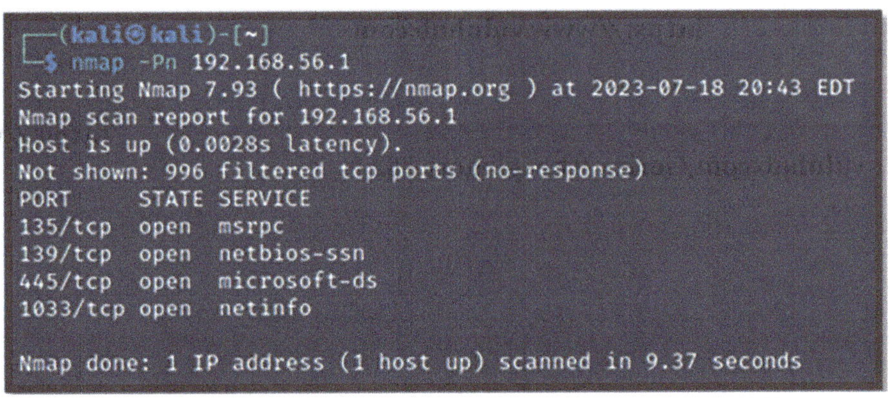

Figure 2.8: *Confirming Network Connectivity via Nmap*

12. Finally, confirm that Legion is installed on the Kali instance by simply opening a command prompt and entering sudo legion. This should open a graphical user interface automatically, as it is a default installation within Kali. However, if for any reason Legion doesn't open, it can be manually installed from GitHub at **https://github.com/GoVanguard/legion.**

13. Similar to Zenmap, Legion is a GUI that will be used to organize Nmap data in later chapters. However, it is distinct from Zenmap in the sense

that Legion provides extensive flexibility in adapting it to fit your specific needs during a penetration testing engagement. It is a highly versatile tool that when combined with advanced Nmap skills can be a powerful asset to any pentester.

At this point, we have successfully set up our scanning hosts. One is a Windows machine with Nmap and Zenmap installed, while the other is a Kali Linux VM with both Nmap and Legion confirmed as installed. From these two endpoints all scanning, examples, and challenges will be possible throughout the entirety of the book.

Setting Up the Target Servers

With the scanners set up, we next have to configure a series of targets for those scans. In the interest of making the lab environment simple yet practical, we will be importing several different VMs to replicate server infrastructure that you may see on real-world penetration tests. Servers of both the Windows and Linux variety will pose not only a diverse target pool for scans but will also be configured with some specific software that will be used in follow-on lab exercises.

Linux

1. Navigate to **https://www.vulnhub.com.** This is a great site for finding and downloading intentionally vulnerable virtual machines to practice your pentesting or capture-the-flag skills. For now, download the zip file for the boxes called The Planets: Earth and Mercury at **https://www.vulnhub.com/series/the-planets,362/**
2. Once unzipped, you will find an `Open Virtualization Format` files, which when double-clicked should import the VM directly into Virtual Box.
3. Open the settings of the new Linux VMs and set the `Network Adapter 1` to `NAT Network: Nmap Lab`.
4. Since these capture the flag (CTF) challenge boxes, you will not have login credentials to sign in. Instead, we need to be creative to determine the IP address. Since we know that they are on the same virtual network as our Kali VM, we have a couple of options. But considering that this is a book all about Nmap, we will simply scan the virtual network for hosts with Nmap:

```
>nmap T5 10.0.2.0/24
```

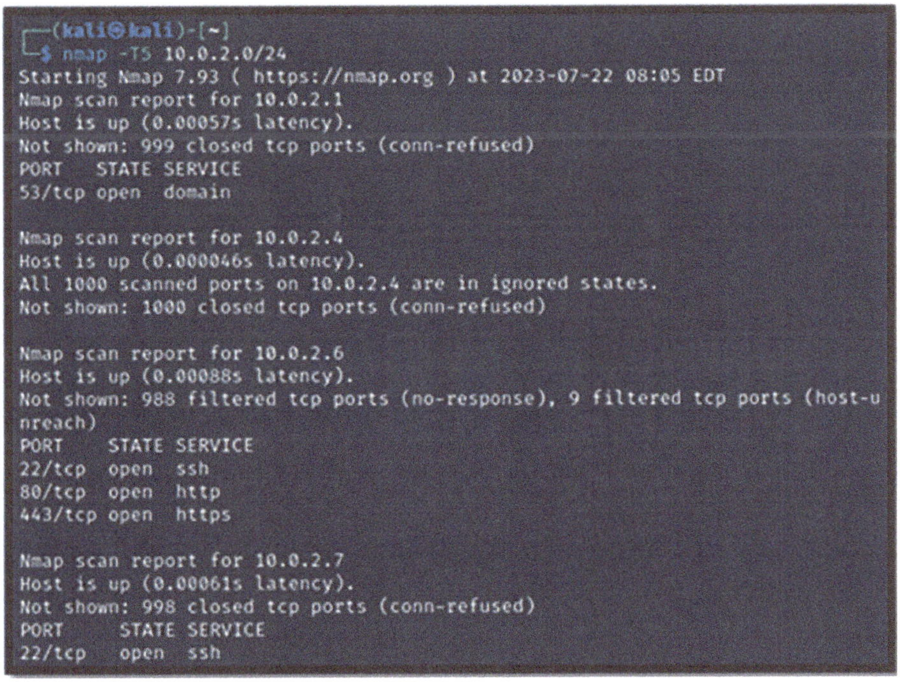

```
┌──(kali㉿kali)-[~]
└─$ nmap -T5 10.0.2.0/24
Starting Nmap 7.93 ( https://nmap.org ) at 2023-07-22 08:05 EDT
Nmap scan report for 10.0.2.1
Host is up (0.00057s latency).
Not shown: 999 closed tcp ports (conn-refused)
PORT   STATE SERVICE
53/tcp open  domain

Nmap scan report for 10.0.2.4
Host is up (0.000046s latency).
All 1000 scanned ports on 10.0.2.4 are in ignored states.
Not shown: 1000 closed tcp ports (conn-refused)

Nmap scan report for 10.0.2.6
Host is up (0.00088s latency).
Not shown: 988 filtered tcp ports (no-response), 9 filtered tcp ports (host-u
nreach)
PORT    STATE SERVICE
22/tcp  open  ssh
80/tcp  open  http
443/tcp open  https

Nmap scan report for 10.0.2.7
Host is up (0.00061s latency).
Not shown: 998 closed tcp ports (conn-refused)
PORT     STATE SERVICE
22/tcp   open  ssh
```

Figure 2.9: *Nmap Scanning of the Subnet*

Here, we can see that there are four identified endpoints on this virtual network. The default gateway, 10.0.2.1, can be ignored. We can confirm through the ifconfig command that 10.0.2.4 is the Kali VM we are scanning from (thus, no ports are being reported). Therefore, 10.0.2.6 and 10.0.2.7 must be the Earth and Mercury virtual machines.

Windows

1. With a Linux server successfully configured, we will now install a Windows server. The easiest way to do this is to utilize Microsoft's official evaluation center and select a trial of Windows Server 2022 at: **https://www.microsoft.com/en-us/evalcenter/evaluate-windows-server-2022.** Download the 64-bit ISO file in your language of choice.
2. Create a new VM in Virtual Box and select Windows 10 64-bit as the operating system, but as of now, leave the ISO file empty.
3. Assign a minimum of 2GB of RAM (although if you can spare the resources, 4GB is preferred). Specify VHD as the file type with Dynamic Allocation selected and a 50GB capacity.

4. Once completed, boot the VM and you will be asked to provide a bootable medium, browse to the ISO file and select **"`Mount and Retry Boot`"**:

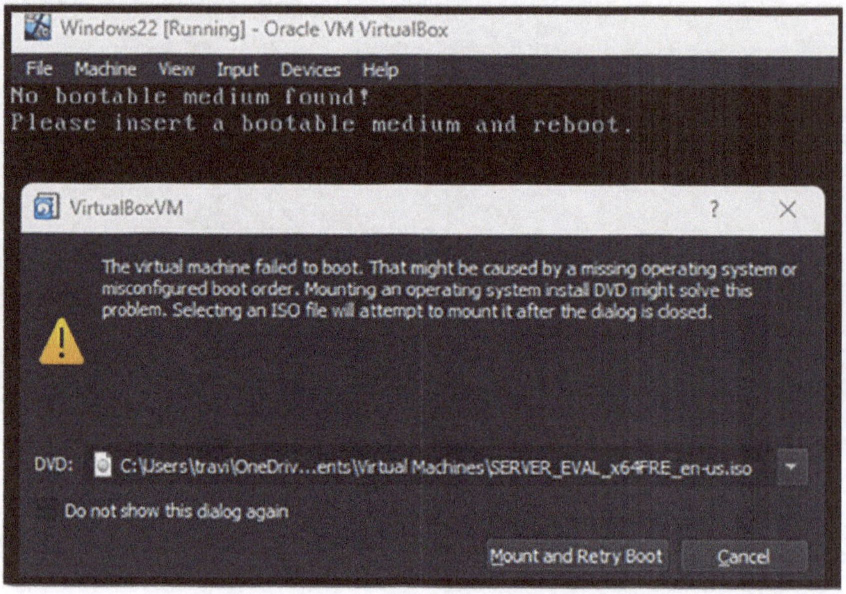

Figure 2.10: *Windows ISO configuration (1 of 3)*

5. Continue the installation process and when prompted to select an operating system, choose "**`Windows Server 2022 Standard Evaluation (Desktop Experience)`**":

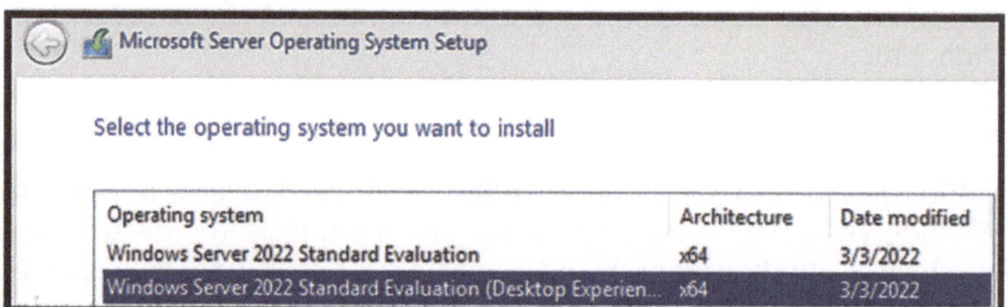

Figure 2.11: *Windows ISO configuration (2 of 3)*

6. Next, we will install an open-source automation server called Jenkins, which is commonly seen in enterprise penetration tests. Specifically, Jenkins is used to automate portions of the building, testing, and deploying processes, which facilitates an important concept called **continuous integration and continuous delivery** (**CICD**) within the **software development lifecycle** (**SDLC**).

7. Jenkins is going to be an important application that we will specifically search for using Nmap later in the book. The installation instructions and Windows download file can be found in Jenkin's official documentation at: **https://www.jenkins.io/doc/book/installing/windows/.**
8. You will most likely also need to install **Java Development Kit** (**JDK**) or **Java Runtime Environment** (**JRE**) during the Jenkins installation process.
9. Once installed, you can confirm that Jenkins is running by checking the Services on the Windows Server as well as navigating to "localhost:8080" in your web browser

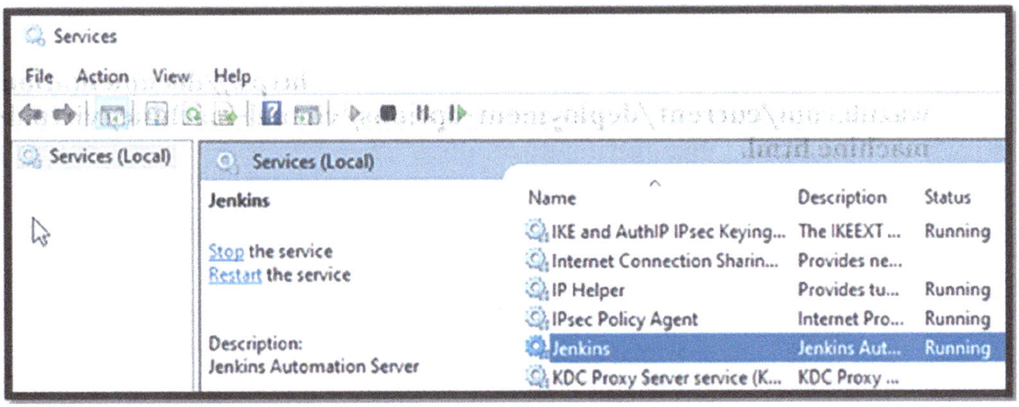

Figure 2.12: *Windows ISO configuration (3 of 3)*

10. Confirm connectivity from the Kali VM by running a default Nmap scan against the Windows Server. You should now see the typical Windows Ports (135, 139, 445, 5357) and the newly added Jenkins Automation Server on port `8080`:

```
┌──(kali㉿kali)-[~]
└─$ nmap 10.0.2.5
Starting Nmap 7.93 ( https://nmap.org ) at 2023-07-22 07:25 EDT
Nmap scan report for 10.0.2.5
Host is up (0.00059s latency).
Not shown: 995 closed tcp ports (conn-refused)
PORT     STATE SERVICE
135/tcp  open  msrpc
139/tcp  open  netbios-ssn
445/tcp  open  microsoft-ds
5357/tcp open  wsdapi
8080/tcp open  http-proxy

Nmap done: 1 IP address (1 host up) scanned in 2.09 seconds
```

Figure 2.13: *Confirming Network Connectivity with Nmap*

Securing the Lab Environment

The final step in setting up our lab at this point will be downloading one more virtual machine. However, instead of purposefully vulnerable machines such as Earth or Mercury, this one will be a security product. We will use Wazuh, which is a completely free and open-source product that has the capabilities of both a **security incident and event management system** (**SIEM**) as well as **extended detection and response** (**XDR**). We will use this as a way to gauge the level of obfuscation during advanced scanning techniques in later chapters.

Anecdotally, Wazuh also makes an excellent security solution to incorporate into your home network. The steps are as follows:

1. To begin, download the prebuilt OVA from **https://documentation.wazuh.com/current/deployment-options/virtual-machine/virtual-machine.html.** Once downloaded, open the OVA file in Virtual Box and select Settings.
2. Under `Network Adapter 1`, set `NAT Network: Nmap Lab`.
3. Under `Network Adapter 2`, set `Bridged Adapter`.
4. Start the Wazuh virtual machine and log in with the provided credentials.
5. Confirm the Wazuh server Ip with the command `ip a`.
6. From any VM in your Nmap Lab network (such as the Windows Server), open a web browser and navigate to the Wazuh Server's IP using HTTPS, and log in with admin/admin:

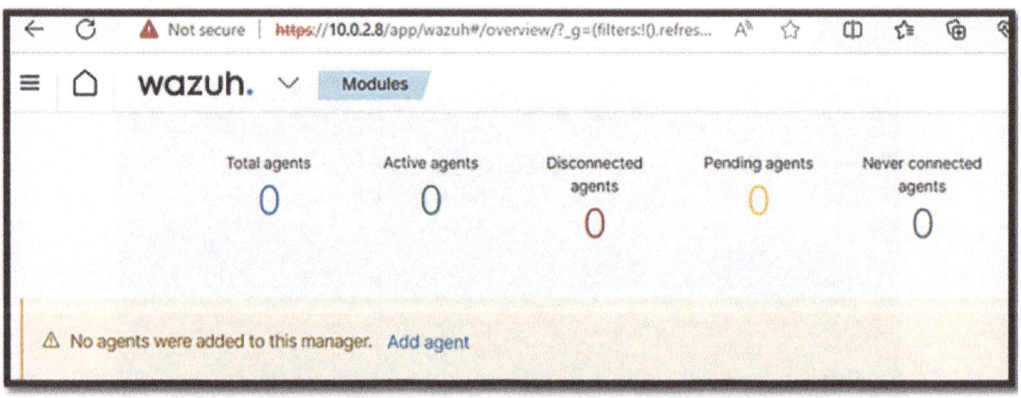

Figure 2.14: *Demonstrating Wazuh Dashboard*

7. From the Add Agent view, select the following options:

   `Windows`

   `Windows Server`

   `i386/x86_64`

   `Add the IP address of the Wazuh Serer (in the preceding example, it would be 10.0.2.8)`

   `Name your agent "WindowsServer2022"`

   `Default group`

8. Next, download the Windows installer package that is provided and then run the generated commands from an administrator PowerShell prompt:

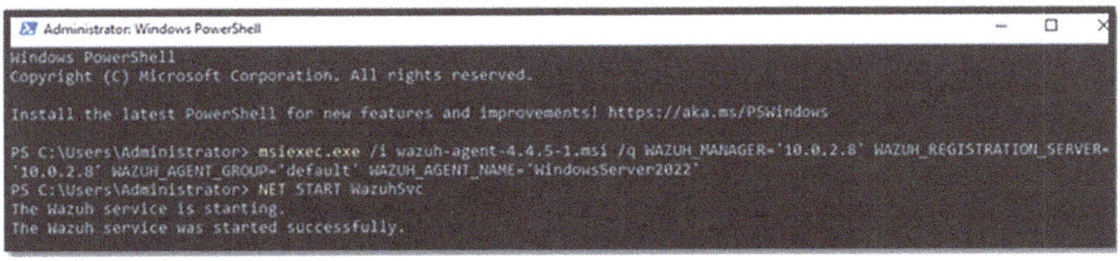

Figure 2.15: *Demonstrating Wazuh Agent Configuration*

9. Refresh the page and you should be able to see the agent listed as active:

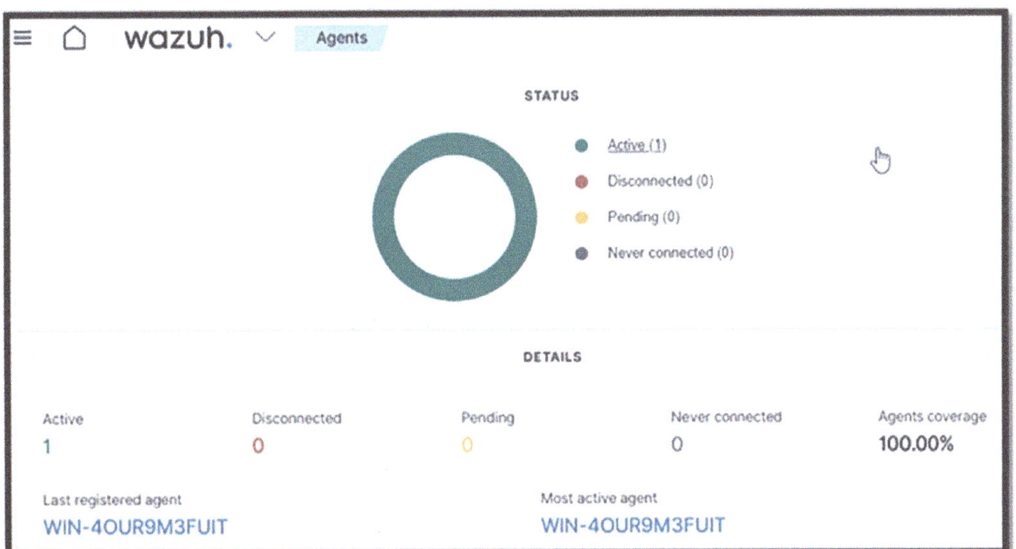

Figure 2.16: *Confirming Agent Connectivity (1 of 2)*

Navigating to the agents interface below should also reflect the newly configured Windows agent:

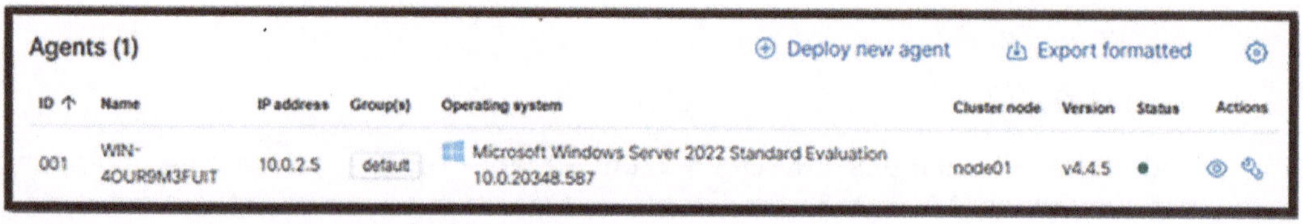

Figure 2.17: *Confirming Agent Connectivity (2 of 2)*

Conclusion

It is a very common, albeit unfortunate, habit for cyber security students to simply read a book, or watch a video, but not practice the techniques themselves. When you see a demonstration, it can appear simpler than it is in practice. If you were to ask a handful of penetration testers how often they have to troubleshoot issues such as installed incorrectly, having dependency issues, or just simply not working as expected, the vast majority would say "every day".

By following along, completing the challenges, and replicating what will be shown over the next several chapters, you will make mistakes, get frustrated, and troubleshoot why things are not working properly. While that isn't the most fun thing at the moment, it is arguably the single most valuable thing you can do to learn a new tool or technique. By forcing yourself out of necessity to dig a little bit deeper, to make sure you have values set properly, and to understand why things are (or are not) coming out as you expect, you will learn in a way that is far more efficient than those who simply read the content.

When most people first start working in cybersecurity, they constantly made the mistake of not doing enough hands-on training. I racked up several degrees and certifications, which helped me learn a lot. However, it was found that whenever something didn't work exactly as expected, I had to seek help from more experienced coworkers. It wasn't until I slowed down on simply ingesting bulk content and spent more time replicating, modifying, and expanding on what I was learning in my lab environment that I truly got comfortable with penetration testing.

So far in the previous chapter, we have touched upon a lot of concepts, learned a lot of definitions, and explored some key differences between security assessments themselves. In this chapter, we built the environment you will need to be successful in working with Nmap and explored all the techniques outlined within the rest of this book. Finally, we are ready to get started.

In the next chapter, we will dive into the basic flags and scans of Nmap and learn about one of the most essential stages of a penetration test – mapping the attack surface. We will discuss what the attack surface is, why it is critical to understand, and how to use Nmap to not only get a snapshot of the attack surface but to maintain an understanding of it over time.

Points to Remember

- Home lab environments are a great way to reinforce the fundamentals of networking by creating and modifying virtual networks.
- By leveraging virtualization technologies such as Virtual Box, Hyper-V, or VMware, you can create modular environments of virtual machines, which can be turned on or off to simulate different scenarios.
- A highly effective lab can be set up for little to no cost. All virtual machines and products outlined in this chapter are free, and the majority of them are open source.
- Cyber security labs do not only have to be focused on penetration testing techniques. By incorporating open-source security products such as a SIEM, IDS, XDR, or Firewall, you can also learn and train on blue and purple team skills.
- Following the techniques and challenges throughout this book in your lab will greatly enhance and reinforce learning.

Challenge 1 - Customize Your Lab

Now that you have seen a few different examples of virtual machines being imported into Virtual Box and configured, the first challenge is to find ways to make the lab even more robust. This is an opportunity for a lot of creativity. Some ideas to get you started could be as follows:

- Download an additional Windows Server and set it up as a Domain Controller for a small Active Directory environment. Active Directory is a massively popular service and will come up in nearly all internal penetration testing engagements. Understanding its intricacies isn't within the scope of Nmap or this book specifically, but is certainly worth considering.
- Configure a LAMP server. This is a popular server configuration that stands for Linux Apache MySQL and PHP. These are another type of server that would be seen fairly often during engagements. In addition, configuring them from scratch is a great way to brush up on your Linux skills.
- Add and configure a firewall. There are many options, but pfSense is recommended. It is a great, free, and open-source firewall with robust features to experiment with.

Multiple Choice Questions

1. **Which of the following is not a virtualization platform?**
    a. Jenkins
    b. Virtual Box
    c. VMware
    d. Hyper-V
2. **Wazuh is an example of which of the following?**
    a. IPS
    b. Firewall
    c. SIEM
    d. Scanner
3. **Jenkins is a popular open-source tool used for what?**
    a. Hosting a website over HTTPS
    b. Facilitating continuous integration and continuous development in the SDLC
    c. Monitoring network traffic for malicious activity
    d. Conducting static application security testing during the SDLC
4. **Which of the following would be a good place to look for free virtual machines designed for penetration testing techniques to be tested on?**
    a. Exploit-db.com
    b. Vulnhub.com
    c. Kali.org
    d. Nmap.org
5. **Which file type is also known as disc images?**
    a. ps1
    b. bat
    c. 7z
    d. Iso

Answers

1. a 2. c 3. b 4. b 5. d

CHAPTER 3
Introduction to Attack Surface Mapping

Introduction

An intricate understanding of the attack surface is core to any assessment of an organization's security posture. The attack surface is something all organizations have and constantly seek to understand, both from the perspective of the red team trying to find and exploit points of weakness and the blue team seeking to defend the perimeter. While this term is thrown around a lot in cyber security training content, let's take a moment to dig into what it means. The National Institute of Standard and Technology (NIST) offers the following definition in Special Publication 800-53 "Security and Privacy Controls for Information Systems and Organizations":

"The set of points on the boundary of a system, a system element, or an environment where an attacker can try to enter, cause an effect on, or extract data from, that system, system element, or environment."

While that does provide a comprehensive and academic explanation, let's look at the idea of an attack surface from a slightly different perspective. Consider your home with all of the possible ways a would-be robber might attempt to break into it. You likely have a few doors and windows, that's obvious; but what about all of the other systems that may lead to a break-in? Do you have a garage with an automatic garage door? That is a system that could be targeted. Do you have a remote garage door opener on the sun visor of your car that is parked in the driveway? Wouldn't a broken car window then lead to the garage door being opened and a robber having a way into the house?

Here we took a simplistic view of only a couple of elements of a potential attack surface, but in reality, the attack surface of your home is far more complex than the majority of people realize. Not only do you have to consider the physical risks of a robber kicking down the door (a metaphorical brute forcing attack), but there are also the less thought technical considerations.

In 2021, I moved into a new home and installed a remote baby monitor in my daughter's room; a pretty simple piece of technology that simply allowed me to monitor for sound and use my phone to get a live feed of her in the crib. After a few weeks, I was curious about the technical attack surface of my new home, so I employed a few different tools. I did some basic Wi-Fi pentesting to test the wireless security, I audited the settings of my router, and I used Nmap to scan my network both from the inside and the out. The decision to scan my network proved to be worthwhile, as I discovered that the new baby monitor had Telnet open.

For those not familiar, Telnet is an ancient and inherently flawed protocol from the early 1970s which allows for remote connection and configuration of systems. What makes this protocol problematic, and an easy target for both penetration testers and malicious actors, is that the vast majority of telnet implementations lack authentication, and the data is not encrypted in transit. This provides a perfect target for a man-in-the-middle attack as anybody on the network could simply use an analyzer, such as Wireshark, and intercept the data. A more secure protocol for a similar function to Telnet would be Secure Shell or SSH.

Seeing Telnet open on the device made me curious about what other security issues might be present on my Internet of Things (IoT) devices, and indeed, I found several other issues I was not aware of with these seemingly simple products, including known vulnerabilities or other inherently weak protocols in use.

The exercise of mapping my personal attack surface was eye-opening and led to me making some very different decisions about what devices I allowed on my network, how I secured and segmented my home network, as well as specific firewall rules I put in place as a result.

Organizations do the same thing, just on a larger scale. As NIST explained, the attack surface is about identifying the boundaries of an environment (application/network/facility, and so on) and pinpointing where a malicious actor may attempt to target in an attack. While this seems like a very obvious thing, akin to making sure you do not have a gaping hole in your fence line, in reality, it can be very challenging for organizations that are complex or experiencing a period of rapid growth.

I have dealt with client organizations that have less than 25 employees, and for them, the attack surface from an external (internet-facing) position is usually quite minimal. It might include a website or two, perhaps a web or mobile application, and their Microsoft Office environment, but not much else. For those organizations, attack surface mapping is easier, though no less important. Contrary to that, I have also had clients with over 30,000 worldwide locations and hundreds of thousands of systems, and countless applications. For organizations like that, the attack surface is so large that it can be overwhelming for the defenders while giving the attackers an advantage.

The attack surface of an organization is important to understand from the point of view of a pentester. You need to understand what you are attacking before you can decide how to attack it. But from the defensive perspective, it is just as important; because without truly understanding all of the possible attack points of the organization, how could you properly deploy the necessary security controls?

In this chapter, we are going to dive deep into understanding the attack surface from the perspective of a penetration tester. Next, we will take the first real steps into Nmap by discussing common flags and scan types and demonstrating in the lab environment how they can be used to map the attack surface both as an attacker and a defender. Finally, we will look at a real-world case study of a relatively small business blue team, that I have worked with, who make excellent use of Nmap to keep their finger on the pulse of organizational changes.

Structure

In this chapter, we will discuss the following topics:

- Understanding Attack Surfaces
- Stages of Penetration Tests
- Fundamental Nmap Flags
- Leveraging Nmap to Map the Attack Surface
- Case Study – Continuous Attack Surface Monitoring of a Small Business
- Challenge – Get Hands-on With Basic Scans
- Challenge – Map the Attack Surface of Your Home Network

Understanding Attack Surfaces

It is often easier to consider multiple different attack surfaces when assessing an organization. For example, each web or mobile application has its own set of unique functions, and from that perspective, would have its specific attack surface. Similarly, on the network side, you will often hear attack surfaces defined as either external or internal as a way of providing more context and focus to the discussion.

External, in this sense, means that it is the attack surface of the organization from outside of their network. In other words, if a remote attacker was doing reconnaissance on the organization from the internet, any websites, VPNs, or other systems would collectively be the external attack surface.

Internal, then, means what an attacker would be able to target from inside the company's network. This could have occurred from a malicious actor who exploited an external vulnerability and gained access to internal systems. But it could also be a disgruntled employee who has easy and legitimate access to the network. It could even be from somebody in the waiting room connecting to the guest Wi-Fi network.

Many organizations have a security posture that resembles the defenses of a turtle. They have a hard-secure shell from the outside, complete with email security solutions to prevent phishing, firewalls, and robust monitoring solutions. But once that shell is cracked, the defenses tend to be far less formidable. While every organization is different, it is easy to understand in general why the external threats would elicit the most investment, both in terms of time and resources. However, given that there are so many different ways to gain a foothold in an internal network, great care must be given there too.

Many organizations have some degree of understanding of their attack surface. They likely have a list of resources, IP addresses, and hostnames, and update that list regularly as systems are routinely spun up or decommissioned. Where organizations sometimes lack specific insight, and why penetration testing is so important, is that there isn't always a real understanding of what ports are open and what services are running on every device. Even if there is a networking understanding, there isn't always an understanding of why some ports and services could be problematic.

One extremely common high-severity vulnerability observed when conducting internal pentests in enterprise environments is port `4786` being open on older Cisco Catalyst switches. Port `4786` is associated with a protocol called Cisco Smart Install, which is a *plug-and-play* protocol used for configuring the device. It also has a very significant vulnerability (CVE-2011-3271), which allows a malicious actor to very easily obtain the configuration file to the device and make changes to it, effectively taking over a critical piece of network infrastructure. This is a vulnerability that will typically get exploited within the first few hours of a pentest.

You may be thinking, why would a vulnerability from 2011 still be commonly present more than a dozen years later? Well, because outdated hardware is still in use in a very widespread way. Technical debt has built up for many organizations over the years when security wasn't prioritized as a critical aspect of the business, and it was challenging for IT and security leaders to get the budget allocation to replace things that were technically still functional.

The shift to the cloud, more servers being cloud-based virtual machines, and the expanding presence of infrastructure as code practices are certainly starting to change this paradigm. But as the saying goes, it takes a long time to turn an aircraft carrier.

Stages of Penetration Tests

A good penetration test is conducted predictably and aligned to known standards and frameworks. This helps ensure that the tester is professional and thorough, as well as provides a way to effectively communicate the process to clients. Two of the more common standards for pentesting include:

- Penetration Testing Execution Standard (**http://www.pentest-standard.org/index.php/Main_Page**)
- NIST SP 800-115: Technical Guide to Information Security Testing and Assessment (**https://csrc.nist.gov/pubs/sp/800/115/final**)

Several frameworks describe the stages of a cyber attack from the perspective of a malicious actor, which can be extremely useful to ensure that accurate and realistic tactics techniques and procedures are being followed. Among these frameworks, we will be focusing on the two most well-known:

- Lockheed Martin Cyber Kill Chain (**https://www.lockheedmartin.com/en-us/capabilities/cyber/cyber-kill-chain.html**)
- MITRE ATT&CK Framework (**https://attack.mitre.org/**)

Each of these resources may use different language and terms for describing the process of a penetration test, but they all generally follow the same core steps, including:

- Conducting reconnaissance
- Exploiting an identified vulnerability to establish an initial foothold

- Establishing persistence on target systems and environment
- Escalating privileges, evading defenses, and conducting lateral movement
- Establishing command and control
- Exfiltrating data and impacting systems

While the terminology used may vary, the idea that you inherently have to start with reconnaissance to understand the target and map their attack surface before progressing into any degree of exploitation is consistent.

The framework preferred to align with is MITRE ATT&CK. The most common component of this framework is an in-depth matrix of **advanced persistent threat** (**APT**) tactics and techniques against enterprises. MITRE ATT&CK is found out to be far more nuanced and detailed in breaking down very specific techniques than the others, which tend to be more high-level. Additionally, a lot of enterprise security products, such as Rapid7 Insight IDR and Microsoft Defender, also map security alerts to MITRE ATT&CK, making it a very well-known, and often requested, framework to use.

Looking at the Matrix for Enterprise, we can see that under the very first tactic, Reconnaissance, there are ten techniques. The first is active scanning, which then has three sub-techniques: Scanning IP Blocks, Vulnerability Scanning, and Wordlist Scanning. Nmap can and often be utilized for each one of these sub-techniques, making it often one of the very first tools utilized by malicious actors and penetration testers.

Fundamental Nmap Flags

We established in *Chapter 1: Introduction to Nmap and Security Assessments* that you can run Nmap without any additional commands (except for the target of course) and expect to determine which of the top 1,000 most common TCP and UDP ports are open. But to do anything more intricate than that, we will have to incorporate additional arguments into the scan called flags. It is important to understand that the flags and their use cases we will go over here are in no way a replacement for the official reference guide (**https://nmap.org/book/man.html**), which will cover many more in great detail. Instead of reinventing the wheel, we are going to focus initially on the 10 flags that are used mostly for simple attack surface analysis during penetration tests.

1. `-sV`: This flag enabled service version detection on the ports that respond as open. Meaning, that in addition to seeing that port `80` is open on a web server, you may also get additional information, such as whether it

is an Apache, Nginx, or IIS web server, as well as what version it is. This additional information can help you determine not only the technology being used in an environment but also start to determine if there are vulnerabilities associated with those services and versions:

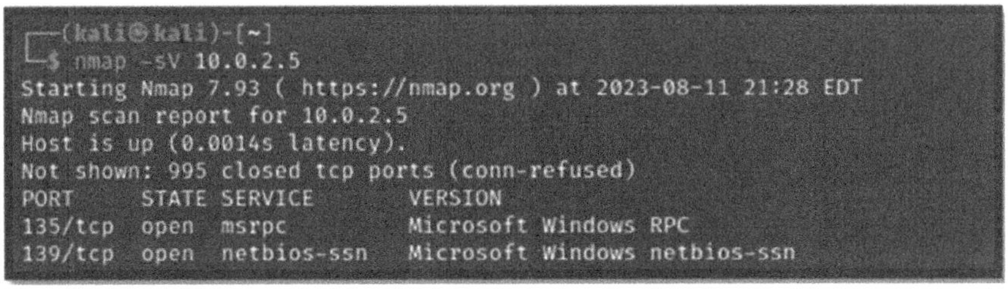

```
┌──(kali㉿kali)-[~]
└─$ nmap -sV 10.0.2.5
Starting Nmap 7.93 ( https://nmap.org ) at 2023-08-11 21:28 EDT
Nmap scan report for 10.0.2.5
Host is up (0.0014s latency).
Not shown: 995 closed tcp ports (conn-refused)
PORT     STATE SERVICE      VERSION
135/tcp  open  msrpc        Microsoft Windows RPC
139/tcp  open  netbios-ssn  Microsoft Windows netbios-ssn
```

Figure 3.1: *Service versioning scan*

2. **`-A`**: This flag enabled operating system detection as well as service versioning on the host. A simple way to remember this one is "**A**" is for "All". You get all the port, service, versioning, and operating system information that Nmap can identify at once:

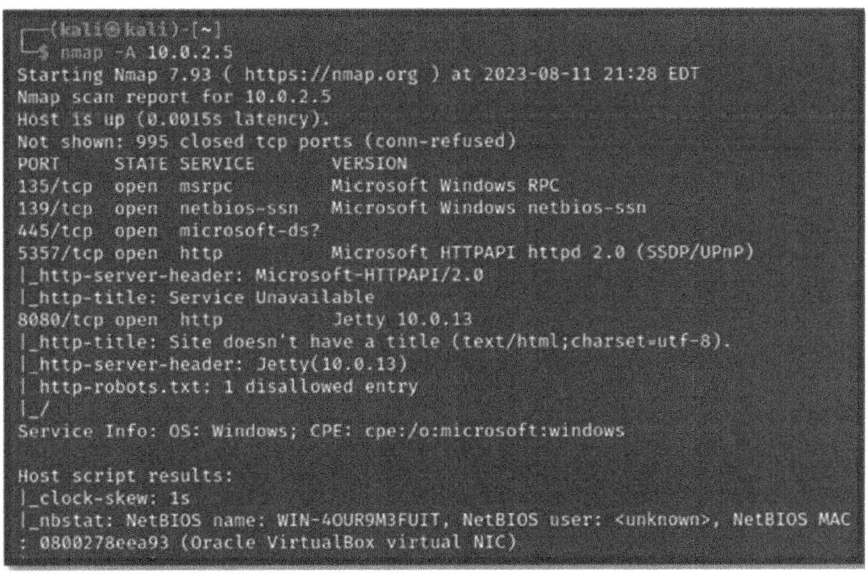

```
┌──(kali㉿kali)-[~]
└─$ nmap -A 10.0.2.5
Starting Nmap 7.93 ( https://nmap.org ) at 2023-08-11 21:28 EDT
Nmap scan report for 10.0.2.5
Host is up (0.0015s latency).
Not shown: 995 closed tcp ports (conn-refused)
PORT     STATE SERVICE      VERSION
135/tcp  open  msrpc        Microsoft Windows RPC
139/tcp  open  netbios-ssn  Microsoft Windows netbios-ssn
445/tcp  open  microsoft-ds?
5357/tcp open  http         Microsoft HTTPAPI httpd 2.0 (SSDP/UPnP)
|_http-server-header: Microsoft-HTTPAPI/2.0
|_http-title: Service Unavailable
8080/tcp open  http         Jetty 10.0.13
|_http-title: Site doesn't have a title (text/html;charset=utf-8).
|_http-server-header: Jetty(10.0.13)
| http-robots.txt: 1 disallowed entry
|_/
Service Info: OS: Windows; CPE: cpe:/o:microsoft:windows

Host script results:
|_clock-skew: 1s
|_nbstat: NetBIOS name: WIN-4OUR9M3FUIT, NetBIOS user: <unknown>, NetBIOS MAC
: 0800278eea93 (Oracle VirtualBox virtual NIC)
```

Figure 3.2: *Service, operating system, and versioning scan*

There are a couple of things to note with `-A`, which are as follows:

- It is redundant and provides more information than `-sV`. It means that there is no reason to combine these flags. The same goes for `-O`, which is operating system versioning; while that flag exists, it is rarely used, as `-A` is considered be a far better alternative.

- It is a much slower scan than `-sV` because it enumerates so much more information. That is why both `-sV` and `-A` are listed here. There will be times when the service versioning information is enough, and you need to speed over the additional information.

3. `-T`: T stands for time; it is the speed at which the scan is conducted, and it comes in six variations, ranging from T0, which is extremely slow, to T5, which is extremely fast. Appropriately, the default of Nmap (if you do not specify otherwise) is T3, quite fast. Depending on if you need to worry about being too noisy and getting detected, or being too aggressive on the network, you may want to manually adjust the speed. I will typically use T2 during most engagements that are not extremely large.

   I recommend experimenting with this, the difference between each of the T-levels is dramatic. In a quick test of scanme.nmap.org with no other flags, you will find that T3+ will complete in probably less than three seconds, but anything below T2 will take several minutes. Depending on your situation, the size of the attack surface, and the length of time you have to scan, it may necessitate adjusting the speed.

4. `-v`: V stands for verbosity; this is a common argument you will find in tools and simply makes the output that is displayed more verbose. It adds additional details to the output and is paired very well with either `-sV` or `-A`. There are also three levels of verbosity: `-v`, `-vv`, and `-vvv`. The more Vs that are added, the more verbose the output will be, but also the longer the scan will take. I have personally rarely found it helpful to use more than a single v when leveraging this flag:

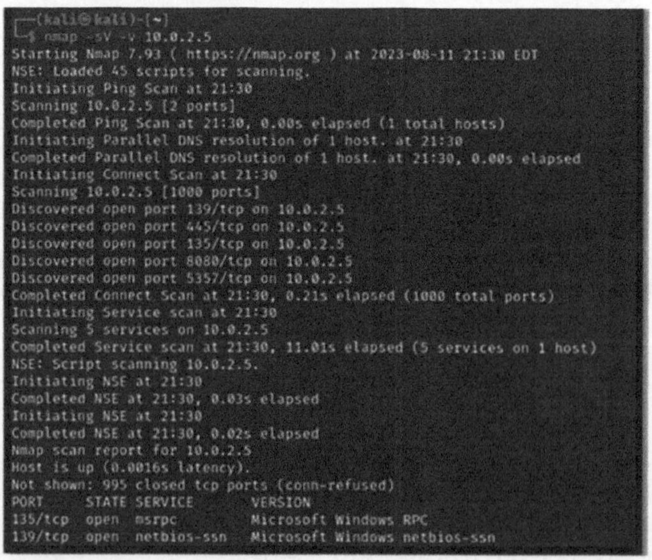

Figure 3.3: *Demonstrating service versioning with verbosity*

5. **-iL**: This flag is "in list", and it is essential for anybody conducting a penetration test of a complex environment. This allows Nmap to read the target list from a txt file rather than scanning one entry or range in the command line. Imagine an engagement where you have dozens if not hundreds of individual external domains and IP addresses; you can put them all into a simple txt file and Nmap will sequentially scan them all at once for you:

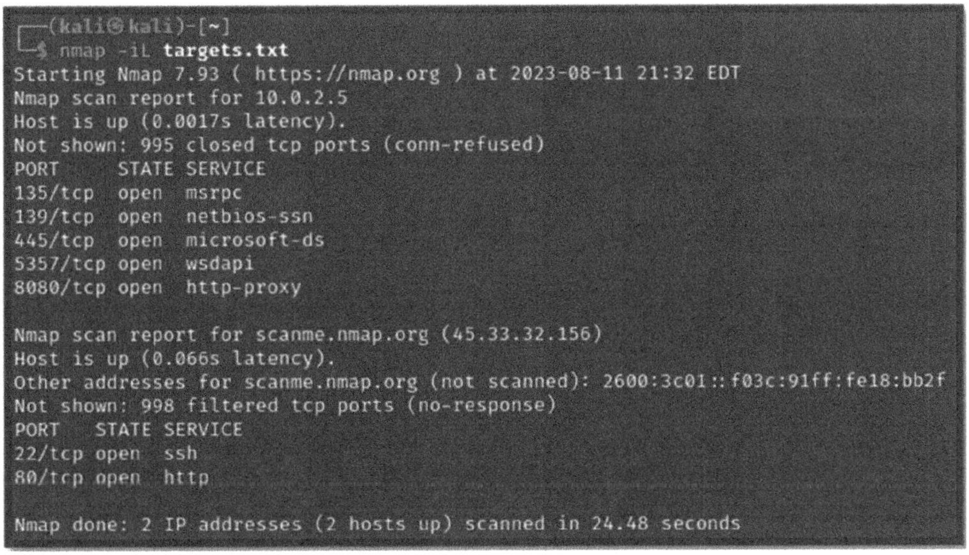

Figure 3.4: *Scanning multiple targets from a source file*

6. **-oX**: This is for Output. There are several options available to save the output to a file, which can be referenced later: `-oG` for Greppable output, `-oN` for normal output, there is even `-oS` for a comical Script Kiddie output riddled with misspellings and crazy capital letters. But I tend to use `-oX`, which outputs to an XML format that is easily imported into additional tools such as Zenmap and Legion.

   Whichever output you prefer (or use `-oA` for all of them), it is strongly recommended to save the output files of your scans so that they can be referenced later. The last thing you want is to spend six hours running a scan overnight just to have the command prompt closed due to the system restarting and losing all of that data. Always save your work.

7. **-p**: P stands for Port. You can specify specific ports that you want to scan that are single, in ranges, or comma-separated like so:
   - `-p 80` (only port 80)
   - `-p 80-443` (every port between 80 and 443)
   - `-p 80,440` (only ports 80 and 443)

This is extremely useful when you are looking for something specific or are just trying to speed up a scan and want to reduce the number of ports from the default of 1,000 down to a handful of the most likely. As additional notes, you can also use -F (fast) to reduce from the top 1,000 to the top 100, or use --allports to scan all 65,535 ports. Keep in mind, scanning tens of thousands of ports does tend to increase the length of the scan fairly significantly.

8. **-sU**: This flag specifies scanning UDP ports as opposed to TCP. When you use the **-p** command, by default, Nmap will assume you mean TCP port X. There may be times when you are explicitly looking for UDP, however, and would need to specify that. One example is if you are looking for the IPMIv2 protocol, which can be hosted on either TCP or UDP port 623. In this instance, you would want to make sure that you check both options, or you could potentially miss a critical vulnerability.

9. **-open**: This flag filters the response and only shows you ports that respond as being "**open**" on the target hosts. This is great for reducing the noise and lengthy output of scans, as well as looking for something specific. Rather than scanning 255 hosts looking for port 4786 (**nmap -p 4786 10.0.0.0/24**) and then having to scroll through all 255 responses to see which ones say "**closed**" and which say "**open**", this flag can be used to do that sorting for me. This is a huge time saver and quality-of-life improvement.

10. **--reason**: This is a flag that most people have never heard of, but it can be really helpful in determining what is going on. It shows the reason why each port is being reported the way that it is. If you are seeing a lot of ports open and they are all coming back Filtered, this is a great flag to add on and rescan the target. While it cannot magically change the status to open, it can display the type of packet that was received from the port when the connection was made:

```
┌──(kali㉿kali)-[~]
└─$ nmap -Pn 192.168.56.1 --reason
Starting Nmap 7.93 ( https://nmap.org ) at 2023-08-11 21:37 EDT
Nmap scan report for 192.168.56.1
Host is up, received user-set (0.0012s latency).
Not shown: 997 filtered tcp ports (no-response)
PORT    STATE SERVICE      REASON
135/tcp open  msrpc        syn-ack
139/tcp open  netbios-ssn  syn-ack
445/tcp open  microsoft-ds syn-ack

Nmap done: 1 IP address (1 host up) scanned in 10.11 seconds
```

Figure 3.5: *Including the reasoning behind the port responses*

There are many more advanced flags we will cover in the following several chapters ,which will incorporate different syntax and naming conventions. While you will naturally start to memorize them with experience, A quick reference guide of all the flags and descriptions we go over in all chapters have been included as an appendix at the end of this book. By strategically combining just these flags, you can efficiently enumerate a lot of information about the systems and, by extension, the attack surface that you are targeting.

Leveraging Nmap to Map the Attack Surface

Internal and external network pentests are the types of security engagements you will most likely be conducting when using Nmap for widespread attack surface mapping. While we have discussed several other use cases for red and purple teaming, we will focus this section on the traditional network pentesting.

Depending on the engagement and the client's preferences you may be provided a full list of IP addresses and domain/subdomains that make up the scope of the test; or, you may be provided only the name of the company and will have to find the assets that they own yourself. The latter is commonly referred to as a *black box* pentest, meaning that you are fully emulating a malicious actor who when targeting an organization has to do all the reconnaissance themselves. In this scenario, there are a couple of things that you will want to do before Nmap gets involved, namely, identifying the systems, domains, and subdomains, which need to be assessed.

Typically, the process begins with subdomain enumeration of the organization's main domain utilizing OWASP Amass (**https://github.com/owasp-amass/amass**), which is **an open-source intelligence** (OSINT) tool designed to aid in external asset discovery:

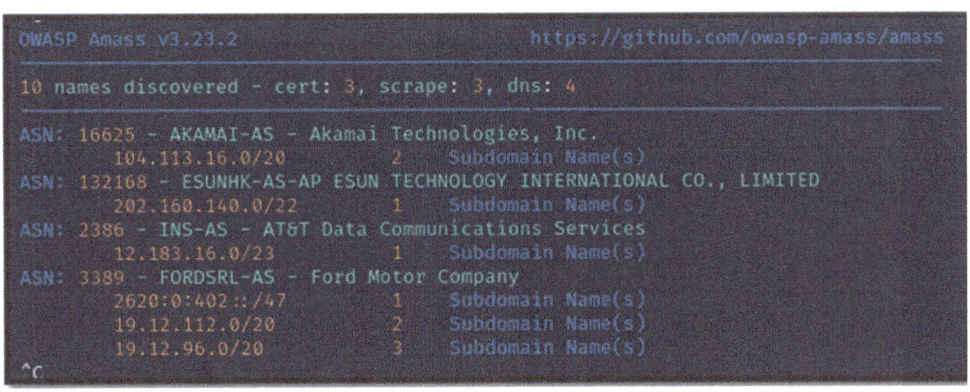

***Figure 3.6**: Demonstrating OWASP amass for subdomain enumeration*

A second tool that is worth utilizing as well is **https://crt.sh**, which looks up subdomains based on the TLS certificates being used:

crt.sh ID	Logged At ⇧	Not Before	Not After	Common Name	Matching Identities
2382034419	2020-01-27	2013-06-25	2016-06-25	fraaa300.nls.ford.com	fraaa300.nls.ford.com
2381949685	2020-01-27	2015-02-08	2015-12-01	www.teamcenter2pdcloc1.ford.com	teamcenter2pdcloc1.ford.com wwwdr.teamcenter2pdcloc1.ford.com www.teamcenter2pdcloc1.ford.com
2381929050	2020-01-27	2013-04-10	2016-04-10	sghaa300.nls.ford.com	sghaa300.nls.ford.com
2381858210	2020-01-27	2014-11-22	2015-11-23	www.teamcenterfoa1pe1.ford.com	teamcenterfoa1pe1.ford.com www.teamcenterfoa1pe1.ford.com
2381858367	2020-01-27	2012-05-27	2015-05-27	www.teamcenterfoe1pe1.ford.com	www.teamcenterfoe1pe1.ford.com
2381715172	2020-01-27	2014-11-24	2015-11-25	www.wsle.ford.com	q1.ford.com wsle.ford.com wwwmg2.wslb2be.ford.com wwwmg2.wslb2b.ford.com wwwmg2.wsle.ford.com wwwmg2.wsl.ford.com

Figure 3.7: *Demonstrating crt.sh for subdomain enumeration*

While the output of both of these tools will often be very much the same; there can occasionally be some important targets that are picked up by one instead of the other. In both cases, this is considered passive reconnaissance as no direct connections are being established.

Once the two outputs are generated, the easiest way to deduplicate them is to paste both lists into Microsoft Excel (or something similar) and use the `deduplicate` function. Now, you have a much more robust set of targets than the main domain name.

Next, take this consolidated list of targets and create a txt file for Nmap to use. In this case, we will use the Nano command and name this as "`targets.txt`":

```
┌──(kali㉿kali)-[~]
└─$ nano targets.txt

┌──(kali㉿kali)-[~]
└─$ cat targets.txt
q1.ford.com
wsle.ford.com
wwwmg2.wslb2be.ford.com
wwwmg2.wslb2b.ford.com
wwwmg2.wsle.ford.com
wwwmg2.wsl.ford.com
www.password.ford.com
www.wslb2be.ford.com
www.wslb2b.ford.com
www.wsle.ford.com
www.wsl.ford.com
```

Figure 3.8: *Creating and reading a target file*

Now we can start to utilize Nmap to dive into the hosts both collectively as well as individually. The strategy tend to be used for this is to first scan the entire target list, looking for ports typically open during this type of engagement. This approach is far quicker and less overt to scan a handful of ports individually rather than the top 1,000 on every host. Then, once the results are analyzed and interesting endpoints are found, the focus will be for more in-depth scans on those devices:

Remember a penetration test is not designed to find every possible vulnerability that exists. The goal is to compromise the external attack surface, gain a foothold on the internal environment, and demonstrate the potential impact of a malicious actor.

```
Nmap -A -T2 --open -p 21,22,25,80,110,179,443,8080,8443 -iL targets.txt
-oX results1.xml
```

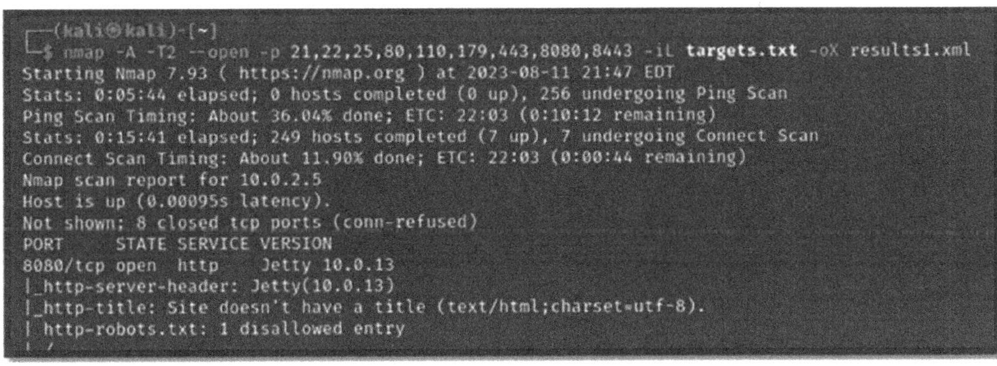

***Figure 3.9**: Initial scan demonstration*

Let's break down what that scan is doing flag by flag:

Flag	Function
`-A`	Fingerprint the operating system and all services and versions
`-T2`	Slow scanning speed
`--open`	Only show results for ports that are returned in the open state
`-p`	A numerical list of the ports to be scanned (refer to *Table* 3.2)
`-iL`	Supplying the targets list "`targets.txt`"
`-oX`	Directing the output to also be piped to the file `results1.xml`

***Table 3.1**: Basic Nmap Flags*

Additionally, we strategically specified several individual ports with the `-p` flag:

Port	Protocol
`21`	FTP – File Transfer Protocol
`22`	SSH – Secure Shell
`25`	SMTP – Simple Mail Transfer Protocol
`80`	HTTP – Hypertext Transfer Protocol
`110`	POP3 – Post Office Protocol version 3
`179`	BGP – Border Gateway Protocol
`443`	HTTPS – Hypertext Transfer Protocol Secure
`8080`	Alternate port for HTTP
`8443`	Alternate port for HTTPS

***Table 3.2:** Basic port to protocol mapping*

These ports can be logically put into three main categories to identify the most commonly seen systems that are externally exposed:

- Web Servers (80,443,8080,8443)
- Mail Servers (25,110)
- File Transfer Servers (21,22)
- Networking Misconfiguration (179)

While these are where I tend to start, remember that it is a starting point only. To conduct a professional quality penetration test, you have to be very thorough and meticulous about details; scanning the entire scope for additional less common ports and services will come after the initial analysis is complete.

As you comb through these results, there are a few key things that you want to be looking for that will help you identify the CPE of each endpoint:

- Specific operating system and version
- What the system is likely used for
- Specific services running on the ports and their associated versions

This is the point where your research skills will become critical to your success as a penetration tester. You will need to systematically determine what vulnerabilities (CVEs) are known that are associated with both the endpoint itself (operating system) and any of the services running on that endpoint. To this end, there are a few great resources that can help you along the way:

Resource	Purpose
Cvedetails.com	This is a free-to-use repository of information on known CVEs, which allows you to search by the CVE ID, product title, vendor, or even vulnerability type.
Cisa.gov	The United States Cybersecurity Infrastructure and Security Agency has a robust database of known exploited vulnerabilities. Once you have identified a vulnerability through cvedetails.com or any other means, this is a great place to check and see if that vulnerability has been exploited in the wild.
Exploit-db.com	This is a database of known exploits, which can be searched by title, system, or CVE ID. Once you have identified an applicable CVE and confirmed that it is being exploited in the wild, this is one area to look into the exploit code.

Table 3.3: *Key resources*

A common question I get asked is, why does it matter if the vulnerability is exploited in the wild? This is somewhat of a philosophical question, but to keep it brief, malicious actors are most often looking for targets of opportunity, not focusing intently on one single organization. During pentests, you are emulating a hacker of moderate sophistication, not a nation-state that has a strategic interest in compromising a very specific system or organization. Most malicious actors will attack the easiest targets rather than investing great sums of time or money into developing a cutting-edge zero-day exploit for a vulnerability that has never been seen before. Taking that one step further, you will find that a large number of known CVEs do not have associated exploits with them; they are essentially theoretical vulnerabilities. This is an important distinction when mapping the attack surface because you need to consider what your potential targets for exploitation are going to be. A high-severity vulnerability that has no known exploit and CISA has never observed it being used by a malicious actor has less value to you as a penetration tester than a moderate-severity issue with known proof of concept exploits that you can leverage.

Don't get me wrong, there are excellent security researchers and pentesters out there who will develop their custom exploits for vulnerabilities that they identify, and that is commendable. But in the scenario of a pentest, you are time bound to have a 1-3 week window where you will have a large number of systems to analyze. It may come to a point where you need to build a custom exploit, but considering the time investment that comes with it, it is best to build out the full attack surface and first determine if there is an easier way.

With the initial group of systems identified you will want to create a second list of targets to dig deeper into the ones that seem to be the most interesting in terms of having outdated services or operating systems. Separating these systems into a `targets2.txt` file, we can then take some of the restrictions off of the scan profile to dig deeper:

```
Nmap -A --version-intensity 9 --allports --open -iL targets2.txt -oX results2.xml
```

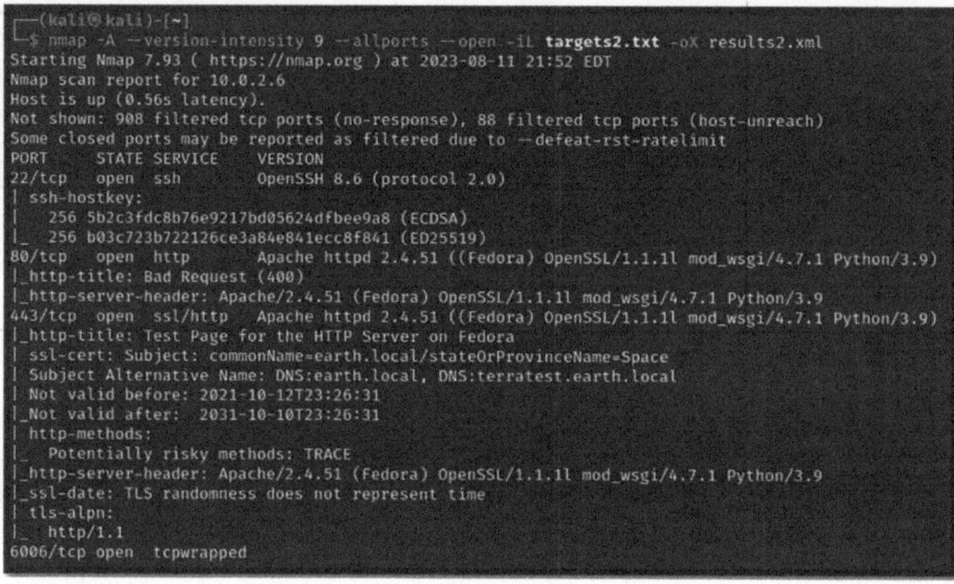

Figure 3.10: *Secondary scan demonstration*

There are two additional flags here not yet discussed: version intensity and all ports. The latter is quite obvious as the "`all ports`" flag simply directs Nmap to query every TCP port that exists. The "`version-intensity`" flag however is slightly more nuanced. Version-intensity is an option that can be given a numerical value from 1 (least intense) to 9 (most intense), which will increase the likelihood of successfully versioning the service at the expense of taking longer to scan.

A default Nmap version scan (`-sV`) will be using a version-intensity rating equivalent to 7, so opting for a lesser value will increase the speed of the scan at the potential cost of detail, while increasing the value to 8 or 9 will have the opposite effect. As an additional note, you can also use the `--version-all` flag as a shorthand alias for "`version-intensity 9`".

This far more in-depth scan of the identified hosts can then be analyzed further to identify first the CPE and then any associated CVEs, allowing you to systematically map the attack surface. This is not unlike how enterprise vulnerability scanners operate to determine the presence of vulnerabilities; however, where you have the edge as a penetration tester is the human ability to consider the context of the whole attack surface when making an assessment.

Vulnerability scanners are very susceptible to both false positive and false negative findings. Any experienced pentester you ask would have countless stories of their vulnerability scanner telling them there is a critical vulnerability in an Apache web server only to find out it was actually Nginx all along. While these systems are getting better with each iteration, and the increased prevalence of artificial intelligence integrations is accelerating this process, the necessity for a discerning professional eye is unlikely to fade anytime soon.

Case Study – Continuous Attack Surface Monitoring of a Small Business

One of my favorite clients I have ever done a penetration test for was a small business of about 20 employees in the financial services sector. Over a couple of years, I did several engagements with them (external pentests, internal pentests, social engineering, and so on), and their security team (of only two people) was always extremely engaged in the process and interested in how the testing was done. At one point, we had the opportunity to train them on some of the red-team tools that were utilized in the engagements; naturally, Nmap was one of them.

As you might guess, with such a small security team, there wasn't a huge budget for enterprise-grade vulnerability management tools, but instead, they got creative with Nmap and used a very simple set of commands to accomplish a few very important things.

First, they built a process with documentation, laying out a few very specific scans that they would run every other Friday. By establishing the process and meticulously documenting how it is meant to run, they were able to keep it regimented and effective.

- They scanned every subnet they had on their internal network, as opposed to just the IP addresses that they knew about. This way, if there were any unexpected "new" devices on the network, they would be able to identify them. This was also a way for them to identify new vulnerabilities.

- They scanned every externally accessible domain and asset the company owned for ports, services, and vulnerabilities.

- They would output the results to XML files, and analyze them for any week-to-week changes using Zenmap.

What was clever about this is that the scan that they used was the same for both internal and external scanning, only the target list had to change. This made it very quick and easy for them to get into the routine of keeping their finger on the pulse of their organization's attack surface.

This is the scan that they used:

```
nmap -A -v -T2 --open --vulners.nse -iL [Internal or External Target List]
-oX [month] [Internal or External]_nmap_results.xml
```

> **I am not claiming Nmap is a replacement for an enterprise solution for continuous vulnerability management solution. But in an instance where budgetary constraints prevent such a purchase, Nmap can be an effective stop-gap measure at zero cost.**

Before utilizing Nmap, they had very little insight into what resources were even externally accessible, let alone specific vulnerabilities associated with them. This additional insight into their attack surface let the security team more aware of their security posture and allowed them to more strategically allocate the resources at their disposal to strengthen that posture.

Challenge 1 - Getting Hands-on with Basic Scans

In this chapter, we have explored a dozen different flags and discussed some use cases for basic scans from an enterprise perspective. Utilize your lab environment to first recreate each of the scans that were demonstrated in this chapter. Next, consider ways to modify some of the scans in your lab environment to elicit different results. While the information necessary can be found in this chapter, don't be afraid to refer and dive into the official documentation at **https://nmap.org/book/man.html**.

Try to accomplish the following with some basic scans:

1. Add additional verbosity beyond `-v`
2. Adjust the speed of the scan by reducing the complexity of service versioning and timing
3. Experiment with outputting different file types
4. Scan specific ports, the top 1000 ports, and all ports on your lab machines

Map the attack surface of the systems in your lab, take note of the CPE of each system, and research any known CVEs associated with them.

Challenge 2 - Map the Attack Surface of Your Home Network

Now that you have some familiarity with Nmap and mapping the attack surface of a lab environment; it is an opportune time to apply this skillset to your life by mapping your personal home network's attack surface. This can most simply be done by scanning the subnet of your main computer (assuming you have not established network segmentation on your home network).

As discussed in the introduction of this chapter, a very similar exercise was eye-opening for me and helped me identify a very troubling security issue with my baby monitor. Perhaps, you will find some similarly concerning items, or (hopefully) confirm the secure state of your network.

As you assess your network's attack surface, consider the following questions:

- Which systems would a malicious actor be most likely to target?
- How can you improve the security of the network? (adding an IDS, Segregating the network, Restricting outbound traffic)
- Are there any systems on your network that you cannot identify?

Add the port TCP 1883 to the scan of your home network. This port is associated with MQ Telemetry Transport (MQTT), which is a lightweight communication protocol very common in IoT devices and is not included in the top 1000 most common ports that a default Nmap scan would pick up.

Conclusion

The ability to accurately and efficiently map an attack surface is essential for a successful penetration tester. While Nmap is not the only tool that is used in the process, it can be a powerful asset for adding important context to the bigger picture. As we have seen, the versatility and power of Nmap truly come alive when leveraging multiple flags in tandem to fine-tune the individual scans.

Attack surface mapping is not only critical for a penetration test but is also a very helpful skill for a blue team cyber security professional. Being able to understand how a malicious actor would analyze an organization or network and try to identify points of weakness will inherently lead to a better understanding of how to protect against such techniques.

This chapter concludes what would generally be considered "basic" Nmap techniques. In the subsequent chapters, we will quickly progress into intermediate and advanced tactics and techniques to fully leverage the capabilities of Nmap in a professional penetration test. To that end, it is highly recommended that you take your time in practicing with the lab environment to build your comfort level with the tool and the basic flags that were discussed in this chapter before progressing to ensure a strong foundation is established.

In the next chapter, we will continue to build on this foundation and dive deeper into using Nmap to identify specific vulnerabilities in systems through in-depth reconnaissance and enumeration techniques. Through additional case studies, more intermediate-level flags, and intricate versioning techniques, we will cover both system fingerprinting and vulnerability analysis in far greater detail.

By the end of the next chapter, you will be going beyond simply mapping the attack surface of your lab environment and home network, and instead identifying specific vulnerabilities that could be exploited against those systems. You will become comfortable researching, confirming, and prioritizing what vulnerabilities to focus on, and perhaps most importantly, how to communicate that information to clients.

Points to Remember

- Everything has an attack surface: every application, every network, and every organization. The attack surface simply refers to the systems or platforms a malicious actor could potentially target for exploitation.

- Mapping an attack surface is the first step to understanding how to allocate resources and properly defend it.

- Nmap is extremely versatile and can be magnified in capacity by utilizing specific commands (flags), in tandem with one other. By strategically leveraging different flags at different times, you can use Nmap for multiple purposes during the attack surface mapping process.

- Focus first on identifying the most interesting or unique systems on the perimeter, then utilize more intricate and in-depth scans to further fingerprint that system.

- A high-severity vulnerability that has no known exploit and CISA has never observed it being used by a malicious actor has less value to you as a penetration tester than a moderate severity issue with known proof of concept exploits that you can leverage.

Multiple Choice Questions

1. **Which of the following flags would be best used to identify both the operating system and the services running on open ports?**
    a. `-A`
    b. `-sV`
    c. `-sU`
    d. `-iL`
2. **Attack surface mapping often begins with organizational reconnaissance of a root domain. Which of the following tools would be best utilized for subdomain enumeration?**
    a. Nmap
    b. OWASP Amass
    c. Metasploit
    d. BurpSuite
3. **An Nmap scan specifying only "`-sV`" will conduct service version enumeration equivalent to what version-intensity rating?**
    a. 2
    b. 5
    c. 7
    d. 9
4. **A default Nmap scan executes at a speed equivalent to which `-T` specification?**
    a. T-2
    b. T-3
    c. T-4
    d. T-5
5. **What flag would you use to output scan results to a .xml file?**
    a. `-oX`
    b. `-oT`
    c. `-oA`
    d. `-oAll`

6. **The following two scans will return the same results. True or false.**

```
Nmap -sV 10.0.0.1 -p 80,443 --open -v
Nmap --open -v -sV -p 80,443 10.0.0.1
```

   a. True
   b. False

7. **This US-based organization maintains a database of known exploited vulnerabilities.**
   a. CIA
   b. CISA
   c. OWASP
   d. MITRE

8. **Which of the following is NOT a port commonly associated with web services?**
   a. 80
   b. 443
   c. 8080
   d. 1883

9. **A ______ pentest describes a scenario in which the penetration tester is emulating a malicious actor who when targeting an organization has to do all the reconnaissance themselves.**
   a. White Box
   b. Black Box
   c. Gray Box

10. **Which is a database of known exploits that can be searched by title, system, or CVE id.**
   a. Exploit-db.com
   b. Cisa.gov
   c. Owasp.org
   d. Attack.mitre.org

Answers

1. a	2. b	3. c	4. b	5. a
6. a	7. b	8. d	9. b	10. a

CHAPTER 4

Identifying Vulnerabilities Through Reconnaissance and Enumeration

Introduction

In the previous chapter, we took a deep dive into how to map an attack surface to understand what systems, ports, and services are exposed within a specified scope. In this chapter, we will take that concept one step further and identify not only the specifics of the endpoints themselves but also how to identify legitimate vulnerabilities that can be exploited.

A penetration test or red teaming engagement has a lot of similarities to a military operation, in that success or failure is often based on the quality of the intelligence available before direct action. The US Army leverages an intelligence cycle which consists of five main (very simplified) phases, including:

1. **Planning**: Identify the final objective and what assets are available to work with.
2. **Collection**: Deploy assets to collect information.
3. **Processing**: Process that information into meaningful intelligence.
4. **Analysis and Production**: Aggregate sources of intelligence and analyze them together to understand the bigger picture, then produce an intelligence estimate of the situation.

5. **Dissemination**: Provide the commander with the final intelligence estimate and recommendations.

Again, this is a very simplified description of a very complex discipline, but the basic structure of the concept is very applicable. To apply this to offensive security, we can consider it this way:

1. Plan the engagement and define the scope.
2. Map the attack surface.
3. Analyze the attack surface to identify applicable vulnerabilities.
4. Conduct targeted exploitation of vulnerable systems.
5. Produce and deliver the final report.

To put it another way, this chapter is going to focus on the reconnaissance, weaponization, delivery, and exploitation phases of the Lockheed Martin Cyber Killchain. To map this to the MITRE ATT&CK framework that would be reconnaissance, resource development, and initial access.

Regardless of the framework utilized, this is the crucial part of a penetration test where you as a cyber security professional have to identify what systems have vulnerabilities and which systems can be practically exploited within the rules of engagement. This is both the most important part of a high-quality pentest and the part that gets the least attention from training materials.

Imagine a situation where a large company pays over $50,000 for a penetration test, only to suffer a data breach due to a malicious actor exploiting a system that wasn't even mentioned in the report, only a month later. Unfortunately, things like this do happen in the industry and it can seriously impact the reputation of your organization. While there are times when a breach is caused by a bleeding edge zero-day exploit like Log4Shell (CVE 2021-44228), which would likely not have been picked up in a pentest before disclosure; most of the time the breach stems from well-known and preventable vulnerabilities.

While it isn't the purview of a penetration test to identify and catalog every single vulnerability on every single in-scope system, it is the responsibility of the tester to ensure no stone goes unturned in identifying the most critical potential attack vectors. This is where the quality of the reconnaissance comes into play.

Through this chapter, we will build on the foundational Nmap knowledge to better understand CPEs and CVEs and how to identify them with custom Nmap scripts, intermediate-level flags, and innovative reconnaissance techniques. We will discuss enumerating systems specifically to identify actionable vulnerabilities, how to research those vulnerabilities, and identify known exploits. We will also analyze a case study that walks through the thought process and strategy of conducting the reconnaissance phase of a network pentest on a medium-sized business and provide two challenges to get hands-on practicing these skills.

Structure

In this chapter, we will discuss the following topics:

- Common Platform Enumeration and Common Vulnerabilities and Exposures
- Introduction to Nmap Scripting Engine
- Intermediate Nmap Flags
- System, Service, and Operating System Enumeration
- Vulnerability Scanning with Nmap
- Case Study – Real-World Internal and External Penetration Test
- Challenge – Fingerprinting Vulnerable Systems
- Challenge – Home Network Vulnerability Scanning

Common Platform Enumeration (CPE) and Common Vulnerabilities and Exposures (CVE)

Common Platform Enumeration (**CPE**) is a standardized way of encoding names of IT products and platforms, which is maintained in a dictionary format by NIST. This convention may seem somewhat confusing at first as the format is really designed to be read and understood by automatable software and hardware inventory management systems rather than rapidly read by engineers. The format of the newest version of CPE (version 2.3) was outlined in the NIST interagency report 7695 as follows:

```
Cpe:[cpe_version]
ype]:[vendor]:[product]:[version]:[update]:[edition]:[language]
```

With this in mind, let's look at the following CPE from the NIST National Vulnerability Database (nvd.nist.gov) for version 3.4.1 of Apache Airflow Providers Microsoft MSSQL:

```
cpe:2.3:a:apache:apache-airflow-providers-microsoft-mssql:3.4.1
```

While it is fairly human-readable, the good news is that many programs and tools, including Nmap, will attempt to identify the CPE through numerous means and output, the most likely result in a far more readable form. To accomplish this, Nmap will combine dozens of operating system versioning and service versioning techniques, which include (among many others):

- Analyzing the TTL of ICMP responses
- Analyzing TCP ISN sampling
- Analyzing IP ID sampling
- Analyzing service headers

With this information, Nmap then queries both the nmap-services and `nmap-os-db` databases, which have a repository of CPEs that are associated with specific indicators. If Nmap is not able to determine a service, operating system, or full CPE, a hyperlink is even provided in the output, so that users may report the correct information (if they can verify it). Considering these databases are in large part community-driven and always expanding, it is yet another reason to ensure you are utilizing the most up-to-date version of Nmap possible.

Experienced penetration testers would caution you to never trust the output of one tool as the complete truth. Nmap is very good at a lot of things, but there have been many instances during penetration tests where experienced engineers have fallen down a rabbit hole due to a mis-enumerated system.

One recent example was a system I was analyzing for a client that Nmap insisted was a Windows 2012R2 server, which reached the end of its life in October of 2023. In reality, that system turned out to be a Windows 2016 server which was fully patched. In my experience, Nmap may not always be 100% accurate on specific versioning, but it does usually get quite close, which still provides a lot of context of the environment.

The next step is to identify the relevant **common vulnerabilities and exposures (CVEs)** that are associated with the established CPE. The concept of CVEs was originally proposed in 1999 and by the early 2000s was in widespread use with adoption by NIST for US government agencies and in 2002 with SP 800-51. Over time, more and more major corporations worldwide began reporting CVE IDs upon discovery of new vulnerabilities to ensure cyber-defenders worldwide had access to the pertinent information as soon as possible. Another critical added benefit is that having a common identifier for a specific vulnerability allows security professionals in different organizations to more easily collaborate on, research, and discuss those unique vulnerabilities.

Vulnerabilities is another word that is used frequently in the information security industry and can have different meanings based on context. When discussing

CVEs always consider the following definition of a vulnerability taken directly from cve.org:

"*A weakness in the computational logic (e.g., code) found in software and hardware components that, when exploited, results in a negative impact to confidentiality, integrity, or availability. Mitigation of the vulnerabilities in this context typically involves coding changes, but could also include specification changes or even specification deprecations (e.g., removal of affected protocols or functionality in their entirety).*"

As briefly discussed previously, the presence of a CVE on a specific system or software does not necessarily mean that it can be meaningfully exploited, it simply means that a security researcher or organization has identified a weakness. While some CVEs such as 2019-0708 (also known as BlueKeep) represent an critical remote code execution vulnerability in some legacy Windows systems that can very easily be exploited; most CVEs do not have nearly as high of a potential impact or ease of exploitation.

To gauge the legitimate impact of a CVE and to aid in prioritizing remediation efforts, many organizations will use what is called the **Common Vulnerability Scoring System** (**CVSS**). The CVSS is a method of qualitatively measuring the severity of a vulnerability from 0 (no impact) to 10 (critical). CVSS is owned and maintained by FIRST, which is a US-based non-profit organization focused on aiding security and incident response teams worldwide. While a 1 to 10 scoring range may seem simple, the calculation is actually quite complex and takes into account many aspects such as attack complexity, impact on the CIA, what privilege level is required for exploitation, and many more.

While the CVSS score certainly is very widely used, one criticism of the system is that it lacks context into the potential impact of the vulnerability. Take for example, two different CVEs with the same CVSS rating of 9.8:

1. **CVE 2018-0171**: A remote code execution in Cisco IOS and IOS XE software that can be exploited to take over networking devices.
2. **CVE 2018-12671**: A remote information disclosure that exposes the password sets within an IP-based camera.

While both of these are individually very severe vulnerabilities that allow a remote attacker to effectively gain control over a device; the real impact to the organization is substantially different. A malicious actor taking over networking equipment such as switches can lead to a devastating cascading compromise of the network, whereas a malicious actor gaining access to a security camera feed is comparatively quite insignificant. The disparity of context regarding practical impact is something to always keep in mind when utilizing CVSS scores.

Introduction to Nmap Scripting Engine

Among the most powerful features Nmap has to assist you in enumerating CPEs, identifying CVEs, and even in some cases exploiting systems is the **Nmap Scripting Engine (NSE)**. This feature enables users to create custom scripts written in Lua. It is no exaggeration to say that there are hundreds of NSE scripts that have been open-sourced and are readily available, the majority of which are included in a database that is available by default when you install Nmap.

While some of the scripts are fairly complex and sophisticated in their functioning, utilizing them is extremely simple, as you just specify the "`--script`" flag followed by the name of the NSE script. To get additional insight into what the script does before running it, using the `-script-help` command is extremely helpful.

In the following example, we can see that the script `vulners.nse` takes the available CPEs and makes a request to the vulners.com API to retrieve and print out information on specific vulnerabilities along with the CVSS score:

```
C:\Users\travi>nmap --script-help vulners.nse
Starting Nmap 7.94 ( https://nmap.org ) at 2023-08-18 21:08 Central Daylight Time

vulners
Categories: vuln safe external
https://nmap.org/nsedoc/scripts/vulners.html
  For each available CPE the script prints out known vulns (links to the correspondent
 info) and correspondent CVSS scores.

  Its work is pretty simple:
  * work only when some software version is identified for an open port
  * take all the known CPEs for that software (from the standard nmap -sV output)
  * make a request to a remote server (vulners.com API) to learn whether any known vul
ns exist for that CPE
  * if no info is found this way, try to get it using the software name alone
  * print the obtained info out
```

Figure 4.1: *Displaying the functionality of vulners.nse*

Also, interesting to point out, the **vulners.nse** script is classified into the categories vuln, safe, and external. At a high level, this indicates that the script is related to identifying vulnerabilities, is safe to run, will not negatively impact the targets, and queries an external data source. There are 13 categories of NSE scripts, which will be discussed in far more detail along with instructions on writing your own custom scripts in *Chapter 8: Leveraging the Nmap Scripting Engine*.

For now, it is sufficient to simply understand that there are a large number of scripts that have added additional features and functionality to Nmap over time; these scripts can be implemented in very creative ways, and they can be combined with additional flags to modify them even further.

Experimenting with and researching different NSE scripts provides an eye-opening experience into seeing how other security researchers have solved individual challenges. Often times, this will lead to solutions to problems that you didn't even realize you had. Throughout the next several chapters, we will be leveraging dozens of individual NSE scripts to accomplish specific objectives.

Intermediate Nmap Flags

The basic flags that we discussed in *Chapter 3: Introduction to Attack Surface Mapping* have provided you with the capability to conduct fundamental scans. We discussed how to adjust the timing, specify which type of enumeration (that is, operating system, ports and services, and so on), adjust verbosity, and utilize input and output files to increase efficiency. However, those represent only a small fraction of the potential modifications you can use to tailor your Nmap scans. The following 12 flags are designed to take your basic scans and bring them up to the next level by adding more capabilities and nuanced control over how they operate:

1. `--script`: Among the most powerful features of Nmap is the **Nmap Scripting Engine** (**NSE**). We have seen a brief display of the different capabilities of NSE scripts already when we analyzed vulnerabilities using the **vulners.nse** script; however, there are hundreds of additional scripts available which dramatically expand the capacity of Nmap. We will be taking a deep dive into NSE scripts and how to write them in Lua in *Chapter 8: Leveraging the Nmap Scripting Engine*:

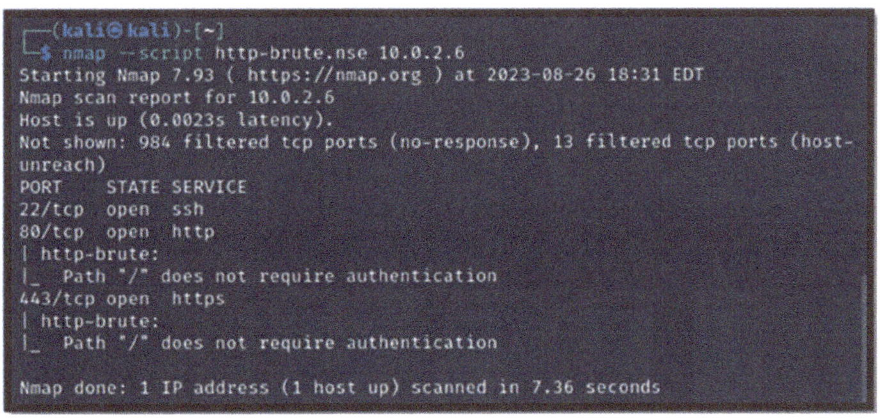

Figure 4.2: *Demonstrating an NSE script*

2. `--script-help`: Due to the sheer number of scripts available, it becomes untenable through rout memorization to keep track of what each one does. While you will naturally lean towards a small handful that suits your particular type of project over time, it is important to explore the

expansive base of scripts. The **`--script-help`** command enables you to do just that by outputting information regarding what the particular scripts do without having to launch them. This lets you verify that the script you have selected is the right tool for the job before use:

```
┌──(kali㉿kali)-[~]
└─$ nmap --script-help http-brute.nse
Starting Nmap 7.93 ( https://nmap.org ) at 2023-08-26 18:32 EDT

http-brute
Categories: intrusive brute
https://nmap.org/nsedoc/scripts/http-brute.html
  Performs brute force password auditing against http basic, digest and ntlm
authentication.

  This script uses the unpwdb and brute libraries to perform password
  guessing. Any successful guesses are stored in the nmap registry, using
  the creds library, for other scripts to use.
```

Figure 4.3: *Demonstrating the --script-help function*

3. **`-6`**: While the vast majority of the time on penetration tests, you are working with IPv4, there is a chance that you will need to scan a specific IPv6 address. Internet Protocol version 6 is not a new concept; it has been the **Internet Engineering Task Force (IETF)**'s solution to IPv4 exhaustion (the concept that there are simply not enough IPv4 addresses for all connected devices) since the late 1990s. That being said, even now, some 25 years later, IPv4 is still far more prevalent. Despite the niche nature, there may be times when you only have access to an IPv6 address, and knowing that Nmap does have the capability to scan such addresses is important to realize.
4. **`-sn`**: During default scanning one of the initial techniques used by Nmap is ICMP probes. These probes are extremely common and are used by Nmap to help ascertain if a host is alive or not. Very simply, if the host replies to the ICMP probe (also known as a ping), then Nmap will recognize that host as alive; if not, it will move on. Although there are other host discovery techniques that Nmap does employ, the ICMP ping tends to occur first. This is commonly known as a ping sweep and is used for large-scope host discovery. This technique will be explored in more depth in *Chapter 5: Mapping a Large Environment*:

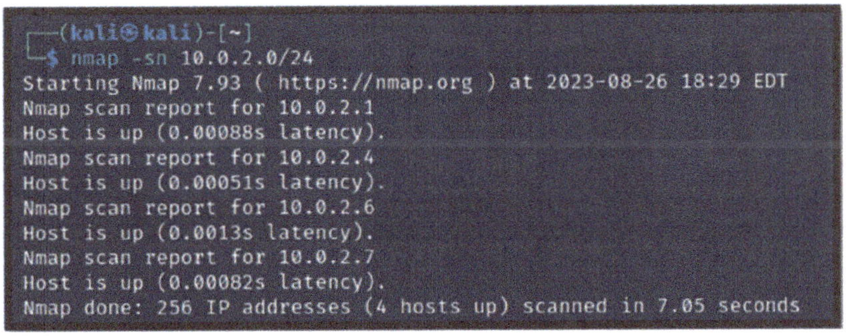

Figure 4.4: *Demonstrating a ping sweep with Nmap*

5. **`-Pn`**: Conversely, to the previous flag, there will also be occasions where you do not want to conduct a ping scan. This becomes problematic in environments that specifically block ICMP traffic. During penetration tests, it is not uncommon to see initial reconnaissance scans come back with no live hosts due to a failure of Nmap to determine hosts were alive because there was no ICMP response. In these instances, it is prudent to disable ICMP and re-scan the targets; more often than not, this will return the expected results. The **`-Pn`** flag is used for exactly this purpose, to disable ICMP (ping) scans.

6. **`-F`**: Think of the `-F` as "Fast", this is a flag that reduces the number of ports scanned from Nmap's default of 1000 to the top 100. This refers to the top 100 most commonly seen ports and services as outlined in the Nmap Well-Known Ports List (https://nmap.org/book/nmap-services.html). While this flag does substantially increase the speed compared to a base scan, it is important to note that very commonly there will be key ports missed. The best way to utilize this scan is as a way to determine which subnets or endpoints of the greater scope should be marked for additional analysis. This is also a technique we will explore further in *Chapter 5: Mapping a Large Environment.*

7. **`--top-ports #`**: We have established that the default of Nmap is to scan the top 1000 ports, and you can use the -F flag to reduce that to the top 100. But what if you want to scan the top 25? Or 50? Or 1000? That is where the `--top-ports` flag comes in; this allows you to specify the exact number to scan, which can help provide a good balance between speed and depth. From numerous interviews with accomplished network penetration testers, the most common specification for this flag seems to be `--top-ports 2500`. This ensures that the vast majority of regularly seen ports are covered while also substantially reducing the time it would take to scan every port.

8. **`--version-intensity #`**: The previous chapter established that the service version could be abled via the `-sV` command, but additional nuance can be added by specifying the intensity of that versioning effort between 0 and 9. This is done by sending a series of probes with assigned values to all identified open ports in an attempt to determine the service running on them. The default value of `-sV` is "7". So, if your objective is to return results quicker, select a lower number, and if you are trying to get a more accurate fingerprint, select the higher value:

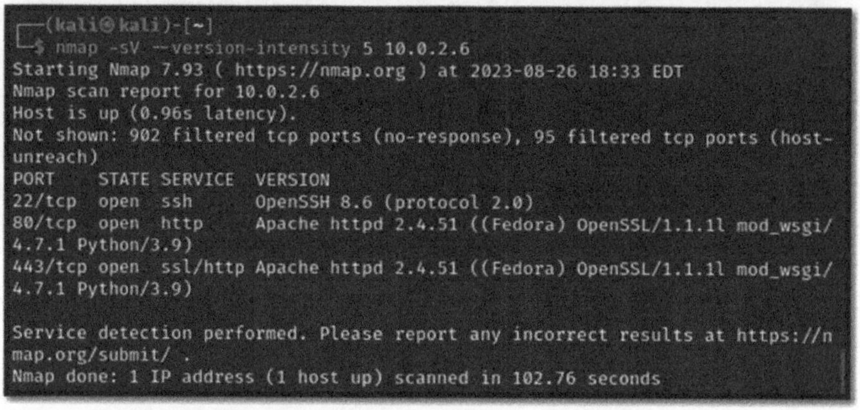

Figure 4.5: *Demonstrating manually setting version intensity*

9. **`--version-light`**: This flag is simply an alias for `--version-intensity 2`. It is a very fast way to conduct scanning when you are less interested in the exact fingerprint of specific services.

10. **`--version-all`**: This is an alias for `--version-intensity 9`, which will make every effort available to Nmap (outside of NSE scripts) to identify the exact version of services. This level of specificity of course comes with the inherent drawback that it will take significantly longer to complete the scan. It is not recommended to use this flag against a scope larger than a /24 subnet, as it will take an egregious amount of time.

11. **`--max-os-tries #`**: When Nmap conducts operating system identification, it will by default attempt five times to determine the exact OS. By specifying a lower value, you can increase the speed of the scan by reducing the attempts to fingerprint the operating system. Alternatively, you can also increase the tries beyond the default of 5 to attempt to better identify the endpoint.

> **Both in my personal experience and in interviews with dozens of network penetration testers, the use case of specifying a `--max-os-tries` value greater than 5 is very rarely done. Most often this is used to reduce the time of scanning while obtaining overt operating system information (that is, Windows or Linux) rather than highly specific fingerprints.**

12. `--exclude-ports #,#`: This is one of the most helpful flags out there for red teaming. During a penetration test, you often do not need to worry about being sneaky or avoiding detection, but in red teaming that is a cornerstone. Many endpoint detection agents, such as SentielOne, CrowdStirke Falcon, and Windows Defender, tend to be very attuned to specific ports being probed such as port 22 (SSH), and 445 (SMB). This flag lets you simply exclude those ports from being scanned, which in some cases is enough to remain under the noise floor in an environment. This technique will be explored in far greater detail in *Chapter 7: Advanced Obfuscation Techniques*.

Exploring the Nmap Scripting Engine

The Nmap Scripting Engine is among the most powerful components of Nmap due to its versatility. Written in the Lua scripting language, these scripts amplify Nmap to be able to fingerprint more specific systems, perform more nuanced scans, exploit known vulnerabilities, and even enumerate firewall rules.

The sheer number of Nmap scripts natively available is staggering. To list them on your Kali machine, simply use the following command:

```
> ls -l /usr/share/nmap/scripts
```

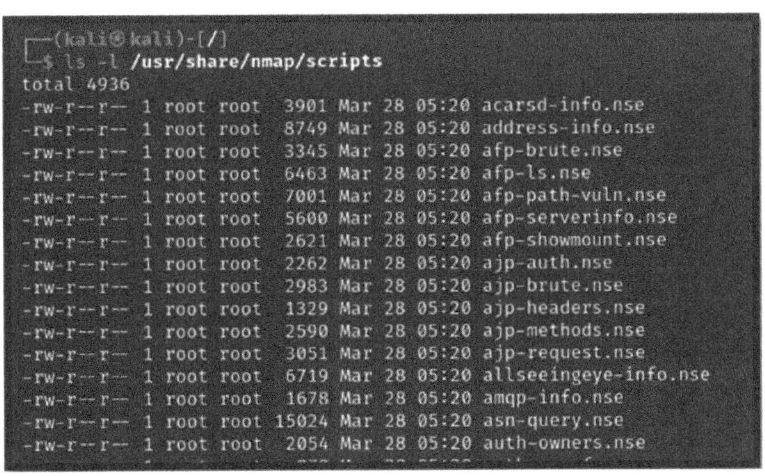

Figure 4.6: *Listing the /usr/share/nmap/scripts directory in Kali Linux*

You can then explore any of them by printing out the file, either via the `cat` command or with a text editor (nano, vi, vim, and so on):

```
>cat /usr/share/nmap/scripts/address-info.nse
```

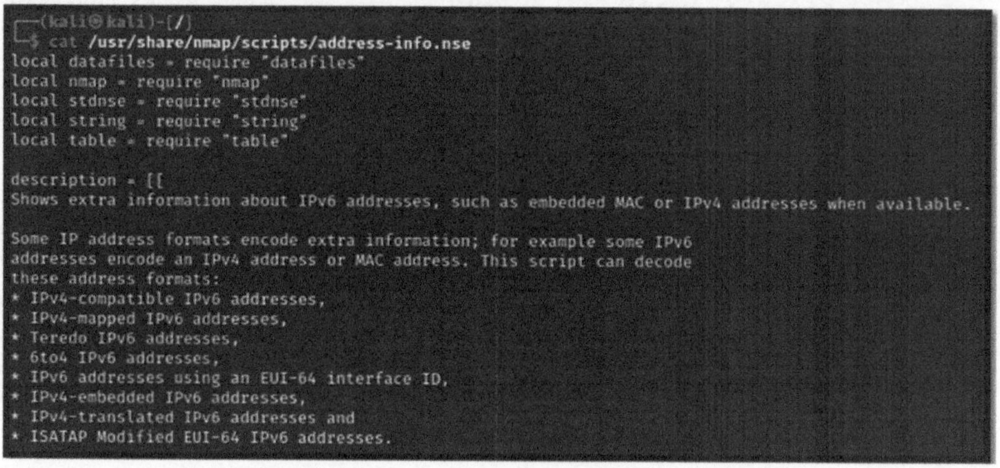

Figure 4.7: *Printing the Lua code of a NSE script*

While there are hundreds of NSE scripts available, as a primer, we will look at 10 that are most often used when conducting enterprise penetration tests of multi-billion dollar corporations:

1. **`Vulners.nse`**: This is one of the handiest scripts available for doing a quick surface-level vulnerability analysis. This script looks at the services being run on the system and queries the vulenrs.com database of vulnerabilities to determine if those services match known vulnerabilities. It will then print out those CVEs to the command prompt along with hyperlinks to their database for additional information. What makes this even more convenient is that Vulners will even define if there is a known exploit available for that vulnerability.

2. **`Ms-exchange-version.nse`**: Outdated versions of on-premises Microsoft Exchange have been riddled with severe vulnerabilities. This script does a better job than even most commercial vulnerability scanners at fingerprinting the exact version of the exchange that is being utilized.

3. **`Smb-security-mode.nse // smb2-security-mode.nse`**: SMB signing not being enabled or required is one of the most common high-severity vulnerabilities seen on internal environments. With this script, you can very rapidly determine if a pass-the-hash attack will be a viable option for lateral movement within the environment.

4. **`Smb-os-discovery.nse`**: Fingerprinting server infrastructure can be challenging, but with Windows 2012R2 recently reaching the end of life (and still very widely used), the opportunity for exploiting these systems is as present as ever. Having the capacity to fingerprint Windows systems via the SMB protocol is essential for any pentester.

5. **`Smb-enum-*`**: This shortcut for running dozens of individual SMB enumeration scripts is a great way to save time on an engagement. When you do not need to worry about being stealthy, throwing everything at a target in the most efficient way is a plus.

6. **`Smb-vuln-*`**: Similar to preceding point, being able to automatically verify susceptibility to a list of high-severity SMB vulnerabilities rapidly can be a great technique, especially in larger scope engagements where efficiency is everything.

7. **`Broadcast-jenkins-discover.nse`**: Jenkins has had countless vulnerabilities over the years and many instances remain tremendously out of date. Being able to identify these systems on the network can provide an early and effective foothold for exploitation.

8. **`Http-wordpress-enum.nse`**: WordPress websites are incredibly common and often make use of many individual plugins, some of which are commercially supported, and others are community-driven. As a result, there have been countless WordPress plugin-specific vulnerabilities over the last decade; many of which do not have patches. This script is a very handy way to fingerprint these plugins and print out any known vulnerabilities associated with them.

9. **`Firewalk.nse`**: Firewalk is a fairly old, but still quite useful script that attempts to determine firewall rules on a specified gateway by analyzing IP time to live (TTL) expirations. Essentially this technique, known as firewalking, sends varying types of probes to the gateway and based on the TTL and reply ascertains if a firewall rule is impacting that port.

   A couple of items to be aware of for this script: first, you need to run it either in an `administrator` or `sudo` command prompt as it needs raw socket access. As a result, this is highly unreliable in **Windows Subsystem for Linux (WSL)**. Second, you also need to include the command "`--traceroute`":

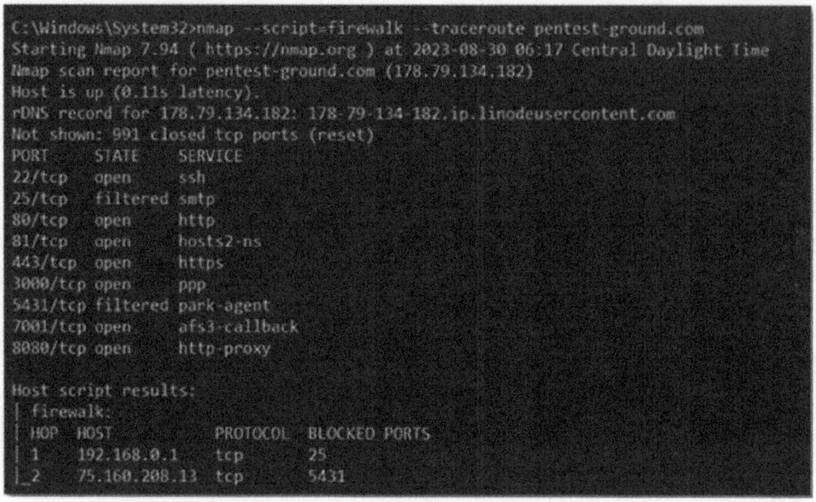

```
C:\Windows\System32>nmap --script=firewalk --traceroute pentest-ground.com
Starting Nmap 7.94 ( https://nmap.org ) at 2023-08-30 06:17 Central Daylight Time
Nmap scan report for pentest-ground.com (178.79.134.182)
Host is up (0.11s latency).
rDNS record for 178.79.134.182: 178-79-134-182.ip.linodeusercontent.com
Not shown: 991 closed tcp ports (reset)
PORT     STATE    SERVICE
22/tcp   open     ssh
25/tcp   filtered smtp
80/tcp   open     http
81/tcp   open     hosts2-ns
443/tcp  open     https
3000/tcp open     ppp
5431/tcp filtered park-agent
7001/tcp open     afs3-callback
8080/tcp open     http-proxy

Host script results:
| firewalk:
| HOP  HOST           PROTOCOL  BLOCKED PORTS
| 1    192.168.0.1    tcp       25
|_2    75.160.208.13  tcp       5431
```

Figure 4.8: *Demonstrating the concept of Firewalking with Nmap*

10. **`Mysql-empty-password.nse`**: This script does exactly what the name would suggest: it checks MySQL servers for default user credentials by attempting to authenticate to the service. While this can be handy, it should be understood that this is both easily detectable and intrusive.

Even more scripts can be found on GitHub where the Infosec community members love to add additional functionality and versatility through custom scripts. We will be deep-diving into NSE scripts, how to write them, how to import new ones, and the best use cases in a later chapter. But for now, the key thing to understand is that NSE scripts are used to expand the functionality of Nmap, are open-source, and are called with the `--script` flag.

NOTE: In 2022, I hosted a live webinar on Cyber-Judo.com on Advanced Nmap Techniques (https://cyber-judo.com/advanced-nmap-techniques), where a major discussion point was different Nmap flags that could be leveraged during penetration tests. I was absolutely shocked by the number of professional penetration testers who reached out to me following the presentation telling me that they had no idea NSE scripts existed.

I kept in touch with many of these engineers and as they explored different NSE scripts they each started incorporating them into their day-to-day pentesting routine and have seen tremendous improvements.

System, Service, and Operating System Enumeration

As we have discussed in the previous chapter, identifying vulnerabilities across environments is conceptually simple. First, you establish the CPE of the system, then through research and additional service enumeration, determine if there are any applicable CVEs that meet the conditions to be meaningfully (and safely) exploited. This is how vulnerability scanners like OpenVas fundamentally operate and quite successfully identify most vulnerabilities. However, during real-world pentests, those easy-to-identify vulnerabilities, which are factored into most open-source and commercial vulnerability scanners, are also typically the issues that the blue team is aware of and have compensating controls to address. More often, true success leading to a cascading compromise within a network environment comes from identifying the vulnerabilities that stem from misconfigurations, inherently flawed protocols, and significant technical debt.

Let's take a moment to explore each of these general categories and break down some examples of how Nmap can contribute to the successful exploitation of them. These examples are meant to serve as both insightful thought exercises and inspiration leading into the challenge presented in this chapter.

Misconfigurations

Security misconfigurations could refer to any number of huge swaths of inadvertent errors when setting up devices. This is such a broad category that in **Open Web Application Security Project** (**OWASP**)'s 2021 edition of Top 10 Vulnerabilities in Web Apps, over 90% of applications had a vulnerability that fell into this category.

A simple way to think about this is that there isn't a problem with the technology, there is a problem with how it was implemented or set up. Think of having a lock on your luggage but forgetting to change the code from 12345. Or, simply not realizing that a default setting is making the whole system less secure, like a baby monitor with telnet open.

Example 1:

The most glaringly obvious example of a security misconfiguration is also extremely common in enterprise networks. If you were to survey a group of network pentesters and ask them "*What is the #1 way you compromise systems on an internal environment*", they will most likely say "default credentials". It is unbelievably common to find printers, phone systems, security cameras, and even significantly more critical devices, such as a Dell iDRAC with their default administrator credentials still active.

For those unfamiliar, a Dell iDRAC is an out of band management platform which provides a central place to manage and configure remote consoles from one interface. Compromising a device such as this almost immediately leads to a cascading compromise of all of the additional remote devices it is configured to manage.

If you ever see one on a pentest, the default credentials are root/calvin.

There are a couple of ways that Nmap can support the auditing of default credentials. The first is the use of a few NSE scripts, which attempt to brute force the devices; a few examples are `citrix-brute-xml.nse`, `ftp-bute.nse`, and `iax2-brute.nse`. While this is one way to go about it, generally it is not recommended to conduct brute force testing without explicit approval from the client due to the potential of disrupting the service. So instead, a somewhat more manual strategy can be employed. Consider using Nmap to scan the subnet for only web servers on the most common ports (80,443,8080,8443):

```
Nmap -p 80,443,8080,8443 -open -iL targets.txt
```

With a list of endpoints that are running web servers, you can then use an open-source tool in Kali Linux called EyeWitness (https://github.com/redsiege/EyeWitness), which can provide a file of targets and will automatically screenshot the websites. The output from EyeWitness is an HTML file that you can then quickly go through and identify which web interfaces look to be unique login fields. A quick Google search will then tell you if there are default credentials that you can try. While this seems extremely simplistic and "*too good to be true*", you will be astounded at how many systems you will get into by just trying "`admin/admin`" as a username and password.

Example 2:

Many systems are set up that, by default, do not have all security systems hardened. The Windows server virtual machine that we put in our lab environment fits this description perfectly. By using the NSE script smb2-security-mode.nse, we can see that SMB signing is enabled but not required. This is a big problem from a security standpoint. SMB signing is a Microsoft feature that signs all SMB messages with both a session key and an encryption algorithm. By doing this, an extremely popular (and old) man-in-the-middle attack called pass-the-hash is largely mitigated. In a pass-the-hash attack, an attacker would acquire the password hash of a valid user, possibly through network traffic poisoning or another vector, and then "pass" that hash to a system not requiring SMB signing to authenticate as that user.

Inherently Flawed Protocols

Some network protocols are designed in such a way that their fundamental implementation presents a vulnerability that can be exploited by an attacker. Two commonly seen examples are **Intelligence Platform Management Interface Version 2 (IPMIv2)** and **MQ Telemetry Transport (MQTT)**. These are very different protocols and are used for completely different purposes, but both offer a very easy path to exploitation once they are identified.

Example 1:

IPMIv2 is a protocol designed to support management and monitoring by system administrators for out-of-band management systems, like an iDRAC, for example. The problem with this protocol is the way it handles authentication and provides a hashed version of the user's password once a username is submitted. This allows attackers to systematically dump all user hashes and attempt to crack them using an offline dictionary or brute force-based means.

Identifying hosts with IPMIv2 with Nmap can be done with one command first identifying hosts with UDP port `623` open, then versioning the service with the `script ipmi-version`:

```
Nmap -sU -p 623 --open --script  ipmi-version.nse -iL targets.txt
```

There are several other tools available which will both scan for and dump the hashes for IPMIv2, such as the Metasploit module auxiliary/scanner/ipmi/ipmi_dumphashes. However, it is almost always quicker and safer to first confirm the use of IPMIv2 using Nmap, and then determine if exploitation is permitted within your rules of engagement.

Example 2:

MQTT is a lightweight messaging protocol most commonly used by IoT devices due to the inherently resource-constrained nature of such devices. In most implementations of MQTT, authentication is completely optional to establish a connection and subscribe to various topics that are published by the MQTT brokers.

To identify and subscribe to various topics for additional system information and enumeration, you can simply scan for systems with port 1833 open and call the `mqtt-subscribe.nse` script:

```
Nmap -p 1883 --open --script mqtt-subscribe -iL targets.txt
```

This is generally a safe script to run and is classified under the Discovery category, although in most cases it would be considered active exploitation. If you wish to subscribe to only a limited number of topics as a proof of concept, a number can be specified with the `mqtt-subscribe.listen-msgs` argument. If you don't specify a number, the default is 100.

Technical Debt

In large enterprises, you will often observe outdated infrastructure and devices. There are a myriad of reasons why this occurs, but most commonly it is because there had been a "if it's not broken don't fix it" mentality to funding infrastructure changes by leadership. Many organizations are now starting to prioritize security as not only a business necessity but also as a key market differentiator to make their offering more appealing to consumers. However, this was not always the case. In many industries, the focus was on profit and revenue growth rather than ensuring systems are kept modern and serviceable. This has resulted in many organizations having extremely out-of-date systems and software in production environments as the funding has just not been allocated to replace them.

Example 1:

Server infrastructure and industrial control devices are typically outdated more often than things like employee workstations in enterprise environments. These devices tend to be far more expensive to replace and have a longer lifetime, which makes them somewhat easier to forget about in the technology refresh cycle. Nmap has many scripts that are excellent at fingerprinting server infrastructure to identify if they are end-of-life or vulnerable to a specific exploit. Some of the most helpful are:

`Ms-sql-info.nse`	`Rdp-vuln-ms12-020.nse`
`Rdp-ntlm-info.nse`	`Realvnc-auth-bypass.nse`
`Smb-os-discovery.nse`	`Rmi-dumpregistry.nse`

These are just a small example of scripts that are available for fingerprinting potentially outdated systems (left-hand column), pinpointing specific vulnerabilities, and even exploiting them (right-hand column).

Example 2:

Common software that is seen out of date is Jenkins, which in older versions is absolutely riddled with vulnerabilities ripe for exploitation. Jenkins is often used in the CI/CD process, but without integrations with third-party applications, it does not have a lot of security controls built in. There are two ways you can easily identify instances of Jenkins on the network.

First, the fact that by default Jenkins hosts a web interface on port `8080` would enable you to simply search for open ports `8080` across the scope. Depending on the number of results, you could either manually check them in a web browser, or use a screenshotting tool like EyeWitness to speed up the process.

Alternatively, you can use a broadcast script built into Nmap called broadcast-jenkins-discover. As a broadcast script, this command does not need to be provided with a specific host or target list to run. However, it does tend to get hung up on a larger environment, so it is recommended to add an additional timeout setting with the `-script-args timeout=` command. This setting will essentially tell Nmap "*if there is no response in X amount of time, move on*":

```
Nmap --script broadcast-jenkins-discover --script-args timeout=15s
```

Once you identify the interface for Jenkins, you can version the portal by triggering an error message when you navigate to a URL that does not exist, such as /error. If the version is particularly old (prior to v2.150.1), there are particularly grave exploits and multiple Metasploit modules associated with it that likely should be reported to the client immediately.

Vulnerability Scanning with Nmap

Nmap is not a replacement for a quality commercial vulnerability scanner. Tools such as Coda, Nessus, Netsparker and others are specifically designed to detect and report vulnerabilities. Even open-source options such as the trail version of OpenVas (**https://openvas.org/**) are better equipped to provide insight as long-term capable vulnerability scanning solutions.

However, there may be instances where you do not have the luxury of installing additional tools in a client environment or are simply trying to remain undetected as you conduct vulnerability scanning. In these instances, `kaliusing Nmap` with some tailored NSE scripts may be the right move.

As we discussed, several NSE scripts relate directly to vulnerability scanning such as `vulners.nse` and `smb-vuln-*`. However, what makes these scripts even more powerful as a vulnerability scanning option is the ability to combine them with additional flags. While we have not touched on the obfuscation techniques that would been commonly leveraged in red teaming (that will be covered in *Chapter 7: Advanced Obfuscation and Firewall Evasion Techniques*), there are still many scan configurations combining vulnerability analysis with fundamental and intermediate flags for the best results.

To illustrate this point, let's break down a few Nmap scans that would be expected of a junior Penetration Tester and analyze how they work for vulnerability analysis:

```
Nmap -Pn --top-ports 500 -T2 -sV --version-all --script vulners.nse -iL
targets.txt -oX results.txt
```

In this scan, the user is attempting to determine an accurate CPE by using the `--version-all` flag, but has reduced the total number of ports from the default of 1,000 to 500. This is likely in an effort to increase the speed of the scan, which is slowed by the `-T2` flag. While these two flags may seem contradictory to one other, there are several instances when a production environment may require both a light touch in terms of impact (`-T2`) and also a rapid assessment (`--top-ports 500`). This service version information is then fed into the `vulners.nse` script, which will look it up against a public vulnerability database. This is a less intrusive method of scanning than often seen with other methods:

Figure 4.9: *Demonstrating a moderately complex versioning scan*

```
Nmap -F -T5 -version-light -sV --script vulners.nse -iL targets.txt -oX
results.txt
```

This scan is clearly focused on speed. The `-F` flag reduces the total ports scanned from 1,000 to 100 and is followed by the maximum speed rating, and the lightest service versioning across the target list before calling `vulners.nse`. This type of scan would be used when the most important thing is identifying both obvious and critical vulnerabilities across in-scope systems. In these cases, there would be no concern of overloading the targets, and there would be enough understanding of the systems to warrant reducing the quality-of-service versioning in favor of sheer speed:

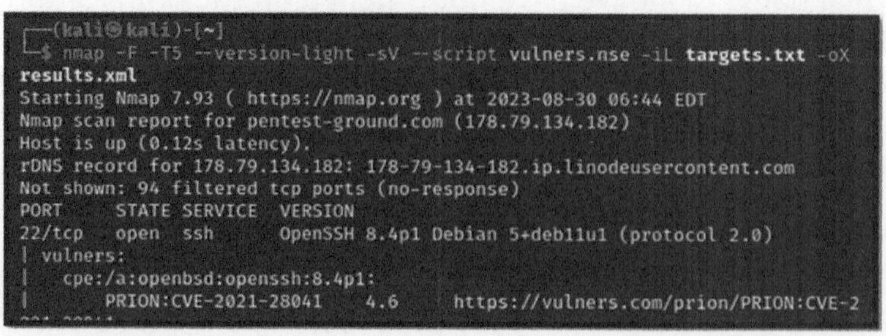

Figure 4.10: *Demonstrating a simple versioning scan*

```
Nmap -p 139,445 --script smb-vun* -iL targets.txt -oX results.txt
```

This scan is focused on SMB vulnerabilities, specifically on Windows hosts. Likely, the user would have identified a subnet or VLAN in the target environment that is used for Windows Servers and is in the stage of the penetration test, where assessing them for major SMB-based vulnerabilities is a prudent next step. While this often results in detection, it is more of a concern in a Red Team engagement than a traditional penetration test:

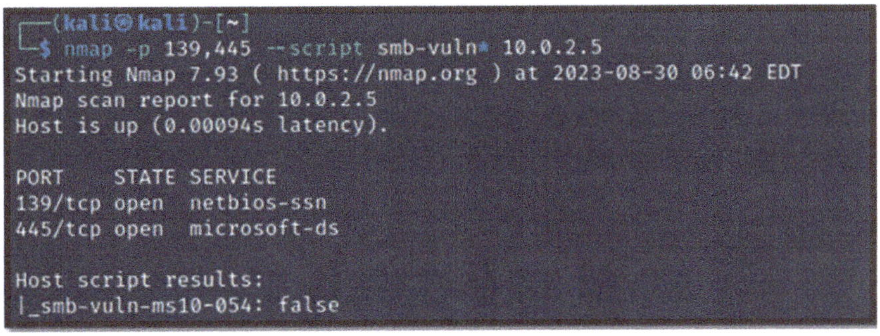

Figure 4.11: *Demonstrating an SMB vulnerability enumeration scan using multiple scripts*

```
Nmap -p 139,445 --open --script smb2-security-mode 10.0.2.5
```

Far less intensive than `smb-vuln-*`, this script is useful in determining if SMB signing is enforced. In this example, we see it being used on a single endpoint, but this is a quick and relatively subtle scan to identify a potentially critical vulnerability that may be used on an entire scope:

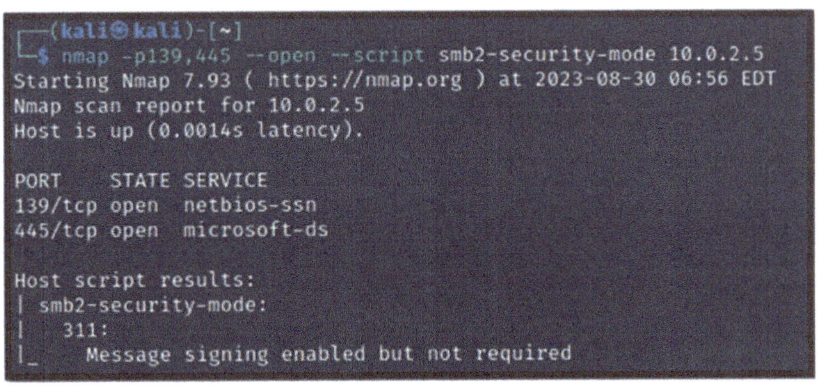

Figure 4.12: *Identifying SMB signing not being required, a high-severity vulnerability*

```
Nmap -p 8080 -script vulners.nse -sV -v -iL targets.txt -oX results.txt
```

While many web servers will run on port `8080`, one specific way to this script is to dive deeper into Jenkins hosts that were identified with the `broadcast-jenkins-discover.nse` script. By scanning a single port that has previous been identified and versioned, the risk of detection is fairly minimal while the opportunity for exploitation is quite high:

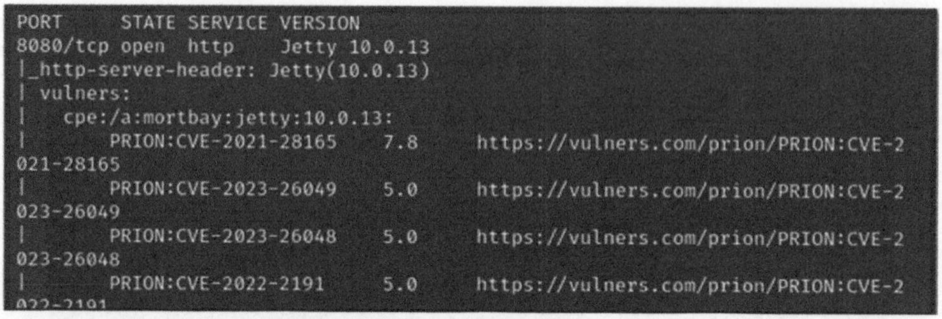

Figure 4.13: *Using the vulners.nse script to print CVEs specific to an outdated version of Jenkins*

```
Nmap -p 80,443 -sV --script http-csrf scanme.nmap.org
```

While Nmap is most commonly considered for its applicability in network pentesting engagement, there are several scripts and options that make it a helpful resource for application-specific vulnerability identification as well. This script in particular does several checks to identify possibilities of **Cross-Site Request Forgery** (**CSRF**) on the target domain(s).

CSRF is an attack by which an attacker forces a user to execute an unwanted action on a web application while authenticated, most typically through social engineering. This Nmap script can help quickly identify areas of user input that may provide a potential initial foothold if leveraged in the right social engineering campaign:

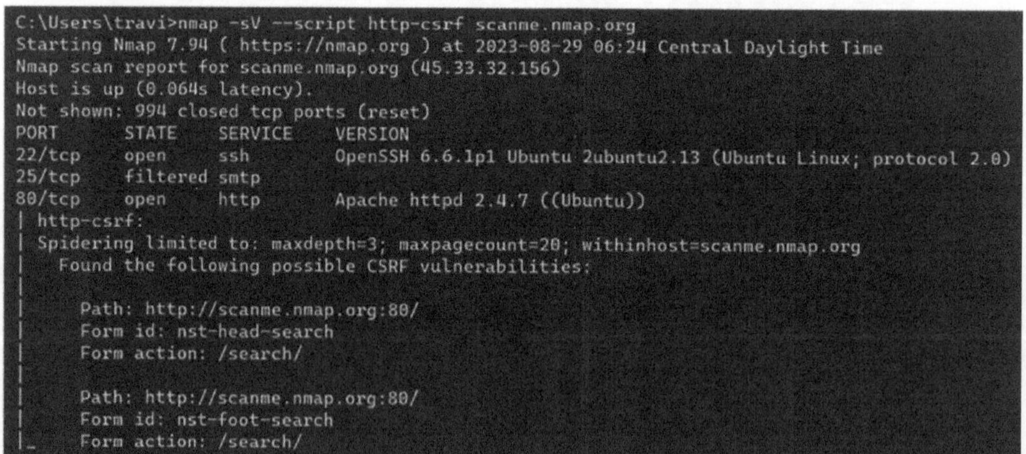

Figure 4.14: *Demonstrating CSRF scanning of a web application with Nmap*

Case Study – Real-World Internal and External Penetration Test

During a combined internal and external penetration test for one of my all-time favorite clients, a multinational financial services organization, I counted the times that I used Nmap just to see how often it would come in handy. When I did this, it wasn't a challenge to see how many times I 'could' use it, but simply to objectively consider how often it was the best tool for the job. The results surprised me in that I used Nmap a total of 19 times during the engagement.

Starting on the external, we were provided a scope that included all of the client's externally facing IP addresses, which essentially allowed me to skip the domain discovery phase. After an initial set of OSINT tasks, I was ready to transition into active reconnaissance and used Nmap to do service versioning and port scanning of the entire scope, outputting the results of course to a .xml for use in Zenmap later. Once the initial scan results came in, a few endpoints using WordPress were observed, so an Nmap script was performed to identify any vulnerabilities with the plugins. Sure enough, there were several. However, there were also some outdated Windows servers externally exposed, which necessitated another set of scans aimed at fingerprinting any Windows server-specific vulnerabilities. By the time the external attack surface had truly been mapped, a total of five scans had been run with Nmap.

On the internal side, I first scanned my local subnet, then did a discovery scan to identify open hosts on a /8 subnet that we were provided (more on enumerating huge scopes like this in the next chapter). With a list of live subnets, I then narrowed it down even more by quickly scanning a select few ports which are often the most interesting. The subnets with the majority of the results then got more intricate scans of all ports and services, SMB-related vulnerabilities, port-specific vulnerabilities like IPMIv2 and MQMT, and broadcast searches for Jenkins servers. By the time the internal attack surface was truly understood, and I moved into the active exploitation phase, I had run a total of 14 Nmap scans.

While at each turn there were technically other tools that I could have used, my comfortability with Nmap let me leverage its versatility to fill the need seamlessly. In this particular example, I was not able to compromise the external perimeter. They were well-secured and the vulnerabilities I found related to WordPress plugins had compensating controls to prevent exploitation. However, the internal environment was a very different story.

Internally, I was able to identify numerous endpoints that had default credentials on them, as well as two different devices with Cisco Smart Install enabled, which enabled pulling the configuration files for Cisco switches. Within those config files were hashed credentials for the network administrator who set up the switches.

These hashes were cracked using `Hashcat` in an offline dictionary attack and then used to conduct a `Kerberoasting` attack against Active Directory, which inevitably led to a complete Active Directory domain compromise.

Nmap wasn't the only tool that was used to achieve AD domain admin access. I used Siet.py to pull the Cisco Smart Install config, `Hashcat` to crack the hash of the network administrator, and several components of `Impacket` to conduct the Kerberoasting attack. However, all of that exploitation was only possible because of a very thorough and strategic mapping of the attack surface using Nmap.

Challenge 1: Fingerprinting Vulnerable Systems

Use every technique and script at your disposal to fully fingerprint every virtual machine in your home lab and at https://pentest-ground.com. Pentest-ground.com is a very well-put-together open target for testing tools and techniques, which is publicly accessible and completely legal to target. It is maintained by the world-class team behind Pentest-tools.com and has several interesting web applications that are ripe for enumeration and exploitation.

Consider writing a report of your findings combining both your home lab environment as well as pentest-ground. Include the scope of your testing, your methodology, and descriptions (with screenshots) of your process from start to finish. This will make a great sample report to demonstrate your skills, which you can post to your blog, GitHub, or LinkedIn account.

Challenge 2: Home Network Vulnerability Scanning

Take the skills you practiced in the previous challenge and turn them inward by conducting a true vulnerability analysis of the systems on your home network. Try to fingerprint each device and determine if there are any vulnerabilities that you were unaware of.

This is another great exercise to chronicle on a blog or write up into a sample report for your GitHub. Having spoken with hundreds of people trying to break into the cyber security industry, I would say less than 5% have ever actually conducted an analysis of their security posture, but it is a great thing to talk about in interviews.

Conclusion

Employing Nmap in a professional penetration test or vulnerability assessment is not a simple checklist. Asking twenty professionals what steps and commands they take will likely yield twenty different (yet similar) answers. Trying to build and follow a checklist is one of the most common pitfalls that people new to cybersecurity will make. This is simply not a career path that can be reduced to checklists.

Instead, it requires a lot of analytical thinking and the ability to pivot based on the situation at hand. This is why so many different methods and techniques for fingerprinting systems, determining the CPEs and eventually the CVEs were presented within this chapter. There will be real-world engagements where you will never use 80% of the commands that were discussed here. But there will very likely also be engagements where you use them all multiple times. No two penetration tests are the same, and when there is that much versatility in potential targets, you need an equal level of versatility in your tools.

Nmap is capable of fingerprinting many systems, identifying and checking for many vulnerabilities, and providing tremendous insight into how systems are configured, but only if you know how to best leverage it. This chapter explored how to dig deep into individual systems and subnets to gather the information necessary to plan the next steps of exploitation.

In the next chapter, we are going to look at one of the most unique and challenging aspects of professional penetration testing, dealing with a huge scope. Most training environments and certification exams consist of only a small handful of systems and allow for a lot of time to dig into the details of every single port and service on those systems. But what happens when you have three weeks to conduct an engagement and the scope is 3 separate /8 subnets? That's 50,331,648 possible IP addresses. If you spent only 1 second on each one, that would be about a year and a half. What do you do when you have that many possible IPs but only three weeks to do the penetration test? That is the question we will answer in *Chapter 5: Mapping a Large Environment.*

Points to Remember

- Most often a cascading compromise within a network environment comes from identifying the vulnerabilities that stem from misconfigurations, inherently flawed protocols, and significant technical debt.
- Nmap scripts are extremely versatile and can be used for very broad things such as vulnerability scanning of all services (`vulners.nse`) as well as very nuanced purposes like identifying instances of Jenkins (`broadcast-jenkins-discover`).

- There are limitless ways to conduct vulnerability scanning with Nmap, the options for adding or subtracting obfuscation, highly detailed probes, and additional context are limited mostly by the creativity of the user.
- Nmap scripts are written in Lua and provide an easy way to add tremendous functionality to suit your individual use case.
- High-quality penetration testing cannot be boiled down to a checklist. Each pentest is different and requires a lot of careful thought and analysis to complete.

Multiple Choice Questions

1. **NSE scripts are written in which language?**
    a. Python
    b. Java
    c. Lua
    d. Ruby
2. **The -F flag indicates Nmap will scan what number of top ports?**
    a. 10
    b. 100
    c. 1,000
    d. 10,000
3. **The Open Web Application Security Project (OWASP)'s 2021 edition of Top 10 Vulnerabilities in Web Apps found that over 90% of applications had a vulnerability in which category?**
    a. Injection
    b. Security Misconfiguration
    c. Cryptographic Failures
    d. Software and Data Integrity Failures
4. **Which technique sends varying types of probes to the gateway and based on the TTL and reply ascertains if a firewall rule is impacting that port?**
    a. ICMP Ping
    b. TCP Port Scan
    c. Firewalking
    d. Firewalling

5. **Typically, before identifying CVEs associated with an endpoint, you should first determine which of the following?**
   a. CVS
   b. CBS
   c. NAT
   d. CPE
6. **True or False: Nmap has invasive and exploitative scripts?**
   a. True
   b. False
7. **Which of the following services is inherently flawed from a security perspective?**
   a. SMB
   b. IPMIv2
   c. SFTP
   d. SMTP

Answers

1. **c**
2. **b**
3. **b**
4. **c**
5. **d**
6. **a**
7. **b**

CHAPTER 5

Mapping a Large Environment

Introduction

An area that is infrequently explored in penetration testing training content is how to operate in a very large enterprise environment. There are several excellent penetration testing courses and certifications, such as the **eLearn Security Junior Penetration Tester** (eJPT) and the **Practical Network Penetration Tester** (PNPT) by TCM Security, that teach network pentesting skills. However, one challenge that both of these, and even the more widely known **Offensive Security Certified Professional** (OSCP), lack is conducting a pentest against a large scope.

It makes perfect sense why most certification exams are conducted in relatively small environments; they are meant to be completed in only a couple of days and having an entire /8 subnet for a lab environment would be exorbitantly expensive and impractical. While the skills needed for pentesting a /24 and a /8 are fundamentally the same, the way that the testing has to be conducted and the hosts prioritized for analysis takes meticulous planning. It is simply impossible to spend the same amount of time on each host in a /16 as you would in a /28.

Don't worry if the CIDR notation of /24, /16, and /8 subnets is confusing, we will cover what that means and why it is important to understand in this chapter.

While the majority of this book focuses on hands-on practice in the lab environment, out of necessity, this chapter is inherently more theory-focused. We will cover the fundamentals of subnets and VLANs as they relate to enterprise environments, and then explore techniques for conducting reconnaissance and enumeration on them. While the individual scans and flags we will discuss will largely be a review (such as a Ping Scan), the strategies for modifying and amplifying those scans for greater efficiency will introduce many new concepts.

Structure

In this chapter, we will discuss the following topics:

- Working with Large Networks
- Black Box Subnet Discovery Techniques and Mass Scanning
- Optimizing Scans for Speed
- Case Study: Real-World Account of Pentesting a Very Large Environment
- Challenge: Optimizing a Custom Scan for Speed

Working with Large Networks

To understand how to work effectively with a large enterprise network, we must first understand the fundamentals of subnetting. Subnetting is essentially the process of subdividing an existing network into smaller individual subnets. There are several reasons to do this, such as the logical and secure organization of different types of equipment (for example, workstations and servers should not be on the same subnet), and the implementation of additional security controls, such as firewall rules restricting access to certain subnets. Subnets can also be used to distinguish networks belonging to different offices within a large organization.

For this book, we will focus less on the intricacies of network architecture and the plethora of blue-team defensive measures that can be implemented, and instead, we will focus on how these types of networks relate to you as a penetration tester. To this end, it is essential to understand the concept of **Classless Inter-Domain Routing (CIDR)** notation. CIDR notation is a way to depict an IP address range with its associated subnet mask, which was first introduced by the Internet Engineering Task Force in the early 1990s.

This is done by using the "/", which in this context is simply called a slash, followed by the subnet mask. For example, the IP range of 10.10.10.0 – 10.10.10.255 would be depicted as 10.10.10.0/24. Since each octet in an IPv4 IP address can have a range between 0 and 255, the "0/24" indicates that the final octet can have any value between 0 and 255. As the /# decreases, the total number of possible IP addresses increases exponentially. While you can subnet all the way down to a /31 network, which is only 1 IP address, by far, the most commonly seen are /24, /16, and /8.

Subnet	IP Range	Total Number of Possible IPs
10.10.10.0/24	10.10.10.0 - 255	256
10.10.0.0/16	10.10.0.0 - 10.10.255.255	65,536
10.0.0.0/8	10.0.0.0 - 10.255.255.255	16,777,216

Table 5.1: *Subnet breakdown by IP address*

You can immediately see that the difference between these subnet sizes is enormous. The good news is that just because a client provides you with a /16 subnet in the scope of your pentest does not mean they have 65 thousand devices. The vast majority of the possible /24 subnets within that /16 will likely be empty. The challenge becomes, how do you figure out where the actual endpoints are in that large range? Certainly, you cannot perform a stealthy port scan of the top 1,000 ports on 65 thousand individual IP addresses; if you tried, the whole engagement would likely be over before the scan finishes! Remember, penetration testers are time-bound in ways that real hackers are not. This inherent limitation necessitates us to be very strategic in how we map the environment.

Different clients will provide different levels of information when defining the scope. In some instances, you will get a very well-defined and labeled spreadsheet of subnets (and/or VLANs) that are organized. In other cases, you may be provided with just a single (or small number of) larger subnet. For example, a client could provide you with the following neat and organized table, or just "10.10.0.0/16":

Office	Network	Purpose
New York	10.10.11.0/24	Workstations
New York	10.10.12.0/24	VOIP
New York	10.10.13.0/24	Servers
Austin	10.10.21.0/24	Workstations
Austin	10.10.22.0/24	VOIP
Austin	10.10.23.0/24	Servers
San Francisco	10.10.31.0/24	Workstations

Office	Network	Purpose
San Francisco	10.10.32.0/24	VOIP
San Francisco	10.10.33.0/24	Servers

Table 5.2: *Ideal scope chart*

In this simplistic example, a /16 would be valid as those /24 subnets are certainly subdivided from the 10.10.0.0/16 subnet; but in reality, only 2295 IP address spaces are being utilized compared to the 65,536 technically possible.

It is much faster and easier when the client simply provides the breakdown, as shown in *Table* 5.2. As a penetration tester, you can then focus on digging as deep as possible into each one of those subnets, knowing that nothing in the scope will be missed entirely. However, every client is different, and occasionally they will want the penetration test to be conducted from a purely black box perspective, where you do not receive any (or very minimal) information about their internal network and have to figure it out on your own. In such cases, one of the very first things you will want to do is start mapping the subnets out into a table or list (similar to *Table* 5.2), so that you can determine which /24 subnets need to be prioritized.

Black Box Subnet Discovery Techniques and Mass Scanning

We have already established that trying to run a basic Nmap scan, even a relatively quick one, on an entire /16 or /8 subnet would take so long that it is highly impractical. First, you need to determine which /24s within those larger subnets have endpoints within them, and one of the easiest ways to do this is to perform a ping sweep of only the gateways. While the gateway can technically be assigned any IP address on a subnet, it is almost always either the .1 or .254 (as in 10.10.10.1 or 10.10.10.254). Instead of performing a ping scan of an entire /16 with Nmap, we can strategically scan the entire range of the third octet while specifying only the .1 or .254 of the fourth octet:

```
Nmap -sn 10.10.0-255.1, 10.10.0-255.254
```

This command will perform a ping scan of all the likely gateways within a /16. Instead of scanning 65 thousand IPs to get the list, only 510 are necessary. This reduces the scan time dramatically, essentially reducing the specified targets from a /16 to the equivalent of 2 × /24s. These will output to two different text files, showing which gateways responded to the ICMP ping. You would then take the IP addresses that responded to the ping sweep and treat them as individual /24s, which need to be analyzed further.

Many users do not realize that Nmap can scan subnets written in both CIDR notation (for example, 10.10.10.0/24) or as octet ranges, as shown earlier. Not to mention that different ranges can be specified in the same scan simply by comma separating them.

One minor inconvenience is that the output of the `-sn` scan is not easily copied and pasted in a way that provides you with one clean list of IP addresses:

Figure 5.1: *Demonstrating the extra characters that return from a ping scan*

Conveniently if you are using Linux, you can pipe together a series of additional commands to turn off name resolution (`-n`), specify a greppable output (`-oG -`), and then filter out the extra information:

```
Nmap -n -sn 10.10.0-255.1, 10.10.0-255.254 -oG - | awk '/Up$/
{print $2}' | > Ping_Sweep.txt
```

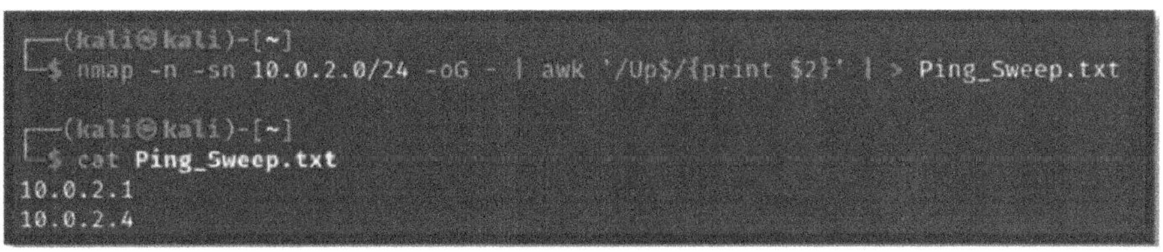

Figure 5.2: *Demonstrating the filtered response*

These examples were given for a /16, but keep in mind that the same technique can be used for a /8 as well by adding a range to the second and third octets (that is, 10.0-255.0-255.1).

Now that you have a set of IPs corresponding to gateways that responded to an ICMP ping, you have a couple of options. You could either conduct another ping scan of all the corresponding alive subnets and print out a file of live targets, which will then become your base target list, or you can scan for a few common ports individually to determine the most interesting subnets. Your choice here may depend on the sheer amount of individuals/24s you are working with, but generally, the former is optimal.

Using the results of your ping sweep, change the final octet on each line to "0/24", and then simply repeat the previous processes by substituting the IP ranges for the `.txt` file:

```
Nmap -n -sn -iL Ping_Sweep.txt -oG - | awk '/Up$/{print $2}' | >
targets.txt
```

Now you have a list of the endpoints that are alive and reachable. If this is a reasonably sized list (a few hundred), then you can treat it in the same way as described in *Chapter 4: Identifying Vulnerabilities Through Reconnaissance and Enumeration*. However, in a large enterprise, this is likely to still be several thousand endpoints. Several thousand is much better than 16 million (assuming it was a /8 to begin with), but still requires additional filtering to be feasible during a typical engagement.

The next step often involves scanning for individual ports one or two at a time to identify systems that may present quick wins with exploitable protocols. Then, progressively transition into scanning for common ports, which will help you identify the purpose of the specific /24s.

Start by scanning for easily exploitable systems for some quick wins, such as Cisco Smart Install, Java RMI, and IPMIv2. Picking up an instance of Cisco Smart Install early in a penetration test can be an absolute game-changer, as the context within the network contained in the device's configuration file is invaluable:

```
Nmap -pn -T4 -iL targets.txt -p 4786 --open -oX smart_install.xml
Nmap -pn -T4 -iL targets.txt -p 1099 --open -oX JavaRMI.xml
Nmap -pn -sU -T4 -iL targets.txt -p 623 --open -oX IPMI.xml
```

There are a couple of things to point out in the preceding commands, specifically the use of the `-pn` and `-T4` flags. We are disabling host discovery (`-pn`) because we have already established that the hosts in targets.txt are alive; thus, sending them additional probes to determine that is a waste of time. The `-T4` flag specifies a fast speed of the scan itself. Combined, these two flags will cut down significantly on the time it takes for results to come back, which is still a very important consideration even after reducing the scope from where it started.

NOTE: It's very important not to forget the --open flag when doing individual port scans, especially for something very specific as shown above. Forgetting this option will result in thousands of results indicating that the port is closed, which will take ages to scroll through.

While there are several other vulnerable ports you could search for at this stage, such as MQTT, those are typically better served for later in the engagement, as the impact and potential for a cascading compromise are less likely than with things like Cisco Smart Install.

Continuing with the process, the next step would be to identify which subnets are utilized primarily for workstation and server infrastructure. Considering the vast majority of organizations utilize Windows devices and servers to some degree, searching for common SMB ports at this stage tends to work well:

```
Nmap -pn -T4 -iL targets.txt -p 139,445 --open -oX SMB_results.
xml
```

Finally, searching for things like web servers and aggregating a list of these devices, which can be automatically enumerated with a screenshot tool such as Eyewitness, is very helpful. This step will take much longer than the previous ones simply because it is scanning four different ports instead of only 1 or 2, which is why collecting the other results first is recommended. You can parse through and analyze the previously collected results while waiting for this scan to finish:

```
Nmap -pn -T4 -iL targets.txt -p 80,443,8080,8443 --open -oX Web_
servers.xml
```

With all this data, you will be able to start piecing together what subnets are used for what types of systems and create your own system for organizing those subnets. Once you have the network generally mapped and understood, then your process of mapping the internal attack surface can begin in earnest.

Optimizing Scans for Speed

Even with the scope reduced as much as reasonably possible, in large enterprise networks, there is still the need to optimize scans for speed to get the results quickly enough to comprehensively analyze the endpoints. In *Chapter 7: Advanced Obfuscation and Firewall Evasion Techniques*, we will look at how to make scans as slow and subtle as possible; here, we need to do the opposite. For this, six additional flags need to be deeply understood:

1. **`--min-hostgroup`**: Nmap scans numerous hosts simultaneously by grouping targets together; with few exceptions, a larger grouping leads to faster overall scans. The drawback here is that no results will be returned until the entirety of the host group has been completed. In most cases, this is not a concern unless you are trying to analyze endpoints that come back in real-time while the scan continues to run. The most common settings here are either `--min-hostgroup 256`, which dictates that networks are scanned in /24 sized groups, or dramatically increasing the size up to `--min-hostgroup 2048`.

2. **`--initial-rtt-timeout`** and **`--max-rtt-timeout`**: Nmap has a complex and variable algorithm for determining the time in which it will await a probe response. The variance is based on several factors, including network latency and in particularly slow networks, this can naturally increase significantly. Specifying a low initial and maximum rtt timeout can cut scan times by a substantial margin. However, there are drawbacks; if you specify settings that are too low, the increase in probes timing out will increase the scan time.

The time specified is measured in milliseconds, so the full flags would look like `--initial-rtt-timeout 300ms` and `--max-rtt-timeout 1000ms`. As a general rule of thumb, keep your `rtt-timeout` range between 250 and 1000 ms for the best results.

Specifying a moderately aggressive rtt-timeout value works phenomenally well for large scale ping sweeps as long as the timeout isn't so low that the network latency is causing the packets to timeout.

3. **`--max-retries`**: The default behavior of Nmap is to retry a port scan 10 times if it does not receive a response on that port's status from the host. This is because a lack of response could indicate that the port is being filtered, or simply that the response was lost; so, in an effort of accuracy, Nmap tries 10 times. In most cases, Nmap will not need 10 tries to get the status of a port. In fact, most responses are returned in just one or two tries. However, on networks with a lot of latency or hosts that are configured with rate limiting, it can be beneficial to reduce the maximum number of retries down to 5 or 3. While there is an inherent risk of losing some information, it is preferable to allow the host timeout to expire and lose all information.

   This is a really useful flag that can be used for both increasing the speed of scans and also adding a degree of obfuscation. While, in this context, we are discussing its capacity to increase the scan speed; in *Chapter 7: Advanced Obfuscation and Firewall Evasion Techniques*, we will explore the same `--max-retries` flag from a completely different perspective.

4. **`--host-timeout`**: Sometimes individual hosts take an extraordinarily long time to scan. This can be caused by a number of factors such as rate limiting or firewalls, and in extreme cases, 1% of the hosts on your target list can take more than 20% of the time of the entire scan. To mitigate this issue, you can specify a host timeout value in minutes, which is the maximum amount of time Nmap will attempt to gather all information before moving on to another host. If Nmap hits the host timeout limit and moves on, you will lose all information on that host. For this reason, do not set an unreasonably low `--host-timeout`, as you will likely miss out on a significant amount of important information. This command is most effective when you are running a scan that will take a very long time (perhaps overnight) and you want to make sure that what should take 8 hours to run doesn't get delayed to 12 hours because of a handful of hosts.

5. **`--defeat-rst-ratelimit`**: Many hosts will reduce the number of ICMP error messages (RST packets) that are sent back when unreachable ports are queried. The implemented rate limits on sending the packets

back to Nmap will impact the adaptive timing nature of Nmap and can significantly slow down the scan as a result. Specifying the `--defeat-rst-ratelimit` will trade accuracy for speed by ignoring the rate limits entirely, which can result in Nmap not waiting long enough for the results to be returned.

6. **`--defeat-icmp-ratelimit`**: Very similar to `--defeat-rst-ratelimit`, the `--defeat-icmp-ratelimit` flag is used to increase the speed of UDP scans specifically. Keep in mind that the same drawbacks to accuracy apply.

We have previously discussed the use of the timing flag (-T1, T2, T3, T4, T5) and established that T3 is Nmap's default and T5 is the maximum speed. Now that you understand the performance flags and their function, it is important to dive deeper into the exact difference between T4 and T5.

As per Nmap's official documentation, T4 leverages the following values:

- `--max-rtt-timeout 1250ms`
- `--min-rtt-timeout 100ms`
- `--initial-rtt-timeout 500ms`
- `--max-retries 6`
- Sets the TCP scan delay to 10ms

While the T5 flag has the following equivalency:

- `--max-rtt-timeout 300ms`
- `--min-rtt-timeout 50ms`
- `--initial-rtt-timeout 250ms`
- `--max-retries 2`
- `--host-timeout 15m`
- `--script-timeout 10m`
- Sets the TCP scan delay to 5ms

You can see that the difference between T4 and T5 is quite significant. So much so that the breakneck speed comes with a significant drawback in accuracy. For this reason, in most cases, using T4 or specifying your performance parameters with the previous flags is optimal. Going fast and collecting data is important but ensuring that the data is accurate is paramount.

Two other flags that are sometimes mentioned when discussing performance are `--min-rate` and `--max-rate`. These are used to manually specify the rate at which packets are sent by Nmap and can be used to either speed up or slow down scans. While this does work well for slowing scans down to avoid detection, it is not the best way to speed them up. Increasing the speed in this way tends to lead to a tremendous decrease in accuracy due to dropped packets. Nmap has an adaptive retransmission algorithm that constantly adjust packet transmission rates based on network latency, and increasing the transmission rate above what the network can handle is detrimental to the integrity of the scan. While there are ways to mitigate this, such as limiting the number of retries per host, it is generally recommended to avoid these flags and increase performance in other ways.

Case Study: Real-World Account of Pentesting a Very Large Environment

When starting a new internal pentest, there are a few initial steps that we almost always do in the same order. We first passively analyze the network traffic on the local subnet with Wireshark to determine if there are any protocols that may be susceptible to poisoning (NBNS, LLMNR). This layer two (of the OSI Model) analysis will often also allow us to determine what type of network infrastructure is in the environment, for example, the presence of **Cisco Discovery Protocol (CDP)**. Next, we typically use a passive ARP scanner such as NetDiscover to determine what type of devices are on the subnet that the penetration testing appliance is on. We follow this by switching from passively gathering information to actively scanning on the local subnet first, then transition into discovery and analysis of the rest of the provided scope.

In most cases, it is best for the client to put the penetration testing device on the same subnet and VLAN as normal user workstations as opposed to something more specific such as a management or ancillary subnet. This better emulates a scenario in which a malicious actor had breached the external perimeter via a compromised user. However, clients do not always follow this recommendation.

One internal network pentesting engagement was particularly memorable for two main reasons. The client provided the scope as five separate /16 subnets, and the subnet that the pentesting appliance was placed on (my starting point) had only one other device on it, which was a printer. As a result, it was necessary to begin discovering other subnets that had active clients on them as quickly as possible.

First, five different target files were created, each one with one of the /16 subnets written in a range that would scan only the gateways (`subnet1.txt`, `subnet2.txt` ... and so on). A simple spreadsheet was also created to help with the organization of which /24s were active within each of the /16s. Taking the extra time to make sure the data could be organized effectively would pay off substantially.

It was then time to start scanning the first /16, and the technique chosen was a ping scan optimized for speed over all else:

```
Nmap -sn -n --defeat-rst-ratelimit --max-rtt-timeout 250ms --max-retries 2 --host-timeout 2m --min-hostgroup 2048 -iL subnet1.txt -oG - | awk '/Up$/{print $2}' | > Ping_Sweep1.txt
```

This scan proved to be a mistake, taking nearly two days of frustration before realizing it was far too aggressive. The settings were tuned higher than even a -T5 scan, especially with only a 2-minute host timeout specification. As a result, only a small handful of successful responses were received on each subnet. The network latency caused most of the packets to be lost, but because some did return successfully, it wasn't immediately apparent that there was an error.

The parameters were substantially reduced by simply replacing most of the custom fields with -T4 and tried again on the same subnets:

```
Nmap -sn -n --defeat-rst-ratelimit -T4 -iL subnet1.txt -oG - | awk '/Up$/{print $2}' | > Ping_Sweep1.txt
```

This time, many more gateways responded; more than 30 subnets were identified in the first /16, as opposed to only 3 or 4 the first time around. As a test case to determine the best speed for the other 4 /16s, this scan was run a third time with the `-T5` setting. Again, it returned only a small handful of results, similar to the first try.

In this case, T4 worked well in the client's environment, but anything more aggressive resulted in a dramatic loss of accuracy and would compromise the integrity and thoroughness of the entire pentest. This taught a valuable lesson that the same optimized scans cannot be used during every pentest; each environment is different and needs to be treated differently. This is why it is so important to understand how the tools work and, whenever possible, avoid relying on checklist-style operations.

Challenge: Optimizing a Custom Scan for Speed

While there is not a good (and legal) way to practice scanning huge subnets within your lab environment, you can experiment with different scan profiles and options and take note of the time that it takes for a scan to return.

First, run a simple service scan on all the targets within your lab environment without specifying any performance-related flags. Take note of the accuracy of the information and the time it took to return results. Next, start adding and experimenting with different combinations of the performance flags discussed in this chapter to determine how fast you can scan in your environment before the accuracy of results is impacted.

Note: Use the -d (debug) flag to see exactly what the scan is doing.

Once you have a scan profile that is working well, experiment with adding different options for additional functionality, such as adding an operating system in addition to service scanning, adding verbosity, including NSE scripts, and so on. Note down the scan options you use and the time they take to return.

This exercise will help you understand the impact of adding and removing options on the overall scan length: Does including verbosity slow the scan down by 5%? Or is it more like 50%? How much does skipping host discovery increase the speed?

Conclusion

Very large networks certainly add a degree of complexity to a penetration test, but it is not an insurmountable challenge. With a well-thought-out playbook, large scopes can be systematically reduced in size and complexity and rebuilt with the hosts that are reachable. While this requires some pre-planning, it can be sequenced and turned into a checklist of sorts that can be replicated in most environments.

Choosing which flags and what values to assign to optimize performance, on the other hand, is a skill that takes a lot of practice. Making the wrong selection can result in scans taking so long to return information that the rest of the penetration test, beyond mapping the attack surface, is rushed. Conversely, wrong selections can also result in incomplete datasets that may provide an inaccurate picture of the attack surface. As a result, performance optimization efforts with Nmap straddle the line between an intermediate and advanced level of skill. Additionally, scanning extremely aggressively can impact the availability of the network, which would undoubtedly violate the rules of engagement.

As with most penetration testing engagements, the biggest challenge is time. Malicious actors who have gained access to an enterprise network can spend many weeks or even months quietly aggregating information before identifying their path of attack. Pentesters, on the other hand, have only a few weeks at most, and that includes the time it takes to furnish a detailed report outlining what was found. Beyond that, it is fairly uncommon for a pentester to work on only one engagement at a time, further reducing the amount of time available.

With these considerations, a pentester must be able to operate in a very efficient manner, and being stuck waiting for hours for scan results to return is certainly not optimally efficient.

In the next chapter, we will explore two additional tools that integrate extremely well with Nmap, especially in larger-scoped environments. These tools, Zenmap and Legion, provide a graphical wrapper on top of Nmap, which can help pentesters visualize and sort the data returned by Nmap. The ability to ingest scan results and provide a more user-friendly way of interacting with the data is critical, especially as those datasets get progressively larger in enterprise environments. Beyond that visualization, we will also see how Legion can be leveraged to trigger additional tools and tests based on the results from those Nmap scans in a semi-autonomous manner.

Points to Remember

- One of the biggest challenges with large networks is that there are so few opportunities to practice specific skills outside of a live enterprise penetration test. This makes planning of truly understanding what your tools are doing essential.
- Understanding subnetting is a fundamental prerequisite for penetration testing. CIDR notation is ubiquitous in the industry and understanding the differences between the level of effort in pentest 5 × /24s versus 2 × /16s is essential.
- Even with the scope reduced as much as reasonably possible, there is still a need to optimize scans for speed in large enterprise networks to get the results quickly enough for comprehensive endpoints analysis.
- Optimizing the performance of Nmap scans requires an intermediate to advanced level of skill, and goes beyond simply setting the timing value.
- Increasing the speed too much can result in a significant loss of accuracy and potentially impact the availability of the network, violating the rules of engagement.

Multiple Choice Questions

1. **Which of the following subnets contain the most possible IP addresses?**
    a. /32
    b. /28
    c. /26
    d. /20

2. **Which of the following options would you use to skip host discovery?**
    a. `-sn`
    b. `-pn`
    c. `-n`
    d. `-nn`
3. **Specifying -T5 sets a --host-timeout value of what?**
    a. 15m
    b. 10m
    c. 5m
    d. 2m
4. **Which of the following is not a drawback of overly aggressive scanning?**
    a. Loss of accuracy
    b. Potential network availability disruption
    c. Potential host availability disruption
    d. Rapid results
5. **By default, how many times will Nmap retry a target port without response before moving on?**
    a. 2
    b. 5
    c. 10
    d. 15

Answers

1. **d**
2. **b**
3. **a**
4. **d**
5. **c**

CHAPTER 6

Leveraging Zenmap and Legion

Introduction

Over the past several chapters we have delved deep into the fundamentals of Nmap, covering basic scanning and vulnerability analysis techniques, and explored intermediate-level techniques surrounding timing and performance optimizations. This chapter explores two main options for adding a **graphical user interface** (**GUI**) on top of Nmap to provide additional context and ease of use. By exploring both Zenmap as well as Legion, we will discuss two options that work well for both Windows and Linux operating systems and demonstrate how each can be used to improve productivity and streamline analysis.

While not technically exclusive to operating system, Zenmap is most often utilized on Windows or macOS systems due to its ease of installation and smooth functionality. On the other hand, Legion is typically associated with Kali Linux. In fact, Legion comes pre-installed on modern versions of Kali, which conveniently makes it functional out of the box!

Nmap on its own is a powerful and highly tailorable tool, but as the size and complexity of the engagements increase, the need to parse the data more efficiently than scrolling in the command line becomes critical. This chapter is all about leveraging these open-source tools to enhance your capability to truly understand the attack surface, strategize, and execute the next steps of the penetration test in the most efficient way possible. By the end of this chapter, you can confidently employ Zenmap and Legion to enhance your penetration testing skills.

Structure

In this chapter, we will discuss the following topics:

- Leveraging Zenmap for Analysis and Scanning
- Leveraging Legion for Analysis and Scanning
- Modifying Legion Configuration Files
- Challenge: Creating a Custom Legion Configuration

Leveraging Zenmap for Analysis and Scanning

For quite some time now, Zenmap has been bundled in the installation executables for Windows and macOS provided on the official Nmap webpage. Essentially meaning, if you have installed Nmap on a Windows system, Zenmap has likely already been configured. If not, simply navigate to https://nmap.org/download#windows and download the latest stable release:

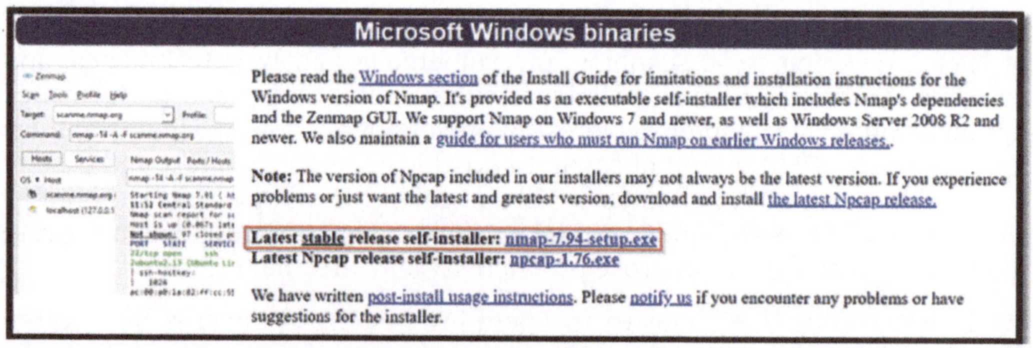

Figure 6.1: *Identifying the Zenmap Installer*

After following the installation wizard, Zenmap will be available and provide a simple, yet sleek interface from which you can either launch scans directly in the command box or select pre-set profiles to use against a given target:

Figure 6.2: *Demonstrating the Zenmap GUI*

By default, there are 10 default scan profiles that can be used, which are:

- Intense Scan
- Intense Scan plus UDP
- Intense Scan, all TCP ports
- Intense Scan, no ping
- Ping Scan
- Quick Scan
- Quick Scan Plus
- Quick traceroute
- Regular scan
- Slow comprehensive Scan

Conveniently, there is no mystery as to what each of these scan profiles does, as the specific Nmap flags are printed in the command box when they are selected, as seen in *Figure* 6.2 for the intense scan.

You can also edit or create entirely new profiles with the Profile tab and save your own custom commands. This is extremely helpful for saving your favorite scan stings to use repeatedly on different targets or engagements. This feature is extremely user-friendly as it provides simple checkboxes to select different features of the scan related to scan functionality, timing options, and even NSE scripts:

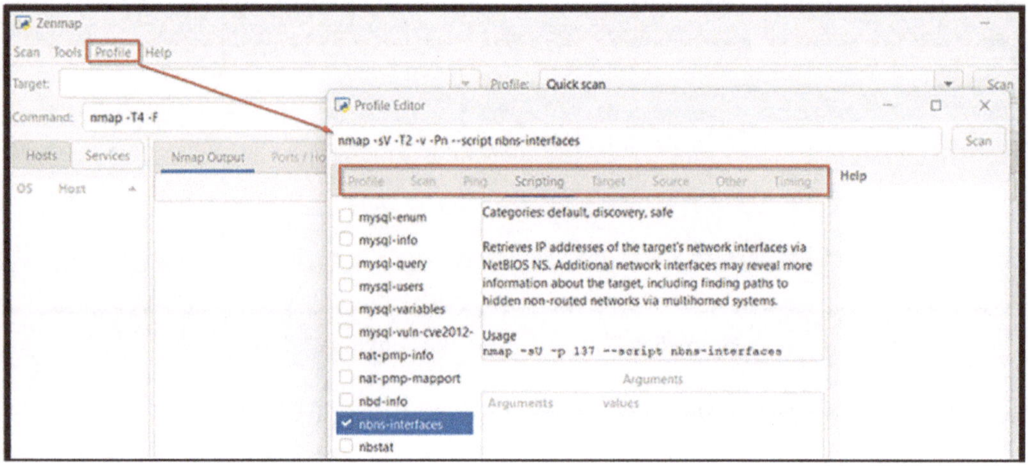

Figure 6.3: *Demonstrating modifying scan profiles in Zenmap*

Once you have your scan syntax set, either with a profile or by putting it in manually, you can launch your scan directly from the GUI by inputting a target and selecting scan. This will not only output the exact same information as the command line version of Nmap but also provide additional sorting options, allowing you to sort the information by Hosts or Services:

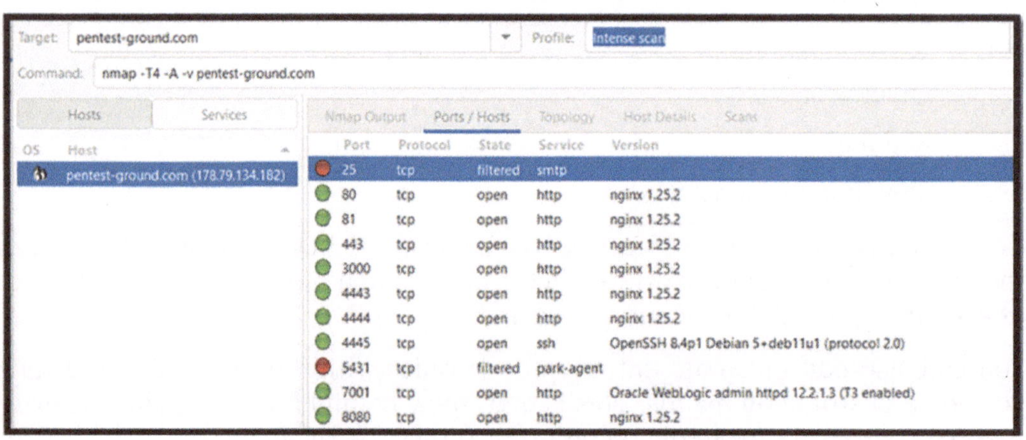

Figure 6.4: *Demonstrating the Legion interface*

While you can scan directly from Zenmap, another excellent feature is the ability to import pre-existing Nmap scan files (in `.xml` format) that you have saved into it as well. To demonstrate this, we can run a scan of both `scanme.nmap.org` and `pentest-ground.com`, then export those results into a `.xml` file:

```
Nmap -sV scanme.nmap.org, pentest-ground.com txt -oX results.xml
```

Under the **Scan** tab in Zenmap, you can now select **Open Scan** and browse to the results.xml file. Once opened, you will see both targets now listed with their corresponding ports and services. By selecting the Service tab and choosing HTTP, you will even see a list of all of the HTTP services running on the various ports across both endpoints:

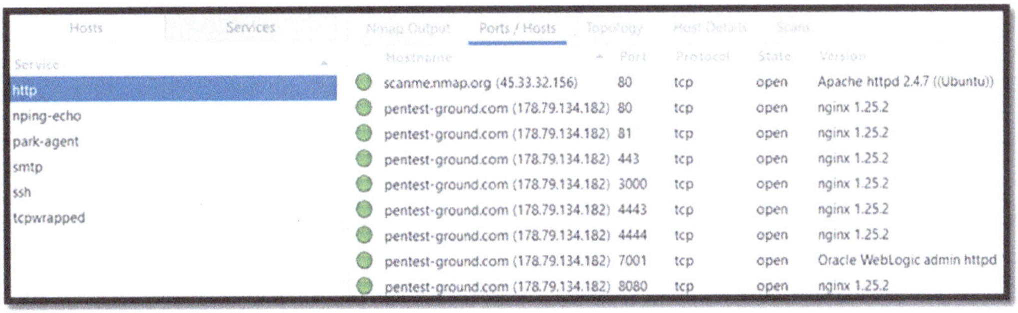

***Figure 6.5:** Demonstrating numerous open ports organized by Legion*

The value here is clear: you can quickly and easily parse through and organize different endpoints in your scope by the ports or services that are open. In a single clean view, you can understand some surface information about their versioning.

Beyond simply sorting by the listed services, Zenmap also has a few additional handy options under the **Tools** tab, which allow you to add custom filters to the dataset and even compare and contrast multiple scan files. The scan comparison feature is particularly helpful when trying to troubleshoot issues that may be impacting the validity of testing. For example, if you are running a scan with particularly slow options and getting only a handful of results back, compared to the same targets returning many results under a different scan profile, it would be indicative of hitting a host timeout rating and losing the data. Comparing results side by side like this can be very helpful in such situations.

As we discussed in *Chapter 5: Mapping a Large Environment*, being able to quickly understand the attack surface and organize the deluge of data that is returned in each stage of scanning is critical to successful network penetration testing. Utilizing Zenmap to speed up this process by organizing the data is not only wise but in many cases simply indispensable.

Leveraging Legion for Analysis and Scanning

Legion at its core is a highly configurable semi-automated penetration testing framework, which aids network penetration testers in reconnaissance, attack surface mapping, and even exploitation of systems. Originally a fork of SECFORCE's tool Sparta, Legion is maintained by Gotham Security and is regularly updated in current releases of Kali Linux.

Legion has many capabilities similar to Zenmap; you can launch scans from it, import Nmap scans into it, and modify how the scans operate. However, what sets the two apart is the ability to couple the results of the Nmap scan with follow-up actions. Consider the convenience of identifying a series of web servers and then automatically capturing screenshots of what the HTTP and HTTPS ports resolve to. Then, you can launch additional tools such as Nikto for web vulnerability scanning on the most interesting of them with just another click.

Legion incorporates dozens of additional open-source tools and more than one hundred scripts into a central suite that naturally integrates with and enhances Nmap. While Nmap is certainly at the core of Legion in terms of ingesting or collecting the initial dataset, being able to take additional action on the endpoints seamlessly is what makes Legion a differentiator.

To begin, start Legion in Kali Linux with the following command:

```
Sudo Legion
```

This will open the GUI and provide you with a clean interface with which you can either configure or launch your own scans with some pre-configured options; or similar to Zenmap, you can import existing Nmap scan results in `.xml` format. First, we will look at how to set up and launch a scan within Legion:

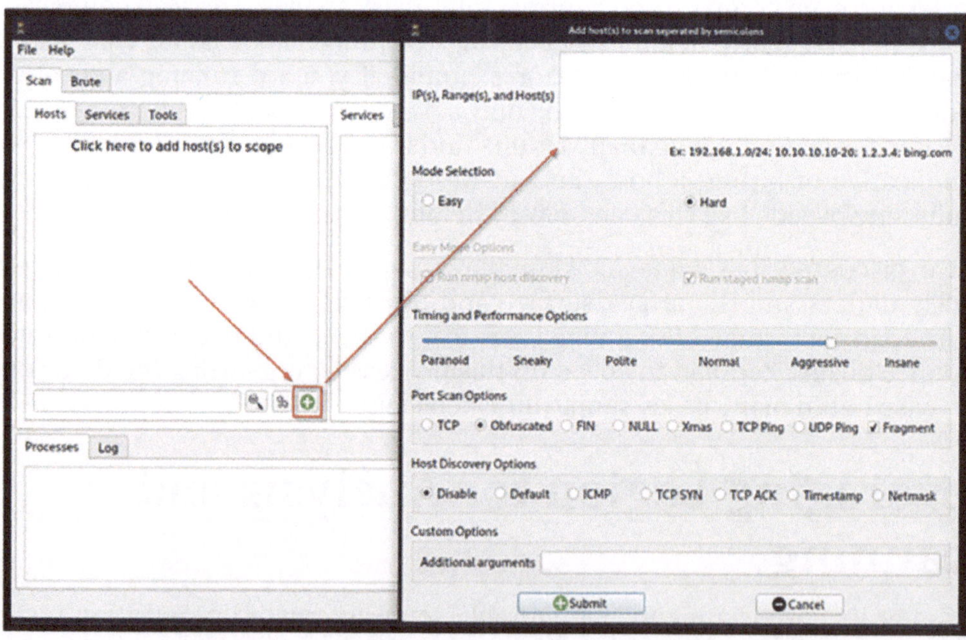

Figure 6.6: *Demonstrating initiating a new scan with Legion*

From here, you have several options to tune your scan. First, the timing and performance section is an exact simulacrum of the T0-T5 speed rating scheme within Nmap. Selecting normal, for example, will result in a T3 setting. Next, under port scan options, several options are available. By default, fragment is selected, which is the `-f` flag, along with obfuscated, which is `--data-length 5 --max-retries 2 --randomize-hosts`. Next are the host discovery options, which default to disable, corresponding to `-Pn`. So, by default, recent versions of Legion are obfuscated by design. You can also add additional arguments (Nmap flags) to the scan profile before launching the scan.

Once initiated, you will see each stage of the scan running within the Legion GUI, and the results will be returned in real-time:

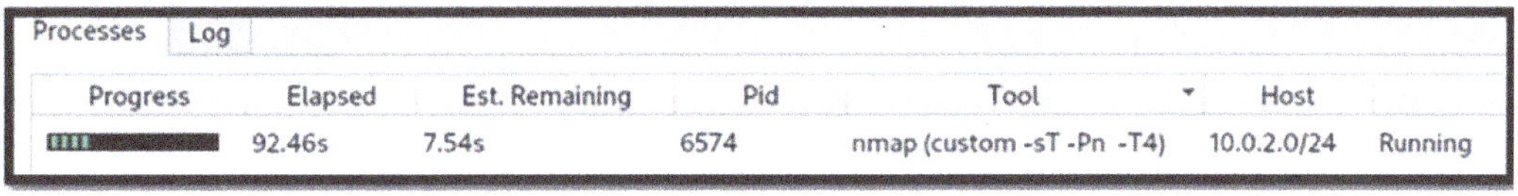

Figure 6.7: *Demonstrating a custom scan running with Legion*

Alternatively, you can also upload a previously completed Nmap scan into Legion by selecting "`file`" and then "`import Nmap scan`":

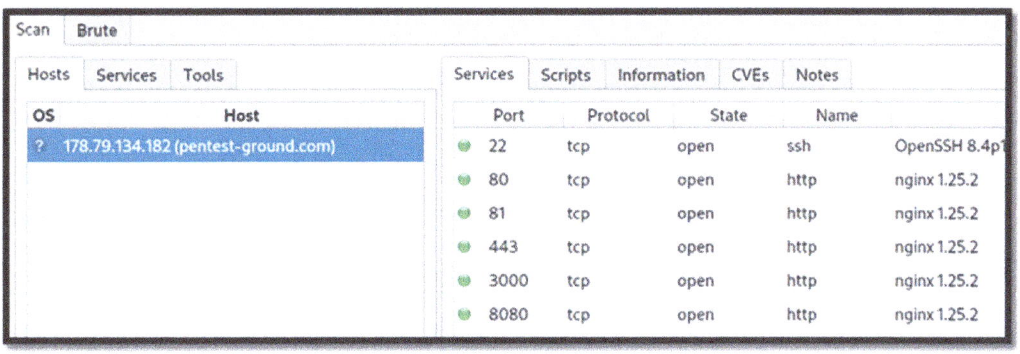

Figure 6.8: *Demonstrating a host organized by services in Legion*

From here, you can sort the results by either hosts or services or launch a litany of additional tools that can aid in the penetration testing process. To initiate additional tools, simply right-click the host or port in question for a curated list of relevant tools. For example, sorting by services and selecting HTTP for pentest-ground.com, then right-clicking, provides the following options:

Figure 6.9: *Demonstrating options following an open HTTP port in Legion*

Dozens of options are available, ranging from taking a screenshot to specific CVE-based NSE scripts, or launching tools such as Nikto or WPscan. The ability of Legion to coordinate this degree of additional analysis within one consolidated platform is what sets it apart from the crowd of other available tools.

Modifying the Legion Configuration File

One of the things that makes Legion so uniquely powerful is the extremely high degree of customization that you can apply to how it operates. By modifying the configuration of the tool, you can specify exactly what occurs at each stage of the scanning process, as well as which follow-up tools to trigger.

First, open an elevated command prompt in Kali and navigate to and open: `/root/.local/share/legion/legion.conf`:

```
sudo -s

nano /root/.local/share/legion/legion.conf
```

This file defines the actions and parameters that Legion abides by when conducting the scans, including lists of default passwords to attempt, host actions, port actions, and much more. However, what we are going to focus on are the three sections at the bottom of the file: `SchedulerSettings`, `StagedNmapSe4ttings`, and `ToolSettings`:

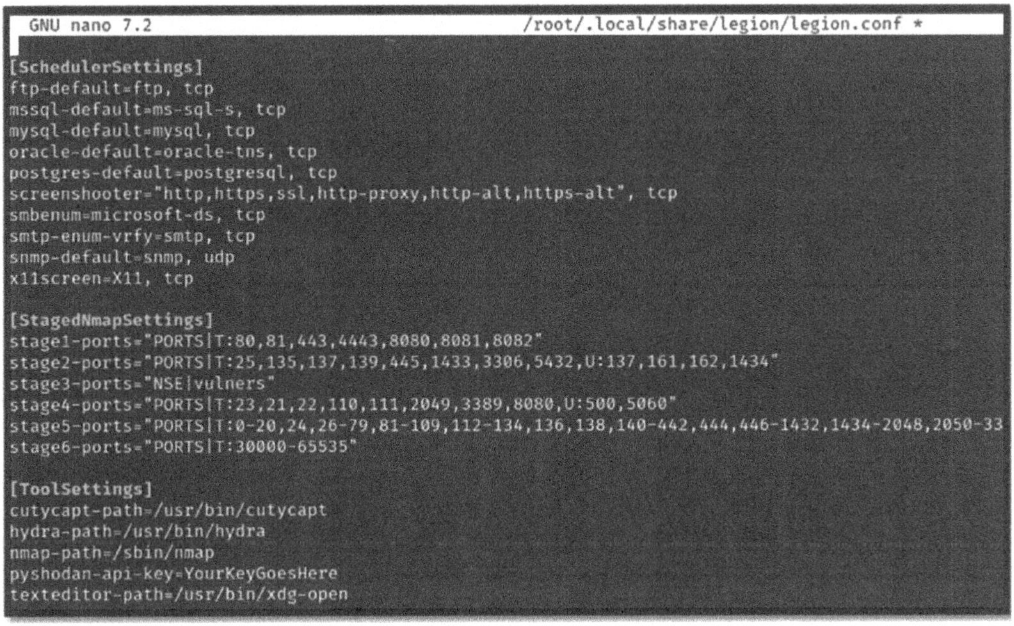

***Figure 6.10**: Viewing the Legion.conf file*

The **`SchedulerSettings`** define what will happen automatically when different conditions are met. For example, the top line in the preceding figure indicates that in a scenario when the **File Transfer Protocol** (**FTP**) is detected, Legion will attempt to authenticate with default credentials. Other default actions include attempting to enumerate SMTP and SNMP information and taking screenshots of identified web pages.

During most engagements, but especially something nuanced like red teaming, blinding attempting default login attempts at scale across tons of systems will likely alert the client's blue team of your activity. If remaining undetected, or at least more subtle, is a concern, removing some of the default scheduler settings can help define the exact actions that are intended. In the event that stealth is a concern, removing all options except for taking screenshots of the web pages would be beneficial:

Figure 6.11: *Identifying the SchedulerSettings and StangedNmapSettings of Legion*

Next, you can adjust the **StagedNmapSettings** to define what occurs at each stage of the Legion scan. This can be defining specific ports or even specific scripts that you want to occur. As scan results populate in the Nmap GUI in real-time as stages progress, this can be set up strategically to trickle in interesting information to analyze while the greater scan is still occurring.

In the preceding image, we can see that stage 1 is focused primarily on web server ports, which are identified and then automatically captured by a screenshot, allowing you to quickly parse through and look at what is being served on each endpoint. The second stage adds a few additional ports, which can be insightful, such as SMTP (port 25), various ports associated with SMB, and others. Then, in stage 3, the vulners.nse script is run on the endpoints, followed by three more stages of progressively more robust scanning, culminating in stage 6, which includes over thirty thousand ports.

While the default scan profile may provide a lot of information, such intensive scanning may also be overkill or simply too noisy for your particular situation. In these instances, modifying the actions at each stage can be extremely helpful.

By default, there are three different custom configurations packaged with Legion on GitHub, each tailored differently for use with a small, medium, or large scope and can be viewed at: https://github.com/GoVanguard/legion/tree/master/custom_configs. Comparing the three, we can see insightful examples of different approaches to the use of Legion scanning based on different situations.

Small Scope:

```
[StagedNmapSettings]

stage1-ports="T:80,88,443,4443,8080,8081,8082"

stage2-ports="T:25,135,137,139,445,1433,3306,5432,U:137,161,162,1434"

stage3-ports="T:23,21,22,110,111,2049,3389,8080,U:500,5060"
```

```
stage4-ports="T:1-20,24,26-79,81-109,112-134,136,138, 140-442,444,446-1432,1434-2048,2050-3305,3307-3388,3390-5431,5433-8079,8081-65535"

stage5-ports="U:1-65535"

stage6-ports="Vulners,CVE"
```

With a small scope, you, as a penetration tester, have the luxury of being able to thoroughly analyze each and every system and make sure that no stone goes unturned. This scan setting will begin, as the default does, with web server ports, but eventually progress to all ports for both TCP and UDP and strategically run the vulners.nse script at the end once all port and service information has been obtained. While this profile is extremely thorough, it is very noisy and extremely slow to finish on anything more than a small handful of hosts.

Medium Scope:

```
[StagedNmapSettings]

stage1-ports="T:23,25,587,80,8080,443,8443, 8081,9443,3389,1099,4786,3306,5432,1521"

stage2-ports="T:135,137,139,445,1433,88"

stage3-ports="U:53,110,161,500, 623"

stage4-ports="T:1-10000"

stage5-ports="Vulners,CVE"

stage6-ports="T:80"
```

In contrast to the small-scoped scan settings, the medium scope reduces the total number of scanned ports to just over 10,000 TCP and a few UDP. Reducing the number of ports to scan by more than 50,000 substantially reduces the duration of the scan; although scanning that many ports will still not be quick. This scope is reasonable for analyzing a few /24 subnets at a time, especially if the rules of engagement allow for scans to run overnight.

Large Scope:

```
[StagedNmapSettings]

stage1-ports="T:23,25,587,80,8080,443,8443, 8081,9443,3389,1099,4786,3306,5432,1521"

stage2-ports="T:135,137,139,445,1433,88"

stage3-ports="U:53,110,161,500"

stage4-ports="Vulners,CVE"

stage5-ports="T:80"

stage6-ports="T:80"
```

This large-scoped scan is much different; considering how many endpoints must be checked, this scan focuses only on the most insightful (or most exploitable) ports. In contrast to the previous two, which focused largely on quantity, this scan profile is far more pinpointed, looking for specific services, which would then warrant deeper investigation.

Finally, the ToolSettings option at the very bottom of legion.conf defines the paths for a few key tools that Legion relies on, such as Nmap, and also provides the opportunity to input a Shodan API key. For those unfamiliar, https://Shodan.io is an extremely useful tool for open-source intelligence gathering. Similar to how search engines like Google and Bing constantly index web pages across the internet, Shodan indexes internet-connected devices and catalogs information about publicly exposed ports and services. While Shodan can be used in the web interface for free, the API key (which is very inexpensive) allows for programmatic usage on a larger scale and is a great investment.

Once you have made the changes you wish to legion.conf, save the file, and restart Legion from the command line. You can then verify that the changes have been honored by selecting Help and Config, which will show you the currently implemented configuration. In the following example, we can see that all except for the screenshot have been removed:

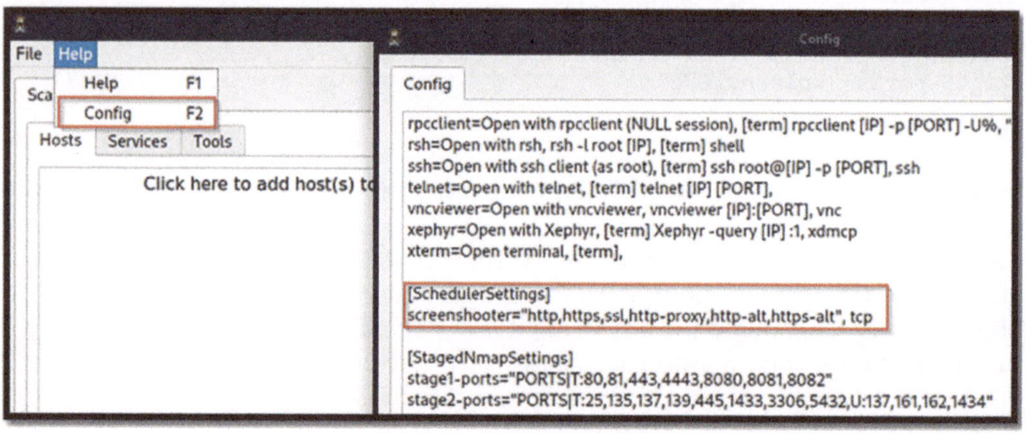

Figure 6.12: *Verifying the changed configuration in Legion*

Challenge: Creating a Custom Legion Configuration and Zenmap Profile

By now, you have undoubtedly started to develop your own set of tactics and techniques when employing Nmap, either with highly specific flags to control the functionality, a sequence of different scans for different phases of the penetration test, or just some quality-of-life options. Take the opportunity to create some custom Legion configurations and Zenmap scan profiles that match your specific use cases. Not only will you have these custom settings for your own use in the future, but they are also a great opportunity to contribute to the cybersecurity community by posting on a blog or GitHub.

Conclusion

Both Zenmap and Legion deserve a place in your penetration testing toolkit. For network pentesting engagements, especially, the ability to quickly ingest and understand the attack surface of an individual subnet or a whole scope is invaluable. While this could certainly be accomplished within the traditional Nmap command line, the interface provides two key benefits. Firstly, you do not have to worry about losing data or missing something important when scrolling through the results in a command prompt. Secondly, and perhaps even more importantly, the scans can be saved and shared amongst your penetration testing team, which enhances collaboration and makes technical review of the findings in your report much more efficient.

While the two tools outlined here are similar, their differences in terms of operating systems and options to go beyond simple port scanning, such as Legion triggering actional tools in a semi-automated fashion, make them distinct. By no means are these the only two tools that natively integrate with Nmap; in fact, there are dozens more that leverage Nmap in some way and provide the opportunity to ingest scan results. Some of these include SpearHead, Defect Dojo, Coda Intelligence, and Attack Forge; however, each of these are far more complex tools used for more intricate attack surface monitoring and reporting. Zenmap and Legion have a few key benefits over others; they are free and open source, can be installed easily, and are intuitive to use without extensive training.

Many people just starting out in penetration testing fail to see the need for ingesting Nmap data into a GUI. This is due to the tendency for pentesting training and certifications to focus on only a small handful of systems instead of a large, robust, and realistic scope. With only a dozen or fewer systems to analyze, there is likely no reason to leave the command line. However, this changes drastically when you have a dozen subnets rather than a dozen endpoints. In those situations, the time that would be wasted by not efficiently organizing the results with these additional tools would be a large impediment to the timeline of the engagement.

In the next chapter, *Chapter 7: Advanced Obfuscation and Firewall Evasion Techniques*, we will build on every introductory and intermediate level skill and technique discussed so far and craft some incredibly intricate and complex scans designed to remain undetected on the network. These techniques do inherently have a more niche use than others, as in the majority of penetration tests, there is not a large emphasis on remaining undetected. Instead, we will discuss and explore these techniques from the perspective of purple and red teaming engagements, where your objective is to bypass security controls and avoid detection.

Points to Remember

- Zenmap and Legion are frameworks with which you can launch custom Nmap scans, open and sort existing Nmap result files, and efficiently comprehend the attack surface.
- Legion also provides the ability to seamlessly trigger additional tools found in Kali Linux based on the results of the Nmap scanning. This ability to chain together conditions, tools, and actions provides a highly flexible semi-autonomous pentesting framework.
- The true value of these tools is when dealing with medium or large scopes where the output in the command line from Nmap would simply be too verbose and inefficient to fully analyze.
- Zenmap is very easy to install on Windows and macOS systems, while Legion is installed in Kali Linux by default.
- Saving organized scan data from Zenmap or Legion allows for convenient collaboration with the rest of your penetration testing team.

Multiple Choice Questions

1. **Which Legion timing option would be most appropriate for a medium to large size scope?**
    a. Aggressive
    b. Polite
    c. Sneaky
    d. Insane
2. **In Zenmap custom scans that can be preconfigured and saved for future use are called what?**
    a. Configs
    b. Profiles
    c. Presets
    d. Quick-Scans

3. **True or false: Legion can be configured to launch NSE scripts automatically?**
    a. True
    b. False
4. **For scanning a large environment with Legion, what changes should you consider making to legion.conf?**
    a. Adjust the `SchedulerSettings` to add additional triggered actions
    b. Adjust the `StagedNmapSettings` to reduce the number of ports scanned
    c. Specify reduced Host Timeout within the `StagedNmapSettings`
    d. Remove all `SchedulersSettings`
5. **Which feature exists only in Zenmap and not Legion?**
    a. Scan results comparison
    b. Importing .xml files
    c. Sorting results by host or service
    d. Adding filters to results
6. **Which feature exists only in Legion and not Zenmap?**
    a. Intuitive interface
    b. Ability to save modified files
    c. Autonomously triggering additional tools
    d. Customized scanning

Answers

1. **a**
2. **b**
3. **a**
4. **b**
5. **a**
6. **c**

Chapter 7

Advanced Obfuscation and Firewall Evasion Techniques

Introduction

Among the most advanced classification of techniques that Nmap excels at is in the domain of stealth. Nmap can add an impressive degree of obfuscation to the scanning process, which in turn can make it very challenging for most **endpoint detection and response** (**EDR**), intrusion detection systems (IDS), and firewalls to identify. However, this is only true when great care and intricate understanding are taken to manipulate the way the scan is conducted.

Evading detection and being the hacking version of a ninja is as much a science of understanding how technology works, as it is an art form in crafting scans with a precise level of subtlety. This balance is what we will explore in this chapter, discussing a range of new flags related to evasion, deception, and obfuscation. We will then take a deeper look at how Nmap works by default; while this has been lightly discussed in previous chapters, understanding how to manipulate parameters is essential for IDS and firewall evasion techniques. Finally, we will explore the common pitfalls that lead to pentesters being detected and how to avoid those mistakes.

Structure

In this chapter, we will discuss the following topics:

- Understanding and Manipulating Default Nmap Scan Parameters
- Advanced Flags for Obfuscation
- Intrusion Detection System (IDS) and Firewall Evasion
- Avoiding Blue Team Detection
- Case Study: Purple Teaming with Nmap
- Case Study: Red Teaming a Bank
- Challenge: Evading Detection in Your Lab Environment
- Challenge: Breaking Down Complex Scans

Understanding and Manipulating Default Nmap Scan Parameters

Letting Nmap scan endpoints in a predictable manner, as expected by security products, can be detrimental to your hopes of avoiding unwanted attention. Everything from the speed of the scan (T0 – T5), to the number of ports scanned, to the order in which hosts are scanned on a subnet, plays a role in detection.

Nmap supports numerous flags that are seldom used by the majority of penetration testers. Ironically, when it comes to avoiding detection, the most often cited flag by cybersecurity training material is **`-sS`**, also known as the Stealth Scan. The stealth scan has been discussed for years, and the concept behind it is very simple – Nmap does not complete the three-way handshake. As you will remember from *Chapter 1: Introduction to Nmap and Security Assessments*, the three-way handshake begins with an SYN packet being sent to the target, the target responds with an acknowledgment (SYN-ACK), and then that acknowledgment is in turn acknowledged back (ACK). When using a stealth scan, Nmap will still send an SYN packet, but once an SYN-ACK is received, Nmap then ends the connection with an RST. By interrupting the three-way handshake, Nmap could still identify if a port was open, but would not establish a full TCP connection, and, in turn, this was helpful in avoiding detection in past years.

However, what many pentesters don't realize is that the **`-sS`** flag is obsolete. It is now (and has been for quite some time) the default behavior of Nmap. In fact, if you wanted to complete a full three-way handshake, you would need to supply a different flag altogether. While it may seem convenient that `-sS` is one less flag to remember, it's important to note that because it has been the default Nmap behavior for so long, security detection products are now trained to associate this type of behavior with Nmap. This effectively negates the actual effect a "*stealth scan*" has on being stealthy.

Another often overlooked default process is the order in which Nmap will scan subnets. By default, Nmap scans in ascending numerical order. This means if you were to scan 10.0.0.0/24, the first endpoint that will be scanned is 10.0.0.0, then 10.0.0.1, then 10.0.0.2, and so on until 10.0.0.255. Heuristically speaking, seeing a single endpoint systematically scanning every single IP in a subnet in order is very obviously a malicious port scan and will likely be identified as such. Detection of this nature is triggered by the nature of the activity (heuristics). The default behavior of scanning the top 1000 ports in a known fixed order also contributes to the probability of heuristic detection.

In contrast to heuristic-based detection, many security products will also employ signature-based detection to identify the activity of specific known malicious tools. Nmap packets, by default, have fixed size and time to live (TTL) values of 40 bytes and 64 seconds, respectively. This means that unless these values are manipulated, the probability of detection is high regardless of how obfuscated the activity is.

As a reminder, Nmap also scans at the T3 speed by default, which is quite fast. Scanning a lot of endpoints very quickly is considered "*noisy*" on the network and is counterproductive to remaining under the noise floor. Being the most flagrant IP address on the network in terms of network traffic will likely raise eyebrows on the networking team and, in turn, the security team.

Thankfully for penetration testers, and much to the chagrin of those selling enterprise security products, every one of these default options can be modified and calibrated to tailor scans that are much more capable of avoiding both heuristic and signature-based detection.

Advanced Flags for Obfuscation

- `-f`: This flag modifies the scan by causing Nmap to employ smaller fragmented packets rather than a complete packet. This helps with the obfuscation of the scan by making it more difficult for intrusion detection systems to identify. While this flag by itself often will not bypassdetection against modern systems, it can be readily combined with many other options when conducting TCP and UDP scans to do so.

  An important thing to note is that packet fragmentation is meant for raw packet frames only. This means that port scans and service versioning will work well, but things like operating system version (`-O`) and most NSE scripts will not support fragmentation.

- **`--randomize-hosts`**: When Nmap operates against a range of endpoints by default, it scans in numerical order. For example, if you were to scan 10.10.10.0/24, the first host scanned would be 10.10.10.0, then 10.10.10.1, 10.10.10.2, and so on up to 10.10.10.255. This creates a distinctly noticeable pattern on the network, which can be easily detected by the IDS. This flag is great for adding entropy to the scan operations by simply picking random endpoints from the list. So, scanning 10.10.10.0/24 with `--randomize-hosts` may start with 10.10.10.47, then 10.10.10.2, followed by 10.10.10.217, and so on.
- **`--data-length #`**: Nmap packets are usually lean, with just simple headers, a fact known by security products. By default, Nmap packets are 40 bytes in length, and ICMP echo requests are 28 bytes; this known length is often used to detect the use of Nmap on the network. The `-data-length` flag allows you to append a random set of data to the end of the packets. This helps make each packet unique and can, when combined with other techniques such as fragmentation, be highly effective in obfuscating the activity.

  Keep in mind that this feature tends to slow the scan down; for this reason, appending a large number of bytes is not recommended. Appending between 5 and 10 bytes will be sufficient for most use cases and strike a balance between speed and stealth.
- **`--exclude-port`**: There may be times when you want to scan a large number of ports but want to exclude one or more specific ones, which often leads to detection. This scenario is when `--exclude-port` comes into play. As we have discussed, the default Nmap scan will utilize the top 1000 most common ports, but there are some ports, such as 22, 139, and 445, which tend to be more sensitive to detection. To exclude these ports, but keep the other 997, you could use the following scan:

  ```
  Nmap --exclude-ports 22,139,445 10.10.10.0/24
  ```
- **`--exclude-host`**: Similarly, to the concept of excluding specific ports, you can also exclude specific hosts in a range of IP addresses. At first, many people consider using this as a way of excluding the gateway when scanning a subnet; however, considering IP address ranges (10.10.10.2-254) can be used, it is only a minimally helpful use case. Instead, host exclusion can be used to avoid scanning yourself on the local subnet or to avoid scanning endpoints that you have identified as security products themselves. For example, if during passive ARP scanning, you identified what appeared to be a Dark Trace listener on 10.10.10.14, you could run the following scan to avoid it:

```
Nmap --exclude-host 10.10.10.14 10.10.10.0/24
```

- **`--discovery-ignore-rst`**: While not technically a means of obfuscation, this flag can be helpful in obtaining better results when facing a firewall. In some situations, firewalls will spoof TCP reset responses to all probes being sent to a disallowed address. Considering the default behavior of Nmap would recognize these RST packets as an indicator that a host is alive, Nmap would then waste an inordinate amount of time scanning things that do not exist. This flag can help in those situations by ignoring the initial RST packet and instead relying on other specified host discovery options.

  In a scenario where you get back a response for a large number of ports or endpoints, all returned as "*filtered*"; this is a good trick to employ.

- **`-Pn`**: This flag simply disables the ICMP ping as part of the host discovery process and instead considers every endpoint as up. In some environments, ICMP will be blocked or detected fairly readily, and this can be a helpful option.

- **`-D`**: This flag is used for decoy scanning, which has a fairly niche place in engagements when detection has occurred, but you are trying to avoid containment by the blue team. By specifying decoys, Nmap can spoof the originating IP address of the scan across multiple provided IPs. The idea here is to hide your true IP that is conducting the scanning from detection by also triggering activation, seeming to originate from other IP addresses.

This function gets a good amount of attention from cybersecurity content creators because it 'seems' like a great idea, like being a needle in a haystack. However, in reality, there are a couple of important considerations before employing this technique:

- If you try to spoof an IP of a host that is down, you may SYN flood the targets.

- If you spoof IPs that don't actually exist, you will still be detected easily.

- If you do this in a production environment, when the client is not expecting the activity, it could be seen as multiple compromised endpoints, which could result in panic and disruption to the organization.

For these reasons, employing decoys is a risky business and may be best suited to collaborative and well-planned purple teaming scenarios.

Intrusion Detection System (IDS) and Firewall Evasion

By now, you have seen dozens of individual Nmap flags, scripts, and techniques that have been introduced to fill a wide variety of use cases in a very scientific manner. However, in the case of evading detection, it becomes more of an art form. No individual flag or script that has been discussed will prove to be a magic bullet that pieces the defenses of client organizations. Instead, they are individual cogs in a complex machinery that you will have to build and tailor to the specific use case by strategically combining these options.

Some of the earlier flags synergize very naturally together. Consider the following scan:

```
Nmap -f --data-length 5 --randomize-hosts 10.0.0.0/24
```

This scan will fragment each packet from the original (usually) 58 bytes into 8 separate packets of 8 bytes or fewer, and then append five additional bytes of random data to the end of each. Now, instead of a single well-known packet length, there are numerous smaller packets, each with unique and seemingly random values. This obfuscates the signature of the tool. Next, the order in which the subnet is scanned becomes randomized, which adds entropy to the process of how Nmap is expected to operate.

This scan is a good start for obfuscation, but several more elements need to be considered, such as the speed of the scan, the necessity for host discovery, the risk of scanning often-detected ports, and the risk of scanning the gateways, just to name a few. Once these elements are added, you will note that the scan becomes somewhat more complex:

```
Nmap -f --data-length 5 --randomize-hosts -T2 -Pn --exclude-ports
22,139, 445 10.0.0.2-254
```

This scan is likely to avoid detection. However, when adding so many options to reduce the speed while still scanning a large number of ports (997 in this case), there will likely be issues related to host timeout. As discussed in *Chapter 5: Mapping a Large Environment*, when scans are conducted too slowly, they can lose accuracy by hitting the host timeout limit default in Nmap. To account for this, additional considerations need to be included, such as specifying the timeout value and defining the number of retries per endpoint. Adding these components makes the scan even more complex:

```
Nmap -f --data-length 5 --randomize-hosts -T2 -Pn --exclude-ports
22,139, 445 --host-timeout 5m --max-retries 3 10.0.0.2-254
```

Here, we have a solution that combines eight individual Nmap flags in a strategic combination with a defined scan range to strike a balance between being obfuscated and efficient. However, keep in mind that this scan results in only a basic port status and prints to the command line. Adding additional options to include service versioning (`-sV`), specifying that only open ports are included (`--open`), or including the reason for statuses (`--reason`), with any degree of verbosity (`-v`), and outputting the results to a saved file (`-oX`), all add additional flags, bringing the total to well over a dozen for a single scan.

Avoiding Blue Team Detection

Time and time again in retrospective analysis and real-time purple teaming engagements, a handful of fairly common mistakes lead to detection by the blue team. Understanding these common pitfalls will allow us to better tailor scan parameters that have a higher probability of remaining undetected:

- **Avoid scanning the gateway**: The gateway is the IP address on a subnet that traffic is directed to when it is in transit outside of the local subnet. This address most often has a switch or a router present, which will then do the necessary routing to forward the traffic to the intended endpoint. These devices also often have the capacity of an **intrusion detection system (IDS)**. By scanning these endpoints deliberately, you are figuratively shooting paintballs at the guard tower.

  In most instances, the gateway will either be at the .1 or the .255 address on a subnet, which should be avoided in most scanning. This can be accomplished best by either defining a specific range 10.10.10.2-254 or by listing the possible gateway address specifically with the `--exclude-host` flag.

- **Avoid scanning ports 22, 139, and 445 until absolutely necessary**: Many security products are particularly sensitive to activity on ports that are often associated with malicious activity, such as SSH (22) and those related to SMB (139,445).

  Starting with SSH, there are many ways in which a penetration tester (or malicious actor) can manipulate outdated implementations of the protocol. Most commonly exploitation is requisite on brute forcing, which is seldom permitted within the rules of engagement, or denial of service, which is virtually never permitted. For this reason, searching for open SSH ports can be deprioritized to the ending stages of the engagement.

  The SMB ports, however, are another matter entirely. There are numerous highly significant and actionable vulnerabilities traditionally associated with SMB, which can be pivotal in offensive security engagements. For this reason, the urge to target these systems right away can seem at times overpowering, especially when there is an indication that there may be outdated server infrastructure in the environment. This allure is recognized by many security products, and as such, there tends to be a more watchful eye on these services in mature environments.

- **Avoid scanning the same endpoint multiple times in a row**: While it may seem obvious, it is worth noting that continuing to hit the same endpoint over and over again is not particularly subtle, and with each additional scan, the likelihood of detection increases. Take care to split up scans into different segments to ensure that analysis can continue in one area while a cool-down period is ongoing in another. This is a very simple way to help avoid breaking the noise floor.

- **Avoid any scripts that attempt default logins**: There are many NSE scripts available that will attempt default or anonymous login attempts on services that are identified. These (usually failed) authentication attempts often have a higher probability of detection than the scan itself.

- **Ensure the speed of the scan is throttled to stay below the noise floor**: You can add all the obfuscation flags you want, but if you forget to reduce the speed of the scan, you will likely be identified as the noisiest endpoint on the network and trigger an investigation. Remember, the default speed of Nmap is (T3), which accomplishes a scan of a local host in roughly a fifth of a second (as per the official documentation). The default is fast.

- **Ensure that there is sufficient entropy in both the packets themselves (signature) and in the way the scan operates (heuristic)**: You must take care to ensure that the packets are obfuscated (consider fragmentation and appending random data) as well as the operations (reducing speed, randomizing endpoints, reducing retries, and more). When both elements are strategically combined, there is a far greater probability of successful evasion than only one technique.

- **Always start on your local subnet before scanning others**: When conducting an internal penetration test, you should begin by fully analyzing the subnet that you are already on. This allows you to scan and gather information on the local endpoints without going through a gateway, which often means sending traffic through an intrusion detection system. This doesn't mean that no obfuscation is necessary, but it does mean that you can lean more toward speed than extreme stealth on the local subnet.

Case Study: Purple Teaming with Nmap

For an organization with a mature security posture, a purple teaming engagement can be one of the most insightful and collaborative opportunities available to fine-tune their security products and defense-in-depth architecture. The fundamental concept of purple teaming is that the red team works in close collaboration with the blue team to conduct specific scenarios and verify the validity of the detection and incident response process. Rather than in a red teaming engagement, where the goal is often thought of as "*beating*" the blue team, purple teaming is an opportunity to foster teamwork and allow each team to learn from one another to better the organization's security posture.

Most purple teaming engagements have several distinctly different scenarios that employ TTPs outlined by major security frameworks, such as MITRE ATT&CK or the **Purple Team Exercise framework** (**PTEF**). One of the most insightful purple team engagements involved leading an extremely large organization with hundreds of locations worldwide and thousands of employees. This engagement was composed of five different scenarios as follows:

- Internal Network Reconnaissance
- Active Directory Exploitation
- Windows Workstation Privilege Escalation
- Windows Server Privilege Escalation and Persistence
- Linux Server Privilege Escalation and Persistence

The majority of the first scenario was conducted with Nmap by using a wide variety of specific scans against different parts of the network scope. The engagement began by establishing a baseline of detection against a default Nmap scan on both the local subnet (10.10.41.0/24) and another subnet hosting server infrastructure (10.10.42.0/24). This activity was detected immediately.

From here, the fun begins by trying to determine the cause of the detection and sequentially adding different techniques and parameters until there is no detection. Considering that even scanning the local workstation subnet was detected, which would not have been routed through an IDS (and the gateway was not scanned), indicating that there was a security product sensor on the local network that detected the activity.

To search for this sensor, an open-source tool called **NetDiscover** was used, which can passively listen to **Address Resolution Protocol** (**ARP**) traffic on the network and then match the MAC addresses in those ARP packets to specific vendors. Sure enough, 10.10.41.117 was identified as a security product. Rescanning the local subnet while excluding 10.10.41.117 allowed the scan to proceed undetected:

```
Nmap -T2 --exclude-host 10.10.41.117 10.10.42.2-254
```

The next step was to achieve the same results on different subnets, meaning Nmap would have to traverse and successfully bypass the client's IDS. Since this was a collaborative process, the strategy of progressively increasing obfuscation while the blue team monitored their detection resources was ideal. This started by reducing the speed and skipping the gateway:

```
Nmap -T2 10.10.42.2-254
```

No change; this was still easily detected by the SOC. The next step was to add more entropy to the heuristics of the scan as well as the signature of the packets. To do this, hosts that were scanned were randomized, host discovery was disabled, packets were fragmented, and 5 bits of random data were appended to the end of each packet fragment, as well as the TTL was reduced from the default of 64 to 58:

```
Nmap -T2 --randomize-hosts -Pn -f --data-length 5 -ttl 58
10.10.42.2-254
```

Despite this, the scan was still detected. Collaborating with the blue team to analyze the results, it became evident that what was being detected in this scenario was not a port scan of the entire subnet, but a port scan of SSH. Relaunching the same scan on a different subnet and excluding port 22 did the trick, with meaningful results and no alerts:

```
Nmap -T2 --randomize-hosts -Pn -f --data-length 5 -ttl 58
--exclude-port 22 10.10.43.2-254
```

Identifying how to bypass the IDS was an important step in the process, but it was not a complete scenario for this engagement. The final step was to begin stripping the different layers of obfuscation to identify the simplest scan that avoided detection. By doing this, it becomes far clearer how to fine-tune the security products to increase the detection capability. Understanding that excluding SSH was key to the process, this was done in two stages: removing the entropy of the scan and removing the entropy of the signature:

- `Nmap -Pn -f --data-length 5 -ttl 58 --exclude-port 22 10.10.43.0/24`
- `Nmap -T2 --randomize-hosts --exclude-port 22 10.10.43.2-254`

Interestingly, both versions of this scan were successful and avoided detection. There was an inherent overreliance on detecting malicious SSH connections as a highly valued anomalous activity by the IDS. While monitoring specific ports deemed impactful for malicious activity is a beneficial practice, other detection settings were reduced to avoid the deluge of false-positive alerts.

This exercise was valuable in identifying specific gaps in the blue team's detection capability and demonstrating the legitimate impact of those gaps. In this case, it demonstrated the potential for a malicious actor who had gained access to the corporate network to conduct reconnaissance.

Case Study: Red Teaming a Bank

Red teaming is among the most advanced and challenging types of engagement within the realm of offensive network security. This type of engagement pits a blue team and a red team directly against each other, with each team operating autonomously. In contrast to purple teaming, where scenarios are carefully curated and coordinated to foster collaboration between the red and the blue teams, red teaming truly emulates a malicious actor intent on breaking into the target organization.

In most red team engagements, there will be a mixture of both traditional penetration testing activities and social engineering components. Most pentesters versed in social engineering will tell you that the often-cited annual statistic from Verizon, which states that greater than 70% of security breaches involved some degree of social engineering, is far from a coincidence. In actuality, social engineering remains among the most effective ways of gaining an initial foothold into an organization from the exterior.

When people hear *social engineering*, one of the first things that come to mind are old-school phishing emails riddled with misspellings and unlikely stories attempting to steal credit card information. However, the reality over the last several years is that malicious actors are employing progressively more sophisticated techniques beyond simple phishing emails. Leveraging enterprise communication platforms such as Slack or Microsoft Teams, impersonating VIPs or support staff on the telephone, sending malicious QR codes, and even utilizing artificial intelligence to spoof the voice of key staff are all techniques being leveraged by malicious actors. In a red team engagement, if it is something malicious actors do, then it is typically fair game, as long as it does not impact the confidentiality, integrity, or availability of systems.

During large-scale red team engagement against a medium-sized bank based out of the United States, initial access was obtained through social engineering. The engagement began as external penetration tests often do, with blind reconnaissance of the organization, its domains and subdomains, exposed assets, personnel, hierarchy, line of business, clients, customers, partners, and products. This context plays a critical role in developing effective social engineering campaigns with believable pretexts.

In this instance, the mail records gave away a key piece of information that led to the successful social engineering, the name of the organization's **IT managed service provider** (**ITMSP**). Considering this client had a mature security posture, it was unlikely that purchasing and utilizing a typo-squatted domain to impersonate key leaders in their organization would be successful (many email security products such as Microsoft 365 and Proofpoint include domain impersonation protections); it was decided to instead impersonate their ITMSP.

For only a few dollars, we were able to purchase a domain very similar to that of the IT provider's domain and created an email account for an IT Support Specialist associated with that organization. Next, instead of simply using this account to send phishing emails (as malicious attachments or hyperlinks would almost certainly be detected and reported), we opted to employ vishing as an attack mechanism. By dialing the company's automated phone line, we determined that there was a dial-by-name option, which meant we could call anybody in the organization without knowing their phone extension or going through a receptionist.

With this context, we built a target list based on the client company's public LinkedIn page, targeting any employee we could find who had been hired within the last 60 days or had their position listed as an intern. New employees were targeted for two main reasons. The first is that they may not have yet built a relationship with specific personnel at their ITMSP and may be more likely to believe our impersonation attempts. The other reason is that new personnel are often given a ton of information all at once in their onboarding and may not be as familiar with how to report suspicious activity, such as a questionable phone call.

With the target list in place, the technique was very simple. We called each new employee and pretended to be a pre-selected Support Specialist from their ITMSP and claimed that their workstation was flagged for not receiving updates and we would need to remotely access their computer to troubleshoot the issue. This is a classic pre-texting technique used by malicious actors and is very similar to the technique that was leveraged in the cyberattack against MGM in September of 2023.

It took several calls to find someone who answered the phone (speaking live is always more effective than leaving voicemails), but eventually, one associate fell for the ploy. We walked this individual through the steps of navigating to an innocent-sounding hyperlink we provided, downloading a remote access software, and inputting a connection code that we provided. In a matter of only a few minutes, we had gained remote access to their workstation; there was no need to try and figure out how to bypass email security controls since we never sent anything. We instructed that employee to get a coffee while we were troubleshooting the issue with their workstation.

The remote access software had two very handy features that we utilized almost immediately: the first was the ability to blank the client's screen (which we warned them would happen so that they were not alarmed) and the second was file transfer capabilities. After blanking their screen, we searched for any VPN profile files, which we were able to find stored on OneDrive. We exfiltrated the VPN information, then un-blanked their screen, and told them that they were all set. After a mutual *thank you for your time*, we ended the call, now in possession of the proverbial keys to the castle, and they hung up none-the-wiser of what had happened.

We were then able to establish a VPN connection to their corporate network from our own penetration testing appliance. With initial access achieved, the next stage of the red teaming followed a very similar pathway to traditional internal-network penetration testing; the main difference being a meticulously stealthy approach to discovery.

We began by analyzing the local subnet to avoid routing through an IDS; but even though it was the local subnet, an abundance of caution was still used to remain undetected:

```
Nmap -T2 --randomize-hosts -Pn -f --data-length 5 -ttl 58 -p
21,25,80,443,8080,8443,4786 --open 10.10.10.2-254 -oX result_
local.xml
```

There is a lot happening in that scan, so let's break it down. We are running a slow-speed (`-T2`) scan of the local subnet, excluding the common gateways. We disabled host discovery via ICMP (`-Pn`), fragmented the packets (`-f`), and appended 5 bits of random data onto each one (`--data-length 5`). We randomized the host selection order (--randomize-hosts) and set a custom time to live (`-ttl`). Finally, we manually selected only seven interesting ports to be scanned for each endpoint (-p) and instructed Nmap to only print open ports (`--open`) and save the results as a `.xml` file (-oX).

Even with scanning only seven ports, this scan took nearly an hour to complete. However, it returned something spectacular. One endpoint on the subnet was an outdated Cisco Catalyst switch with port `4786`, also known as Cisco Smart Install in an open state. For a network pentester, this is nearly as exciting as finding vulnerable NBNS traffic on the network. Within minutes, we leveraged an open-source tool called Siet.py to pull the configuration file from that switch. While a malicious actor would likely modify the config and push it back to the switch and trigger a restart, which was outside the rules of engagement, as it would cause a network disruption. However, what we could glean from the configuration file was the hashed password of the switch admin account, a breakdown of subnets in use, as well as the SNMP community strings being employed.

This password hash was successfully cracked offline, revealing a relatively weak administrator password. While we had both the user and password in plaintext, it was not an active directory account, so the usage possibilities were limited at this point.

Continuing the discovery, we determined that we needed to expand the analysis to other subnets that were identified in the Catalyst switch config. These became the target list for the next stage of scans, which was done against no more than 2 x /24 subnets at a time:

```
Nmap -T2 --randomize-hosts -Pn -f --data-length 5 -ttl 58
--exclude-port 22,139,445 -iL targets1.txt -oX results1.xml
```

The only real difference between this scan and the first one is that, this time, rather than specifying a few specific ports, we are instead excluding ones that often lead to detection (`--exclude-port`).

We repeated this scan, switching in additional subnets, for the next several hours before calling it a day. The next morning, when we went to resume the activity, we found that the VPN connection had been severed. Evidently, the blue team had detected the scans at some point, quickly investigated, and contained the threat (us). It was a frankly impressive response time when we looked at the logs of when the connection was severed, and made a point of praising that response process in the formal report.

This engagement was insightful to the client for a number of reasons:

- It demonstrated a social engineering technique that was not covered in their end-user security awareness training (vishing).
- It demonstrated the speed at which a malicious actor could take over network infrastructure (the Catalyst switch).
- It demonstrated a highly capable blue team with an efficient playbook for triaging alerts and containing threats.

NOTE: In retrospect, it would have been wiser to scan only a small handful of ports at a time when transitioning to other subnets rather than simply excluding a few.

Challenge: Evading Detection in Your Lab Environment

Recreate the sequence of scans outlined in the Purple Teaming section (and copied below for your convenience) from the vantage point of both inside your lab environment and from your host machine. Compare and contrast the point at which you notice the detection in Wazuh, and then craft your own custom scan that strikes a balance between sufficient obfuscation and efficient speed:

```
Nmap -iL targets.txt

Nmap -T2 -iL targets.txt

Nmap -T2 --randomize-hosts -Pn -f --data-length 5 -ttl 58

Nmap -T2 --randomize-hosts -Pn -f --data-length 5 -ttl 58
--exclude-port 22
```

Next, analyze the difference with the complex scan from the section on IDS and Firewall Evasion:

```
Nmap -f --data-length 5 --randomize-hosts -T2 -Pn --exclude-ports
22,139, 445 --host-timeout 5m --max-retries 3
```

Challenge: Breaking Down Complex Scans

Analyze the following three complex scans and try to break down what each scan is doing, as well as the scenario in which you would consider using it.

Assume in each of the following scans your IP address is 10.12.50.16:

```
Nmap -f --data-length 5 --randomize-hosts -T2 -Pn --exclude-ports
22,139, 445 --host-timeout 5m --max-retries 3 -iL targets.txt -oX
results.xml
```

```
Nmap -T4 --randomize-hosts -Pn --exclude-host 10.12.50.16 10.12.50.2-254
-host-timeout -oX results.xml
```

```
Nmap -D 10.12.50.15, 10.12.15.17, 10.12.15.41 --exclude-host
10.12.50.16, 10.12.50.1, 10.12.50.255 --randomize-hosts 10.12.50.0/24
```

Conclusion

In this chapter, we have explored many individual flags and techniques that can be chained together to obfuscate your scanning activity from detection. By manipulating both the signature of the tool as well as the heuristics of its operation, Nmap offers numerous options for evasion. These flags and techniques are considered to be at an advanced practitioner level, requiring not only a high level of fundamental knowledge in how Nmap and port scanning work to understand their functionality, but also an understanding of their relatively niche use cases. Finding the sweet spot between a sufficient amount of obfuscation and a functional level of speed to complete the engagement within the set timeline is a delicate balancing act that requires experience, experimentation, and finesse.

In the next chapter, we will wrap up our deep dive into Nmap skills by exploring the intricacies of the Nmap Scripting Engine (NSE). This chapter will bring all of the skills we have been working on full circle and provide you with the tools and opportunity to create entirely new functions for Nmap that suit your particular workflow and use case.

Points to Remember

- Effective obfuscation is a combination of modifying the signature of Nmap as well as the way that the scan functions. Both elements need to be considered and employed for optimal success.
- Adding advanced obfuscation and timing modification requires a delicate balance between using just enough stealth to suffice while still scanning quickly enough to avoid losing data.
- Obfuscation is primarily a concern in red teaming and purple teaming engagements rather than traditional penetration testing.
- Nmap can be effectively used to progressively test detection capabilities during purple teaming scenarios.
- Bypassing detection gets progressively more difficult as security products become more adept at identifying malicious activity. This moving target is why an intricate understanding of how Nmap functions is pivotal to success in this regard.

Multiple Choice Questions

1. **Which of the following ports has a higher probability of detection?**
   a. 80
   b. 53
   c. 21
   d. 445
2. **Which of the following scans will fragment individual packets, append random data to the end of them, and throttle speed?**
   a. `-f --randomize-hosts`
   b. `-T4 -f –randomize-hosts --discovery-ignore-rst`
   c. `--data-length 5 --script firewalk.nse`
   d. `-f --data-length 10 -T2`
3. **Which of the following is not a concern when employing decoy scanning?**
   a. Causing an SYN flood
   b. Causing panic in a production environment
   c. Reducing the speed of results
   d. Selecting non-existent hosts

4. **Which of the following is not a common mistake that leads to detection?**
    a. Scanning the gateway
    b. Scanning to slowly
    c. Scanning too quickly
    d. Obfuscating only the signature

5. **Which type of engagements are you most likely to employ advanced obfuscation techniques? (select all that apply)**
    a. Network Penetration Test
    b. Red Teaming
    c. Web Application Penetration Test
    d. Purple Teaming

Answers

1. **d**
2. **d**
3. **c**
4. **b**
5. **b, d**

CHAPTER 8

Leveraging the Nmap Scripting Engine

Introduction

The Nmap Scripting Engine (NSE) has been alluded to several times in previous chapters and presented as a means of invoking creative and powerful additional functionality within Nmap. We have discussed examples of using scripts for both broad-based vulnerability scanning as well as more targeted verification of specific vulnerabilities. With hundreds of NSE scripts available and the relative ease of creating new ones, the options are vast. This chapter is dedicated to enhancing your understanding of how NSE scripts work, enabling you to utilize them to the fullest potential in professional penetration tests.

We will first understand what the NSE is and how it fundamentally works. We will then explore its syntax and best practices of usage. Next, we will discuss how to identify which scripts are included in your version of Nmap and how to add additional ones to your arsenal. Finally, we will explore the Lua scripting language and break down how to create your own NSE script. By the end of this chapter, you will have accumulated all the skills necessary to employ Nmap at an advanced level for professional cybersecurity engagements.

Structure

In this chapter, we will discuss the following topics:

- Introduction to Nmap Scripting Engine (NSE)
- Script Syntax and Usage
- Locating, Modifying, and Adding NSE Scripts
- Introduction to NSE Scripting
- Challenge: Create a custom NSE script and post it to GitHub
- Challenge: Test and refine the custom script in a lab environment
- Challenge: Scanning with multiple concurrent scripts

Introduction to Nmap Scripting Engine (NSE)

The scripting engine is widely considered to be Nmap's most powerful and customizable feature. It enables nuanced functionality that goes far beyond simple port scanning to provide a significantly increased suite of capabilities. This is possible through the Lua scripting language, a powerful scripting language designed and maintained by the PUC-Rio team at the Pontifical Catholic University of Rio de Janeiro, Brazil. Beyond Nmap, Lua has been utilized in many mainstream applications and games such as Adobe Photoshop Lightroom, World of Warcraft, and Angry Birds.

Through the development of Nmap, Gordon Lyon (the creator of Nmap) designated 14 distinct categories of NSE scripts as follows [Usage and Examples | Nmap Network Scanning (https://nmap.org/book/nse-usage.html#nse-categories)]:

1. **Auth**: This category broadly encompasses any script that deals with the authentication of the target system. Scripts where you supply credentials, use default credentials, or entirely bypass authentication would generally fall in this category.

2. **Broadcast**: Broadcast scripts are most often used for the discovery of additional or specific systems by broadcasting on the local network. One very handy example of this is the script `broadcast-jenkins-discover`, which identifies instances of Jenkins servers on the LAN via a broadcast probe. While broadcast scripts are not as widely used compared to some other categories, such as discovery, they do have niche use cases.

3. **Brute**: True to its name, this category encompasses all scripts that use brute-force style techniques. This could be for specific services like HTTP

or SNMP or for particular software such as Oracle or VmWare. Be very careful with these types of scripts as brute forcing can unintentionally take down systems or lock out user accounts.

4. **Default**: The default category is the list of scripts that are called when using either the `-sC` or the `-A` flags. In order to be included in the default category, by default, there are six categories that are considered: speed, usefulness, verbosity, reliability, intrusiveness, and privacy. While these categories for consideration are helpful to be aware of, they are also inherently subjective, as such it is recommended to be very deliberate about what scripts you are calling.

5. **Discovery**: These scripts are used for active reconnaissance and discovering specific information on the network. This could be a script to discover all systems with a particular service, such as SNMPv1, or it could be more specific and discover additional information on a specified target. An example of the latter would be the script `smb-enum-shares`, which enumerates Windows shares on the specified target. Discovery scripts are among the most helpful categories of NSE scripts, as they tend to be very specific, safe to run, and produce clear and concise output.

6. **DoS**: This category includes all scripts that may, intentionally or otherwise, crash systems and cause denial of service conditions. Unless specifically load testing or conducting an experiment in a lab environment, there is little reason to use these scripts in a professional capacity.

7. **Exploit**: These scripts actively exploit particular vulnerabilities. While there aren't a huge number of these compared to more broad categories such as discovery, the ones that are included tend to be quite effective. Some major vulnerabilities that can be exploited with these scripts include Shellshock and MS17-010 (Eternal Blue). These scripts are often adaptations of well-known exploit code, and in many cases, there are also equivalent modules in tools such as Metasploit, which depending on the situation may be more beneficial due to the availability of post-exploitation options.

8. **External**: External scripts are relatively few and far between and refer to scripts that send data outside the typical scanner-target relationship. For example, the `vulners.nse` script falls into this category, as the software and versions are used to query the third-party Vulners database to retrieve vulnerability information. Another example includes the script `whois-ip`, which does a simple WHOIS lookup.

9. **Fuzzer**: Fuzzing scripts send copious packets to the target server typically with unexpected or randomized values. While there are some

situations in which fuzzing is useful for identifying vulnerabilities, it is also an extremely arduous process with Nmap.

> **NOTE: Nmap does a lot of things really well, but in my opinion, fuzzing is not one of them. There are plenty of other open-source tools out there that are more specifically designed for fuzzing, and it is generally recommended to use those instead.**

10. **Malware**: These scripts can be used to detect targets that are infected by malware. A well-known example of this would be the `smtp-strangeport` script, which looks for SMTP servers running on an obscure port. These scripts can be interesting to experiment with but are in no way a replacement for a dedicated **endpoint detection and response** (**EDR**) or antivirus solution.

11. **Vuln**: These scripts simply check for very specific vulnerabilities. Similar to the exploit category, the automatic exploitation is not executed.

12. **Intrusive**: Scripts are always categorized into one of three categories of their function: intrusive, safe, and version. Intrusive scripts are those that have an elevated probability of crashing target systems and thus cannot be classified as 'safe'. Generally speaking, these scripts should not be used in a professional penetration test in most scenarios.

13. **Safe**: In contrast to intrusive, safe scripts are designed not to exploit anything, not to crash systems, and not to be associated with using huge amounts of bandwidth. These are the scripts that you will want to make the most use of.

14. **Version**: This is a special categorization that is largely indistinguishable from the regular version detection capabilities that would be seen with the `-sV` flag. While there are some very niche scripts in this category that can be helpful, they are seldom used.

Beyond the categories, there are also four types of scripts to be aware of:

1. **Prerule**: Scripts that run before Nmap's scanning phase. These are useful especially for broadcast scripts, which are designed to identify and pull in additional targets (use the `flag -newtargets` to do this) prior to scanning.

2. **Host**: Scripts that run during Nmap's scanning phase individually on each host.

3. **Service**: This is the most common script type and runs when the condition of a specific service is identified. For example, a web server on port 80 would elicit more than a dozen additional discovery scripts associated

with HTTP. If the same endpoint had another HTTP service on port 8080, then those same service scripts would be run a second time on that port.

4. **Postrule**: Scripts that run after Nmap have scanned all of the targets.

These types of scripts are not something you need to worry about specifying when using NSE scripts; rather they will come into play when you are writing your own.

Script Syntax and Usage

The usage of scripts within Nmap is quite intuitive; in fact, there are only three main flags to be aware of for common usage:

1. **`--script`**: This is the primary command to specify a script by file name or category as has been exemplified numerous times throughout previous chapters. While `--script` itself is simple, there are several sub-commands that should be understood for more advanced operations:

   a. **`--script "keyword-*"`**: By specifying a specific quoted string after the script flag followed by an asterisk, you can direct Nmap to run every NSE script, which begins with "`smb`". In this example, such a command would launch dozens of SMB-specific scripts ranging from simple enumeration to brute forcing, and even significant exploits such as Eternal Blue (`smb-vuln-ms17-010.nse`):

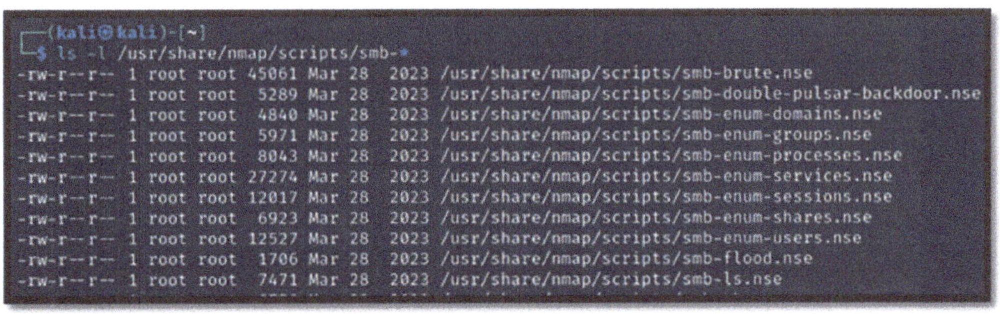

***Figure 8.1:** Searching NSE Script Library via wildcard*

   As you can see, specifying too broad of a categorization of scripts could lead to unintended consequences. To minimize this risk, consider adding more context to the command, such as specifying `--script "smb-enum-*"`, to filter out the more aggressive scripts in favor of enumeration.

   b. **`--script "category"`**: Any of the script categories described in the previous section can be specified or excluded with this option. For example, `--script "safe"` would run all the scripts in the safe category. Inversely, `--script "not brute"` would run all scripts except those in the brute category.

Both the keywords and categories can be combined together in some niche circumstances. Consider a scenario where you want to safely analyze a group of systems but avoid SMB-related scripts to reduce the probability of detection. In such a situation, you could run `--script "safe and not smb-*"`:

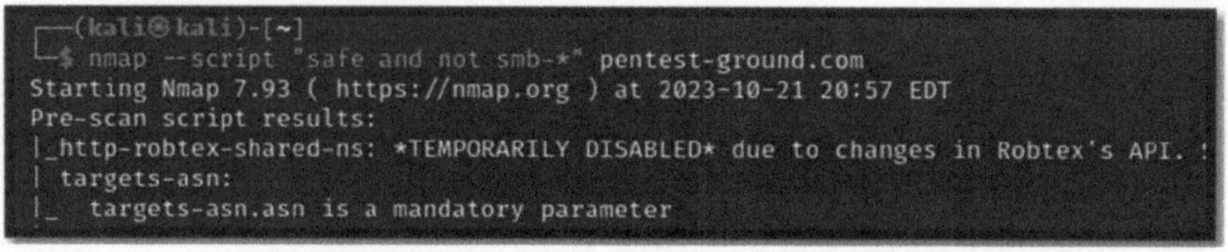

***Figure 8.2**: Scanning by category and exception*

c. **`script + [name of script]`**: Prefixing the "+" before the name of the script will force Nmap to run the script even if normally it would not meet the criteria. For example, if you were searching for SMB signing with the `--smb-security-mode` script, but ports 139 and 445 came back filtered instead of open, Nmap would stop and avoid running the script. The "+" prefix would override this behavior and force the execution.

Technically, you can also run "--script all" to run every script in every category.

It is highly recommended that you never do this unless experimenting with detection capabilities in your lab. Running hundreds of random scripts on targets in a client network is never a good idea.

2. **`-sC`**: This flag is a shortcut for `--script=default`, which would launch a "script scan" of all the scripts in the default category. Considering many of these are inherently intrusive, it is generally not recommended outside of a lab environment. Instead, a more nuanced approach to using more specific scripts or script categories should be employed.

3. **`--script-args`**: This flag allows you to specify arguments to existing scripts that are configured to support them. A simple example of this could be a script to enumerate SMB file shares that may support a username and password argument being provided to do authenticated enumeration. In such case, `--script-args 'user=admin,pass=welcome123'` could be used to support authentication.

Consult the Nmap documentation portal (https://nmap.org/nsedoc/scripts/) for a searchable repository listing all of the arguments that each of the, at the time of writing, 604 nse scripts built into Nmap accepts.

Be very careful using "`--script-args=unsafe=#`". Running scans with the unsafe argument has a chance to crash systems or services.

Locating, Modifying, and Adding NSE Scripts

There is a plethora of NSE scripts that are included by default in Nmap, which can be explored either on the official website (https://nmap.org/book.nse.html) or locally. If using Kali Linux, the command to list out all pre-installed Nmap scripts would be:

- **`ls -l /usr/share/nmap/scripts`**:

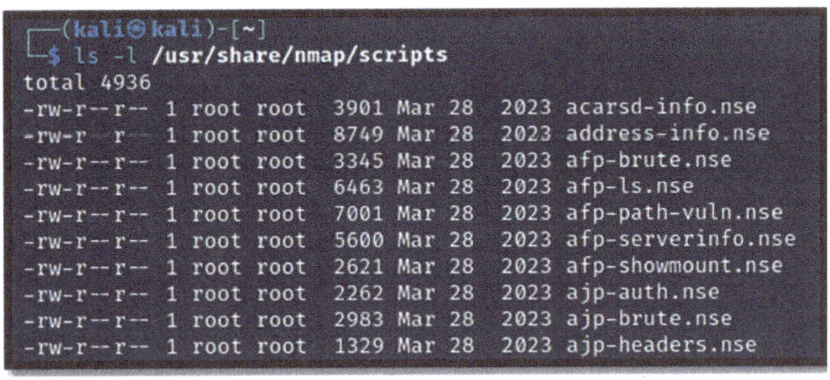

***Figure 8.3**: Locating NSE scripts in Kali Linux*

In addition to the scripts included with Nmap by default, there are hundreds of others that have been created by the community and shared on GitHub. Adding one of these scripts can be accomplished by navigating to the script that you want and copying it into a `.nse` file using a built-in text editor such as `nano`, `vi`, `gedit`, or `vim`.

For example, to import a script that would specifically add checks to fingerprint the version and patch level of Microsoft Exchange servers, follow these steps:

1. Navigate to the relevant GitHub page, which in this case can be found at ms-exchange-version-nse/ms-exchange-version.nse at main · righel/ ms-exchange-version-nse · GitHub; then copy the entirety of the script to your clipboard.

2. Create a file in the `/usr/share/nmap/scripts` directory called `ms-exchange-version.nse` using a text editor and paste the script:

```
sudo -s
cd usr/share/nmap/scripts
nano ms-exchange-versions.nse
Paste the script
Ctrl+x
y
```

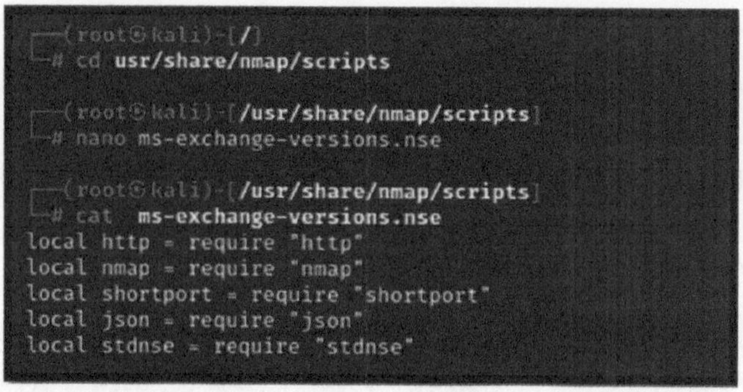

Figure 8.4: *Demonstrating syntax to save additional NSE scripts*

3. The script can now be run from any directory:

- `Nmap --script=ms-exchange-version.nse [target]`

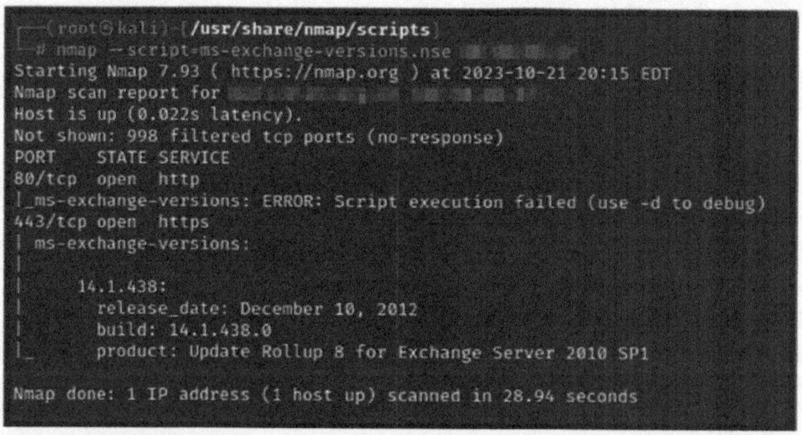

Figure 8.5: *Demonstrating imported NSE script usage*

In this example, we can see that the script attempted to version Microsoft Exchange on port 80 and failed, but it succeeded in identifying an impressively old version on port 443.

You could certainly clone the entire GitHub repo, but the drawback is that to run the script, you would need to be in that specific file. For example, if we were to clone the repository for `ms-exchange-version.nse` and attempt to run the script directly, it would fail. Instead, we would need to change directories to the newly created `/ms-exchange-version-nse` before it would run successfully.

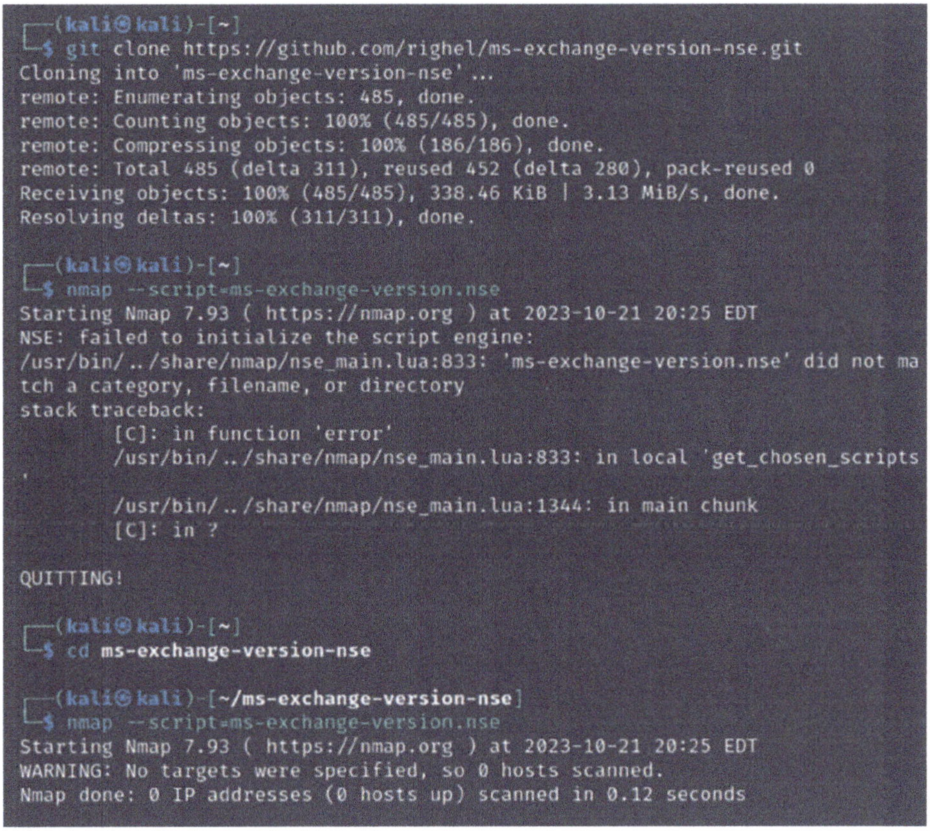

Figure 8.6: *Illustrating the pitfall of cloning a script into a new directory*

By placing the script directly into `/usr/share/nmap/scripts`, Nmap inherently knows where to look for it regardless of where you are in the file system.

In the event that you have already cloned the repository, or forgot to do this initially, the scripts can be easily moved to `/usr/share/nmap/scripts` with the following command:

- **sudo mv [script file] /usr/share/nmap/scripts**:

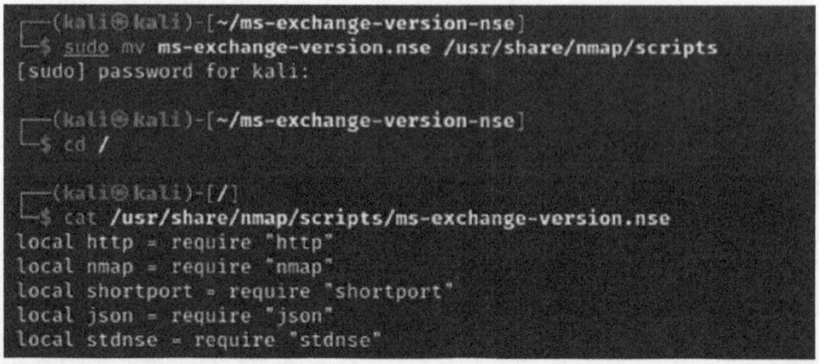

Figure 8.7: *Demonstrating moving a script into the proper directory via command line*

Introduction to NSE Scripting

As briefly mentioned, NSE scripts are written in the Lua scripting language, which is a relatively straightforward and flexible language. In this section, we will take a look at the components of a script designed to check for an indicator of compromise associated with exploitation of CVE-2023-20198. This CVE refers to a CVSS 10.0 critical vulnerability with Cisco IOS XE, which allowed an unauthenticated remote user to bypass authentication and create a local administrator user. This CVE was released in October of 2023 and was known to have been widely exploited. A popular method of maintaining persistence after exploitation was to use an available implant; thus, the script we will create here will be meant to check for the implant, rather than the vulnerability itself.

CVE-2023-20198 was a particularly dangerous vulnerability because it was so trivial to exploit, literally a single line curl command was able to create the local user account. Similarly, the associated implant could also be identified with a curl command. This simplicity enables this **indicator of compromise** (**IoC**) to be an excellent example of simple things that can be semi-automated with NSE scripts.

First, there is a commonly used format for NSE scripts, which includes a description and administrative information such as the author, license, NSE categories, and usage. We will start with these items at the top of the script:

```
description = [[
This script checks for the presence of an implant that has been associated
with the exploitation of CVE-2023-20198 which allows an unauthenticated
user to create a local user of the highest privilege level on Cisco IOS
XE Web Management User Interface. It should be noted, this script checks
for the commonly used implant to identify an indicator of compromise (IoC)
```

```
it does not determine the target's vulnerability to the exploit itself.
]]

author = "Travis DeForge"
license = "Same as Nmap--See https://nmap.org/book/man-legal.html"
categories = {"malware", "safe"}

-- @usage
-- nmap --script CVE-2023-20198-Implant-Checker.nse <target(s)>
```

With those administrative details out of the way, the actual script can be provided. In this instance, we simply need Nmap to run `curl -k -x POST <target>/webui/logoutconfirm.html?logon_hash=1` and print the output for us. To do this, we will first define the action, and then specify the target IP address within the URL path:

```
-- Define the action function
action = function(host, port)
      local target_ip = host.ip
       -- Define the URL with the target IP addresses
local url = "https://" .. target_ip .. "/webui/logoutconfirm.html?logon_
hash=1"
```

To finish the NSE script, now we just need to define the command to execute and print the results for analysis:

```
-- Execute
  local command = 'curl -k -X POST "' .. url .. '"'
  local handle = io.popen(command)
  local result = handle:read("*a")
  handle:close()

  -- Print the server response
  return result
end
```

While this is an extremely niche and very simple example of what can be converted into an NSE script; it is meant to be used as inspiration for you to identify other actions within your own workflows, which could be better optimized with Nmap.

Challenge: Create a Custom NSE Script and Post it to GitHub

Throughout this book, you have used Nmap for a wide swath of use cases and been exposed to the nearly limitless combination of different functions within it. Take the opportunity to reflect on some of the operations you have experimented with and how you could expand, simplify, or automate some of those operations into a consolidated NSE script of your own.

Posting scripts of this nature on your GitHub account will not only provide more credibility to yourself as a security engineer, but it will also help out the rest of the security community. It's a win-win.

Challenge: Test and Refine a Custom Script in the Lab environment

Once you have your custom script created, regardless of whether it is an adaptation of CVE-2023-20198 or something different entirely, experiment with ways to iteratively improve the initial version. Experiment with methods of building obfuscation into the script, optimizing the timing profiles, or refining the output.

This can also be done by forking new versions of existing scripts and making your own modifications. This is meant to be an exercise in recognizing that you are not limited in your capacity with Nmap just because a script doesn't currently do what you need. You have the capability to modify, improve, and create additional functionality through NSE scripts at any time.

As always, don't forget to add the new version to your GitHub!

Challenge: Scanning with Multiple Concurrent Scripts

For this challenge, determine a combination of scripts that synergize well together, which you may want to call during the same scan. This could be something as simple as using a prerule broadcast script with the `--newtargets` flag to populate a target list and then using the postrule vulners.nse script to identify vulnerability information on those systems.

Keep in mind the order in which the scans will be conducted, the types of scans they are, and whether the output from one will be the input for another (if necessary). By identifying the combinations of concurrent scripts that fit your preferences and use cases, you will rapidly assemble a catalog of go-to Nmap commands that you will be able to use time and time again on different engagements.

Conclusion

Throughout this book, we have seen numerous examples of Nmap being leveraged to do powerful things, from obfuscation to optimization and everything in between. Undoubtedly one of the most powerful aspects of Nmap is the scripting engine. By understanding how the NSE scripts work, where to find them, how to incorporate them into your workflow, and even how to create custom ones yourself, you will be able to elevate your penetration testing skills to the next level.

In this chapter, we took a deeper look at the components of NSE scripts, how they work, what rules govern their function, and even how to construct your first custom script. With these tools at your disposal, the potential is limited only by your creativity.

In the next chapter, we will wrap up our Nmap deep dive by exploring industry best practices related to port and vulnerability scanning. We will cover verification of findings to reduce the rate of false positive and false negative results, communicating results to clients, as well as common mistakes made by inexperienced practitioners.

Points to Remember

- The Nmap scripting engine (NSE) is widely considered to be Nmap's most powerful feature, enabling users to customize their own functionality to fit their workflows and preferences using the Lua scripting language.

- The categories of NSE scripts are extremely important to understand and check before running scripts. This can be the difference between ensuring the script you run is safe or accidentally causing a denial-of-service condition in a production environment.

- NSE scripts can run at varying times in relation to the standard scanning function of Nmap, including prerule and postrule. Understanding when specific scripts run will be important for any troubleshooting or to ensure that you are not getting a false positive or false negative result.

- If you choose to write custom NSE scripts, strongly consider posting them to a public GitHub repository with a comprehensive description. This is a simple but impactful way to give back to the information security community.

Multiple Choice Questions

1. **NSE scripts are written in which language?**
   a. Rust
   b. Python
   c. C#
   d. Lua
2. **Which category of NSE scripts are most closely associated with active reconnaissance?**
   a. Default
   b. Safe
   c. Discovery
   d. External
3. **Which category of NSE scripts would be used to identify indicators of compromise on a system?**
   a. Exploit
   b. Auth
   c. Intrusive
   d. Malware
4. **Which categories of NSE scripts have the greatest probability of causing a system to go offline (Choose 4)?**
   a. `Auth`
   b. `Broadcast`
   c. `Brute`
   d. **`Default`**
   e. `Discovery`
   f. `DoS`
   g. `Exploit`
   h. `External`
   i. `Fuzzer`
   j. `Malware`
   h. `Vuln`
   i. `Intrusive`
   j. `Safe`
   k. `Version`

5. **Scripts that run before Nmap's scanning phase are referred to as what type of NSE script?**
   a. `Prerule`
   b. `Host`
   c. `Service`
   d. `Postrule`
6. **Scripts that run individually on each host are referred to as what type of NSE script?**
   a. `Prerule`
   b. `Host`
   c. `Service`
   d. `Postrule`
7. **What is the most common type of NSE script?**
   a. `Prerule`
   b. `Host`
   c. `Service`
   d. `Postrule`
8. **Which of the following is the proper syntax to run all scripts in the Safe and Discovery category against the post scanme.nmap.org?**
   a. `Nmap --script safe & discovery scanme.nmap.org`
   b. `Nmap --script "safe & discovery" scanme.nmap.org`
   c. `Nmap --script safe and discovery scanme.nmap.org`
   d. `Nmap --script "safe and discovery" scanme.nmap.org`
9. **In Kali Linux, where in the file system can you find the NSE scripts by default?**
   a. `/usr/share/nmap/scripts`
   b. `/home/nmap/scripts`
   c. `/root/nmap/scripts`
   d. `/etc/shadow`
10. **Which of the following is generally not included in the administrative section of an NSE script?**
    a. Description
    b. Author
    c. License
    d. Nmap Version

Answers

1. **d**
2. **c**
3. **d**
4. **c, f, h, l**
5. **a**
6. **b**
7. **c**
8. **d**
9. **a**
10. **d**

Chapter 9

Best Practices and Considerations

Introduction

The previous eight chapters have provided an in-depth look into the function and optimized usage of Nmap, its role in offensive security, and how to become a power-user of the tool. In this chapter, we will conclude our deep dive by discussing some important do's and don'ts as it relates to employing Nmap in a professional capacity.

First, we will discuss considerations for determining which type of scan is appropriate for particular situations. In many instances, understanding both the scope and the intent of the penetration test will provide the insight needed to identify the degree to which your Nmap scans must be obfuscated or optimized. Understanding how to translate those rules of engagement into the intent of the engagement, and ultimately into how to conduct the penetration test, is a skill in itself that must be trained.

Next, we will discuss the major considerations that must be considered to avoid negatively impacting a client's systems. Even the best penetration test and the most thorough report will be overshadowed by accidently taking down client systems. Thus, understanding the potential impact will empower you to make an informed decision every step of the way.

Finally, we will conclude with a discussion on how to best communicate results to clients. At the end of the day, in penetration testing, the technical "*hacking*" is only one piece of the puzzle, the communication piece plays a huge role. Clients pay tens of thousands of dollars for penetration tests not just for the pentester to identify vulnerabilities, but also for the partnership in understanding how to best remediate those issues. As a result, understanding how best to communicate your testing results is an essential skill for any pentester.

Structure

In this chapter, we will discuss the following topics:

- Identifying the Right Scan at the Right Time
- Key Considerations to Avoid a Negative Impact on Client Systems
- Effective Communication of Results

Identifying the Right Scan at the Right Time

Understanding the intent of the engagement is of paramount importance in any project, be it a penetration test, purple team, or red team engagement. The rules of engagement and discussions with the client will provide you with a lot of insight into the particular needs of that customer. In cybersecurity, and especially in penetration testing, it is not a one-size-fits-all offering. Organizations that offer one specific package with pre-defined parameters for a penetration test are likely not taking into consideration the specific nuances of client environments or the unique needs of each customer. While there may be large security organizations for which it makes business sense not to customize their service offerings, for the majority, this narrow-mindedness introduces a disservice to customers.

A common misconception is that a penetration test exists to 'beat up' the client and showcase all of their shortcomings. In some organizations, penetration testers are expected to (and shamed if they do not) obtain domain administrator access in every engagement. However, the idea that your objective is to "*win*" is short-sighted and misguided. As a professional penetration tester, your objective is to accurately provide a snapshot of the security posture of the environment that you are testing, both the good and the bad. This may seem like a broad mandate, but, in actuality, it also must be in accordance with the objective of the test to start with.

Understanding the reasoning behind why a client is seeking a penetration test is absolutely critical in meeting (and exceeding) the expectations of the engagement. Some clients will inevitably be engaging in, to quote Christian Scott (Chief Operating Officer and Chief Information Security Office of Gotham Security, and my personal mentor), "*compliance theater*". This means that the purpose of the penetration test is simply that their organization is required to have them; the clients aren't particularly concerned with the findings or the insights and simply need the "*box checked for the year*".

In contrast, the best clients will be extremely involved and interested in the insight that comes from the penetration test. Their objective is not to look good on paper with a clean report but to holistically understand the true attack surface of the organization they defend. These are the clients who are the best to collaborate with and typically have a more robust security program.

In either case, there are specific outcomes and methodologies that the client is expecting. While their expectations should never bias you into any form of misrepresentation, knowing the objectives will help frame the narrative of the pentesting report. Many pentesting training courses emphasize the importance of "*rooting boxes*" and getting "*domain admin access*". While these occurrences are certainly considered wins, your fundamental objective as a pentester is not simply to hack into everything. Instead, it is to emulate a malicious actor, demonstrate the overall security posture of the environment, and safely demonstrate the potential impact of identified vulnerabilities most accurately. While this mission statement may seem redundant and analogous to simply "rooting boxes", the importance is in the nuance of understanding your responsibility to avoid impacting the confidentiality, integrity, or availability of systems.

This fundamental requirement to accurately portray a sophisticated hacker while being cognizant of both unintended impact and the client's objectives can, at times, present a challenging line to walk. This challenge exists both from a high-level strategy of the engagement perspective and at the ground level of knowing what scans to use at what time. To illustrate the importance of considering these aspects, we will look at three hypothetical client situations and determine which types of scans should be used:

1. Client A is conducting an external penetration test against all internet-facing corporate systems, including their Microsoft 365 environment. It is December 8th, and Client A is required to have an annual penetration test completed every year. In the past, they have contracted pentesting companies which accidentally locked out dozens of user email accounts and caused a large disruption, which has negatively impacted the executive leadership's view of penetration testing.

In this scenario, it seems likely that Client A is engaging in a third-party penetration test mostly because they are required to prior to the end of the calendar year. Due to poor experiences in the past with pentesters not properly considering the impact of their actions, the client is (understandably) skeptical about the value of the test as a whole. In this situation, it will be absolutely critical to ensure that none of the actions you take cause a negative impact on the CIA or any systems, which means reducing the speed of scans to avoid accidentally causing a denial-of-service (DoS) on systems, avoiding intrusive, DoS, and brute NSE scripts, and limiting the number of systems scanned at one time to reduce the noise.

Additionally, it may be beneficial to customize the report for this client to illustrate the great care you took in protecting the confidentiality, availability, and integrity of their systems. A successful engagement of this nature may help restore Client A's faith in the penetration testing process over time.

2. Client B is conducting an internal network penetration test to test the validity of security controls that have been implemented at the conclusion of a network segmentation initiative. While there is an interest in ensuring that the environment is compliant with the **Payment Card Industry Data Security Standard (PCI-DSS)**, the greater emphasis is on ensuring that standard users are unable to access sensitive infrastructure.

   Client B has a very different perspective and is contracting an internal pentest to validate the usefulness of newly implemented security controls. While they are beholden to PCI-DSS, which includes a degree of network segmentation, the overall purpose is to verify that users placed on the standard user VLAN (or the employee wireless network) cannot access sensitive infrastructure. There are a few things to consider here. First, can those security controls be bypassed through obfuscation? Using the stealthy Nmap scans discussed in previous chapters, are you able to interact with the sensitive systems? Next, can you compromise other (less sensitive) systems and then pivot to the sensitive ones?

   Both of these high-level strategies must be very thoroughly analyzed and addressed deliberately in the report and status updates to Client B. Additionally, since the ultimate targets are sensitive systems, taking great care to ensure that those systems are not negatively impacted is essential. In this case, it may be beneficial to keep Client B up to date in real-time when any degree of access to those systems is achieved. Based on the Client's comfort level, simply being able to interact with the sensitive systems may be impactful enough, and attempting further exploitation may not be wanted. In these situations, clear communication is critical

3. Client C is conducting both an internal and external network penetration test coupled with social engineering. This is the standard type of engagement that Client C executes twice annually and rotates third-party testing firms each year.

   Client C appears to be an organization that takes security very seriously by incorporating not only technical penetration testing but also social engineering on a twice-annual basis. Additionally, the practice of rotating pentesting vendors is not uncommon as different teams will use different techniques, different tools, and perhaps different fundamental methodologies. This suggests that the security program of Client C is likely fairly mature, or at least the security team is working hard on increasing its maturity level.

   The type of scans you select in this scenario may be more complex in nature as it is likely you will need a deeper level of analysis to identify core issues that have not previously been discovered due to the frequency of testing. Remember, the more intricate and in-depth the scan (usually), the longer it will take to complete. So be cognizant of combining flags to achieve a balance of both depth of analysis and optimized speed of results. Considering Client C receives pentesting reports frequently, and from a variety of vendors, taking care to document your process every step of the way to demonstrate thoroughness of the test will be important.

As you can see, while there are some commonalities across each scenario, such as avoiding impacting the CIA triad, there are nuances to each client that should be considered. Good penetration testing is not one-size-fits-all; taking the time to speak with and understand the client will best set you up for success in delivering a stellar report.

Key Considerations to Avoid a Negative Impact on Client Systems

From a high-level and academic vantage point, the concept of not impacting the CIA triad seems to be common sense and almost a red teaming trope. However, in practice, when trying to creatively identify and exploit vulnerable systems, it can happen unintentionally, even to experienced practitioners. In a similar vein to understanding the goals of the engagement from the client's perspective, understanding the nuances of the environment and the systems themselves is equally important. While it is infeasible to expect to become an expert on every system that you may find in a real-world engagement, there are a few general guidelines that can help minimize the potential impact:

1. Once you fingerprint a system or service, understand how it works before attempting to exploit it.

   Once you have conducted a few penetration tests, most systems that you run into will be relatively familiar. You will come across a lot of Windows workstations, Windows and Linux servers, databases such as SQL and MSSQL, web servers like Apache, Microsoft IIS, and Nginx, and some ancillary (yet common) systems like Jenkins, IDRACs, and the like. However, in most engagements, you will encounter at least a couple of systems or services that you have never heard of before. It could be a fairly uncommon (in enterprise settings) service related to IoS devices like MQTT, or it could be an obscure implementation of SSH that you are unfamiliar with. It could even be a strange Linux system that turns out to be the audio system in the executive conference room. The point is, there will always be something that will require additional research.

   The responsible penetration tester embraces the necessity of research and understands what the systems are for, and generally how they work, before launching any intrusive tools at them. Failure to do so can turn even a seemingly benign script into a potential denial-of-service catalyst.

   Consider, for example, old versions of Pure-FTPd (think v1.0.48 and older); there is a very important nuance in this implementation of FTP – a maximum number of connections is possible. This means that if a tool or script makes a connection over port 21 to this service repeatedly without closing the connection, all the possible connections to the server can be used up. When all the connections are used up, there is effectively a denial-of-service condition where the system is not offline, but legitimate users would be unable to connect to it. This information can be quickly identified by searching vulnerabilities related to PureFTPd but would require the pentester to look into a vulnerability specifically related to DoS.

   This illustrates an important concept when conducting vulnerability research. If there are vulnerabilities related to a destructive activity, such as DoS, on the system you are targeting, make sure you understand how that exploit works. In the case of PureFTPd, it can be fairly easy to accidentally cause that DoS condition with scripts that on other implementations of FTP would be perfectly fine.

2. Understand the criticality of systems prior to aggressively targeting them.

   In 2021, a penetration test was conducted that identified a Windows 2003 server in a production environment. It was egregious to see a system so incredibly outdated. To put it into perspective just how old that is, Windows 2003 servers supported a maximum of 2 GB of RAM. What's worse is that this server was running business-critical operations for the client. Even though there were numerous exploits available that could have been used to take over this system (and likely by extension the rest of the environment), the sheer age and importance made it far too risky to attempt. In fact, for fear of accidentally overwhelming it and taking it offline, removing this system from any future scans in the environment was opted. In this instance, it was an easy decision that the client ended up appreciating.

3. If in doubt, ask for clarification from the project point of contact.

   This guideline supplements #2 in seeking additional clarification from your points of contact when something seems unusual. In the aforementioned scenario, the only reason the nearly two-decade-old Windows server was indentified as business critical was because the point of contact was asked. Inquiring about such a system because it was so unusual compared to the rest of the environment, the client was happy to provide some additional context.

   If you are in a situation where something seems odd, asking for clarification before proceeding is often a wise strategy. The great thing about network penetration testing is that you can easily set a system aside while asking for more context and work on a different part of the environment in the meantime.

4. Clarify with the client if there are any systems that should not be targeted on specific days or at specific times.

   It isn't particularly common, but in some instances, there will be a certain subset of systems (often a particular VLAN) that is under additional load or is more important to the client at particular peak times during the day. It may be a requirement to scan and analyze these systems during off hours, or in specific periods. While this would usually be directed within the rules of engagement document, it is a good practice to proactively ask the client if any systems have such restrictions. They will likely appreciate your attention to detail and consideration, and you may avoid an unforeseen disruption.

5. Never test something new for the first time in a client environment.

   It doesn't matter if it is a new commercial tool, a new open-source tool, an NSE script, or even an NSE script you wrote; always test it in a lab environment first. There can easily be unexpected and unintended consequences on target systems, and understanding what those are prior to choosing to use them in a live environment is critical. Launching unknown or untested scripts in a client's environment is both dangerous and irresponsible.

6. Know when to move on to another target.

   This is perhaps the most challenging aspect of penetration testing for people new to the field; knowing when to move on. Many training platforms like Tryhackme or HackTheBox have specifically vulnerable machines that are made to be exploited. Even the ones that are quite difficult can, somehow, be compromised. This can lead to junior pentesters thinking that any system can be compromised if they dig into it long enough. While there may be some philosophical truth to that, in reality, penetration tests are time-bound and require the tester to move relatively quickly. Additionally, it is far more likely that a malicious actor will target simple low-hanging fruit for a quick win rather than spending a tremendous amount of time and resources developing a zero-day exploit.

   Despite the logic of that premise, it can be very hard to move on from a system that you feel may be vulnerable. As a result, a common mistake is to continue to conduct more and more aggressive scans on the system and even remove safeguards to get results faster out of frustration. Rather than letting frustration take hold, consider setting the system aside for additional analysis and moving on to the next part of the scope. Exactly how long you should dig before considering moving on is highly dependent on the situation (the size of the environment, the length of the engagement, and so on).

Effective Communication of Results

For some, communication comes extremely naturally, and providing regular status updates to clients is a walk in the park. But for others, it can be challenging to switch context from in-depth technical analysis to communicating over the high-level overview and back again. Penetration testing is an activity where most seem to prefer a degree of immersion, meaning extended periods of time where you are able to remain engaged and focused on the task at hand. Having to stop mid-thought to reach out to a client is, fundamentally, disruptive. However, disruptive or not, it is an extremely important part of the process.

Providing regular status updates has many benefits, to name just a few:

- It ensures the client is on the same page with the state of the environment. Surprises are rarely a good thing in cybersecurity, so if the client has been kept abreast of the progress and major findings throughout the engagement, the presentation is often far more cordial.

- It provides the opportunity to call out major findings in near-real time. Imagine you were the client and had just started a four-week penetration test only to find out on the last day there was a critical vulnerability that could have been fixed a month ago. That would be extremely frustrating. Regular status updates allow you to keep the client updated with major findings throughout the process. Remember, your goal is to help the client understand and improve their security posture, not to "win".
- You can ask clarification questions. Sometimes additional context into what systems are used for, or what VLANs are expected to be reachable from certain pivot points, can be highly beneficial.

For most engagements, reaching out to clients is beneficial at the very beginning of the project, when a high-severity vulnerability is identified, when there are important clarification questions, when you have gained access to specific systems, and when reaching approximately 25%, 50%, and 75% of project completion. While some clients will want more or less touchpoints, these milestones provide an effective baseline to work from.

Conclusion

At this point, we have explored each of the major features and functions of Nmap, how to employ them efficiently in a professional setting, and how to use those skills to amplify your capabilities as a penetration tester. This final chapter has laid out a series of best practices and considerations when employing these skills and techniques to ensure you have a successful outcome.

Ultimately, the key to using Nmap in any capacity is to research how it works and how it can be used to accomplish the specific function that you need. A deviously simple concept, but truly core to the story, as the versatility of Nmap is extremely vast, as has been extensively demonstrated. This concept of understanding the how and the why behind what you are doing is what truly separates good penetration testers from great ones. While following a checklist is helpful for learning the basics, once you progress beyond those basics, the nuances of the environment, your tooling, and the objectives of the engagement begin to play a major role.

With the skills you have learned in this book, paired with the lab environment that you have set up, you have everything you need to become an expert at employing Nmap in penetration tests, purple, and red teaming engagements. You have also been exposed to many key ideas related to ethics, best practices, and common pitfalls in offensive security engagements.

The final pages of this book encompass two distinct appendices that may be used and referenced to expand your depth of understanding of Nmap. The first is an additional collection of Nmap-related questions and answers, which are entirely distinct from the set found at the end of the preceding chapters. These can be used as a 'final exam', so to speak, to gauge your degree of understanding of the material presented. The second appendix is a quick reference guide that has each of the Nmap scans discussed throughout all chapters collectively organized based on purpose. This is meant to serve as a quick reference guide so that you may rapidly find the scan syntax you are looking for without having to endlessly dig for it. Use these resources to further solidify your comfortability and expertise with Nmap.

Points to Remember

- Every client is different, and as a result, every engagement will have distinct and important nuances that make it different. A great penetration tester will take these additional considerations in stride and ensure that their methodology and actions are appropriate to the client's goals. Remember, penetration tests are not one-size-fits-all.
- Great care must be taken to avoid negatively impacting client systems. There are a lot of factors that go into this, but at its core, it boils down to maintaining clear lines of communication with the client and understanding the systems that you are targeting. In either case, the additional context will often help avoid disruption.
- Surprises in cybersecurity are never a good thing. By providing regular status updates on both a periodic basis and when significant findings are identified, you can ensure that the client is not surprised by the results when they receive the final report.

APPENDIX A
Additional Questions

Multiple Choice Questions

1. **This type of engagement involves the offensive and defensive teams purposefully working against one another and is often employed by organizations with mature security programs.**
    a. Penetration Test
    b. Purple Teaming
    c. Vulnerability Scan
    d. Red Teaming
2. **This service can be considered a search engine for internet-connected devices and can be used to obtain information about externally accessible systems passively.**
    a. Google
    b. Shodan
    c. ChatGPT
    d. DnsTwist.io

3. **This practice typically involves an automated process that seeks to identify vulnerabilities, often on a recurring basis.**
    a. Vulnerability Scan
    b. Purple Teaming
    c. Penetration Test
    d. Red Teaming
4. **This type of engagement seeks to enumerate a real-world malicious actor using known malicious actor tactics, techniques, and procedures (TTPs) to actively exploit the target systems or network.**
    a. Penetration Test
    b. Purple Teaming
    c. Vulnerability Scanning
    d. Red Teaming
5. **This status means the port is accessible, but Nmap cannot determine if it is open or closed.**
    a. Filtered
    b. Unfiltered
    c. Open | Filtered
    d. Closed | Filtered
6. **This model is a framework to describe how computer systems can communicate with one another, from the physical layer that involves cables and electrical signals, to the application layer where the user directly interacts**
    a. MITRE ATT&CK
    b. MITRE D3FEND
    c. OSI Model
    d. Lockheed Martin Kill Chain
7. **Who was the original creator and maintainer of Nmap?**
    a. Gordon Lyon
    b. Kevin Mitnick
    c. Alan Woodward
    d. Brian Krebs

8. **Intelligence Platform Management Interface (IPMI) is most commonly seen on which UDP port?**
   a. 443
   b. 8080
   c. 445
   d. 623
9. **What is the second step of the TCP three-way handshake?**
   a. ACK
   b. RST
   c. SYN-ACK
   d. SYN
10. **This type of penetration test takes the perspective of a malicious actor with inside knowledge of, and access to, the client's infrastructure.**
    a. White Box
    b. Black Box
    c. Red Box
    d. Purple Box
11. **Nmap can be installed on which of the following?**
    a. Hyper-V
    b. VMware
    c. Virtual Box
    d. All of the Above
12. **Wazuh is an open source _____? (Choose two)**
    a. SIEM
    b. Firewall
    c. IDS
    d. XDR
13. **Which of the following firewalls can be incorporated into your home or lab environment for free?**
    a. Aruba Networks
    b. Cisco Meraki
    c. Zscaler
    d. pfSense

14. New tools, techniques, and scripts should be tested in a lab environment before being executed in a client's network.

   a. True
   b. False

15. In a lab environment, implementing a security tool such as Wazuh can be beneficial in which way?

   a. To gauge the level of obfuscation during advanced scanning techniques
   b. To understand the level of noise generated during scanning
   c. To experiment with detection and response configurations
   d. All of the Above

16. Which of the following tools provides an interactive graphical user interface (GUI) for Nmap? (Choose Two)

   a. LAMP
   b. Legion
   c. Zenmap
   d. Bloodhound

17. Which of the following flags are used to specify a target file?

   a. `-iL`
   b. `-oX`
   c. `--target-file`
   d. `-T`

18. Which of the following flags are used to adjust the amount of information returned by Nmap?

   a. `-v`
   b. `--script`
   c. `-reason`
   d. `-oX`

19. This flag is utilized to specify that UDP should be utilized rather than TCP.

   a. `-sU`
   b. `-Pn`
   c. `-UDP`
   d. `-6`

20. **What is the proper syntax for scanning the following address: 9e1c:2591:09d0:767e:4592:0a60:dee4:07de**
    a. `Nmap -6 9e1c:2591:09d0:767e:4592:0a60:dee4:07de`
    b. `Nmap -p 80,443 9e1c:2591:09d0:767e:4592:0a60:dee4:07de`
    c. `Nmap -A 9e1c:2591:09d0:767e:4592:0a60:dee4:07de`
    d. `Nmap -Pn 9e1c:2591:09d0:767e:4592:0a60:dee4:07de`
21. **By default, Nmap will scan how many TCP ports on a target system?**
    a. 10
    b. 100
    c. 1000
    d. 10000
22. **This flag, often used for troubleshooting, shows the reason why Nmap reported the status of each open port.**
    a. `--Open`
    b. `--Reason`
    c. `--Why`
    d. `-vv`
23. **To exclude ports that are closed, filtered, or unknown from the Nmap results, you would include which flag?**
    a. `--alive`
    b. `-oX`
    c. `-X`
    d. `-open`
24. **Which TCP port is most commonly associated with Border Gateway Protocol (BGP)?**
    a. 22
    b. 25
    c. 179
    d. 1433
25. **Which TCP port is most commonly associated with Simple Mail Transfer Protocol (SMTP)?**
    a. 22
    b. 25
    c. 179
    d. 1433

26. **Which of the following pieces of information are beneficial in determining the CPE of a system?**
    a. Specific operating system and version
    b. What the system is likely used for
    c. Specific services running on the ports and their associated versions
    d. All of the above
27. **In addition to ports 80 and 443, which of the following TCP ports is also commonly associated with web servers?**
    a. 8080
    b. 4786
    c. 1433
    d. 9001
28. **This is a free-to-use repository of information on known CVEs which allows you to search by the CVE ID, product title, vendor, or even vulnerability type.**
    a. Cisa.gov
    b. Attack.mitre.org
    c. Exploit-db.com
    d. Cvedetails.com
29. **What is the version intensity of a default Nmap scan?**
    a. 6
    b. 7
    c. 8
    d. 9
30. **What is one unique benefit of outputting Nmap results into the .xml format?**
    a. The results are easier to read
    b. The results can be imported into Legion
    c. The results are more accurate
    d. The scan will finish faster

31. This Nmap script queries a third-party vulnerability database and outputs CVEs that are associated with the target system following enumeration.

a. `Cve.nse`

b. `Vulners.nse`

c. `Searchsploit`

d. `Firewalk.nse`

32. Increasing verbosity will have what effect on the duration of the Nmap scan?

a. There will be no change to the duration

b. The scan will finish more quickly

c. The scan will take longer to finish

33. Which of the following is not an output option for Nmap scan results?

a. Greppable

b. XML

c. Normal

d. Abridged

34. Every organization inherently has some degree of an attack surface.

a. True

b. False

35. _____ is a standardized way of encoding names of IT products and platforms and is maintained in a dictionary format by NIST.

a. CVE

b. CPE

c. CWE

d. OSCP

36. Which of the following is not one of the service versioning techniques utilized by Nmap by default?

a. Analyzing the TTL of ICMP responses

b. Analyzing service headers

c. Querying the NIST API for product and platform information

d. Analyzing TCP ISN sampling

37. This common designation for specific vulnerabilities allows security professionals in different organizations to more easily collaborate.

   a. CVE
   b. CPE
   c. CWE
   d. OSCP

38. What is the proper syntax to provide a description and example usage of a specific NSE script?

   a. `-script -help`
   b. `--script-help`
   c. `--help-script`
   d. `-script-h`

39. Which flag would be utilized to conduct a ping sweep with Nmap?

   a. `-Pn`
   b. `-sn`
   c. `--ping`
   d. `-h`

40. Which of the following flags reduces the total number of ports scanned from 1000 to a base of 100?

   a. `-F`
   b. `-sV`
   c. `-T5`
   d. `-s`

41. Which of the following subnets contains the fewest possible IP addresses?

   a. /32
   b. /30
   c. /16
   d. /8

42. Which of the following is a commonly specified value for grouping targets for concurrent scanning with the `--min-hostgroup` flag?

   a. 256
   b. 3
   c. 10,00
   d. 257

43. Time values specified in both the `--initial-rtt-timeout` and `--max-rtt-timeout` flags are specified in what measurement?

a. Seconds
b. Minutes
c. Milliseconds
d. Hours

44. What is an important consideration to keep in mind when using the `--defeat-rst-limit` command to ignore rate limits on the host?

a. The scans will take much longer to complete
b. The scans will take less time to complete
c. The scans will take much longer to complete and be more accurate
d. The scans will take less time to complete and be less accurate

45. What value for `--max-retries` is set when specifying the `-T5` flag?

a. 8
b. 6
c. 4
d. 2

46. Which of the following open-source tools is commonly used before Nmap on an internal network penetration test to passively scan ARP traffic for initial host discovery?

a. Legion
b. NetDiscover
c. Zenmap
d. Zmap

47. Which operating system comes with Legion preinstalled?

a. Windows
b. MacOS
c. Red Hat Enterprise Linux
d. Kali Linux

48. Which of the following is not a benefit of using Zenmap?

a. The ability to import scan files
b. A GUI to organize and visualize the data
c. The ability to launch additional scans
d. The ability to trigger additional tools automatically

49. **Which of the following is not a default scan profile built into Zenmap?**
    a. Intense Scan
    b. Ping Scan
    c. Quick Scan
    d. Stealth Scan

50. **In Kali Linux, the Legion configuration file would be found in which directory by default?**
    a. /root/.local/home/legion
    b. /root/.local/share/legion
    c. /root/.local/etc/legion
    d. /root/.local/opt/legion

51. **In the Legion configuration, what do the `SchedulerSettings` specify?**
    a. The sequence of each stage of scanning
    b. The ports that should be scanned in each stage
    c. Definitions of available options
    d. Additional actions taken when specific results are identified

52. **The following Legion Settings would be most appropriate for what sized scope?**

```
[StagedNmapSettings]
stage1-ports="T:23,25,587,80,8080,443, 8443,8081,9443,3389,1099,4786,3306,5432,1521"
stage2-ports="T:135,137,139,445,1433,88"
stage3-ports="U:53,110,161,500, 623"
stage4-ports="T:1-10000"
stage5-ports="Vulners,CVE"
stage6-ports="T:80"
```

    a. Small
    b. Medium
    c. Large
    d. Very Large

53. **Which of the following is not a key benefit of both Zenmap and Legion?**
    a. Free and open-source
    b. Quick and easy instillation

c. Intuitive to use
d. Fully replaces commercial vulnerability scanners

54. Which of the following commonly referenced flags are considered obsolete and included in all modern versions of Nmap scans by default?

a. `-A`
b. `-sV`
c. `-sS`
d. `-S`

55. Which of the following flags can be used to fragment raw packet frames?

a. `-f`
b. `-F`
c. `--data-length`
d. `-Pn`

56. Which option would be most beneficial in a scenario where your initial scan returned a large number of hosts as "Filtered"?

a. `--randomize-hosts`
b. `--discovery-ignore-rst`
c. `-D`
d. `--exclude-host`

57. Which of the following does not help avoid blue team detection?

a. Avoiding scanning gateways
b. Avoiding scanning the same endpoint repeatedly
c. Adding obfuscation to scans
d. Scanning as quickly as possible

58. Which of the following is not a standard category of NSE scripts?

a. Spider
b. Auth
c. Broadcast
d. Exploit

59. Which of the following is the proper syntax to run all scripts except those in the Brute category?

a. `--script "not brute"`

b. `--script "safe"`

c. `--script * and not brute`

d. `--script "safe and not brute"`

60. Which of the following flags allows you to specify additional arguments related to the script?

a. `-script-args`

b. `-sC`

c. `-script "keyword"`

d. `-D +`

Answers

1. d
2. b
3. a
4. a
5. c
6. a
7. d
8. c
9. d
10. a,d
11. d
12. a
13. d
14. b,c
15. a
16. a
17. a
18. a
19. c
20. b
21. d
22. c
23. b
24. d
25. a
26. d
27. a
28. b
29. c
30. b
31. b
32. c
33. d
34. a
35. b
36. c
37. a
38. b
39. b
40. a
41. a
42. a
43. c
44. d
45. d
46. b
47. d
48. d
49. d
50. b
51. d
52. b
53. d
54. c
55. b
56. d
57. d
58. a
59. a
60. a

Appendix B
Nmap Quick Reference Guide

Port States

Open	The port is actively accepting connections
Closed	The port is accessible but there is no application listening on it
Filtered	Nmap cannot tell if it is opened or closed, often due to a firewall
Unfiltered	The port is accessible, but Nmap cannot tell if it is open or closed. This status is rarely seen unless you are doing a very specific type of scanning to map firewall rulesets
Open|Filtered	Nmap cannot tell if it is Open or Filtered, possibly because of a lack of response
Closed|Filtered	Nmap cannot tell if it is Closed or Filtered

Flags for Basic Scanning

Flag	Function
`-sV`	Enables service version detection on the ports that respond as open
`-A`	Enables operating system detection as well as service versioning on the target
`-v`	Adds additional details to the output and is paired ery well with either -sV or -A
`-p`	Specify specific port(s) to scan
`-sU`	Specify UDP scanning rather than TCP
`-iL`	Read the target list from a .txt file
`-oX`	Output scan results to a .xml file
`-sn`	Ping scan
`-6`	Specify IPv6 scanning
`-F`	Reduces the number of ports scanned from the top 1,000 TCP to the top 100 TCP
`--top-ports`	Specifies a provided number of ports to scan
`--open`	Filters results to only ports recognized as "open"
`--reason`	Shows the reason why each port is being reported the way that it is
`--script`	Specify the provided NSE script(s)
`--script-help`	Display details and usage of a specified NSE script
`--script-args-timeout`	Specifies the amount of time Nmap can spend attempting to get a result from a script before moving on to the next target

Mapping the Attack Surface

Purpose:

A slow and comprehensive scan of a few of the most common interesting ports, which outputs to an XML file.

Syntax:

```
Nmap -A -T2 --open -p 21,22,25,80,110,179,443,8080,8443 -iL targets.txt
-oX results1.xml
```

Purpose:

A slow and comprehensive scan of all ports with higher emphasis on service versioning, which outputs to an XML file.

Syntax:

```
Nmap -A --version-intensity 9 --allports --open -iL targets2.txt -oX
results2.xml
```

Purpose:

A slow scan, with ICMP ping disabled, of the top 500 ports with service versioning that will also return vulnerability information.

Syntax:

```
Nmap Pn --top-ports 500 -T2 -sV --version-all --script vulners.nse -iL
targets.txt -oX results.xml
```

Purpose:

A fast scan of the top 100 ports with light emphasis on service versioning, which will return vulnerability information for fingerprinted services.

Syntax:

```
Nmap -F -T5 -version-light -sV --script vulners.nse -iL targets.txt -oX
results.txt
```

Purpose:

A broadcast script to identify instances of Jenkins on an internal network.

Syntax:

```
Nmap --script broadcast-jenkins-discover --script-args timeout=15s
```

Purpose:

Identifying vulnerabilities related to SMB on Windows Systems.

Syntax:

```
Nmap -p 139,445 --script smb-vun* -iL targets.txt -oX results.txt
```

Purpose:

Identifying if SMB signing is enabled and required on specified hosts via SMBv2.

Syntax:

```
Nmap -p 139,445 --open --script smb2-securtity-mode
```

Purpose:

Scanning for cross-site request forgery vulnerabilities on web servers.

Syntax:

```
Nmap -p 80,443 -sV --script http-csrf
```

Purpose:

A fast scan to identify and output a list of targets with ports associated with SMB open.

Syntax:

```
Nmap -pn -T4 -iL targets.txt -p 139,445 --open -oX SMB_results.xml
```

Purpose:

A fast UDP scan to identify and output a list of targets with the port associated with IPMI open.

Syntax:

```
Nmap -pn -sU -T4 -iL targets.txt -p 623 --open -oX IPMI.xml
```

Purpose:

A fast scan to identify and output a list of targets with a port associated with JavaRMI open.

Syntax:

```
Nmap pn -T4 -iL targets.txt -p 1099 --open -oX JavaRMI.xml
```

Purpose:

A fast scan to identify and output a list of targets with a port associated with Cisco Smart Install open.

Syntax:

```
Nmap -pn -T4 -iL targets.txt -p 4786 --open -oX smart_install.xml
```

Timing and Performance

Flag	Function
`-T`	Specifies the speed of scanning from T0 (slowest) to T5 (fastest)
`--version-intensity`	Specifies the intensity of service versioning efforts from 0 (lightest) to 9 (most intense)
`--max-os-tries`	Specifies the number of times Nmap will attempt to fingerprint the operating system
`--max-retries`	Specify the number of times Nmap will attempt to scan a host before moving on to another
`--discovery-ignore-rst`	Prevents Nmap from considering a host down based on an RST response to a probe
`--min-hostgroup`	Specifies the size of target groups to scan concurrently
`--initial-rtt-timeout`	Specifies a minimum rtt timeout rate in milliseconds
`--max-rtt-timeout`	Specifies a maximum rtt timeout rate in milliseconds
`--host-timeout`	Specify a host timeout value in minutes, which is the maximum amount of time Nmap will attempt to gather all information before moving on to another host
`--defeat-icmp-ratelimit`	Used to increase the speed of UDP scans specifically
`--defeat-rst-ratelimit`	Trade accuracy for speed by ignoring the rate limits entirely, which can result in Nmap not waiting long enough for the results to be returned

Scanning Large Scopes

Purpose:

A simple ping sweep of subnets listed in a target file, which will output a sanitized list of live endpoints to a target file.

Syntax:

```
Nmap -n -sn -iL Ping_Sweep.txt -oG - | awk '/Up$/{print $2}' | >
targets.txt
```

Purpose:

A ping sweep, optimized for speed, which will output a sanitized list of live endpoints to a target file.

Note: This is designed for extremely large scopes, with an emphasis on finding the /24 subnets that are in use, rather than accurately identifying every single live endpoint. This scan trades accuracy for speed.

Syntax:

```
Nmap -sn -n --defeat-rst-ratelimit --max-rtt-timeout 250ms --max-retries
2 --host-timeout 2m --min-hostgroup 2048 -iL subnet1.txt -oG - | awk '/
Up$/{print $2}' | > Ping_Sweep1.txt
```

Purpose:

A fast scan to identify targets with ports commonly associated with web servers open.

Syntax:

```
Nmap -pn -T4 -iL targets.txt -p 80,443,8080,8443 --open -oX Web_servers.
xml
```

Obfuscation

Flag	Function
`--exclude-ports`	Specifies ports that should not be scanned
`--exclude-host`	Specifies hosts that should not be scanned in a given range
`-Pn`	Disable Ping
`--randomize-hosts`	Modifies the default scanning behavior of targets selected from a sequential range to a random one
`--data-length`	Appends a specified number of bits of random data to the end of each packet
`-D`	Decoy scanning
`-f`	Fragments packets to add more entropy
`-ttl`	Specifies a given time to live

Stealth Scanning

Purpose:

A somewhat stealthy scan that fragments packets, adds entropy to the packets, and randomizes the hosts targeted.

Syntax:

```
Nmap -f --data-length 5 --randomize-hosts
```

Purpose:

A moderately stealthy scan that fragments packets, adds entropy to the packets, randomizes hosts, disables ping, throttles the speed, and excludes commonly detected ports for SSH and SMB.

Syntax:

```
Nmap -f --data-length 5 --randomize-hosts -T2 -Pn --exclude-ports
22,139, 445
```

Purpose:

A moderately stealthy scan that fragments packets, adds entropy to the packets, randomizes hosts, disables ping, throttles the speed, and modifies the default ttl of packets.

Syntax:

```
Nmap -T2 --randomize-hosts -Pn -f --data-length 5 -ttl 58
```

Purpose:

A stealthy scan that fragments packets, adds entropy to the packets, randomizes hosts, disables ping, throttles the speed, excludes commonly detected ports for SSH and SMB, and puts reduced limits on the host timeout and maximum retries of each host.

Syntax:

```
Nmap -f --data-length 5 --randomize-hosts -T2 -Pn --exclude-ports
22,139, 445 --host-timeout 5m --max-retries 3
```

Purpose:

A slow scan that employs numerous complementary obfuscation techniques while specifically scanning targets for susceptibility to `pass-the-hash` attacks by checking SMB signing.

Syntax:

```
sudo nmap -p 139,445 -Pn --disable-arp-ping --discovery-ignore-rst
--open --randomize-hosts -T2 --data-length 5 --max-retries 2 --host-
timeout 5s --script smb-security-mode,smb2-security-mode -iL targets.txt
```

Nmap Scripting Engine

Script Category	Description
Auth	Script that deals with the authentication of the target system
Broadcast	Scripts used for the discovery of additional or specific systems by broadcasting on the local network
Brute	Scripts that use brute-force style techniques
Default	The default category is the list of scripts that are called when using either the `-sC` or the `-A` flags
Discovery	Scripts that are used for active reconnaissance and discovering specific information on the network
DoS	Scripts that may, intentionally or otherwise, crash systems and cause denial of service conditions
Exploit	Scripts that actively exploit particular vulnerabilities
External	Scripts that send data outside of the typical scanner – target relationship
Fuzzer	Scripts used to "`Fuzz`" servers or services to identify hidden resources
Malware	Scripts can be used to detect targets that are infected by malware
Vuln	Scripts that check for very specific vulnerabilities
Intrusive	Scripts that have an elevated probability of crashing target systems and thus cannot be classified as 'safe'
Safe	Scripts are designed not to exploit anything, not to crash systems, and not to be associated with using huge amounts of bandwidth
Version	Scripts that are related to service versioning

Top 10 Handy NSE Scripts

Script	Function
`Vulners.nse`	Looks at the services being run on the system and queries the vulenrs.com database of vulnerabilities to determine if those services match known vulnerabilities
`Ms-exchange-version.nse`	Fingerprints and identifies vulnerabilities associated specifically with on-premises Microsoft Exchange servers
`Smb-security-mode.nse`	Identifies if SMB signing is enabled on the target(s) via SMB version 1
`Smb2-security-mode.nse`	Identifies if SMB signing is enabled on the target(s) via SMB version 2
`Smb-os-discovery.nse`	Fingerprint Windows systems via the SMB protocol
`Smb-enum-*`	Shortcut for running dozens of individual SMB enumeration scripts
`Smb-vuln-*`	Shortcut for running dozens of individual SMB vulnerability discovery scripts
`Broadcast-jenkins-discover.nse`	Broadcasts a probe to identify instances of Jenkins on the network
`Http-wordpress-enum.nse`	Fingerprints WordPress plugins and prints vulnerabilities associated with them
`Firewalk.nse`	Sends varying types of probes to the gateway and based on the TTL and reply ascertains if a firewall rule is impacting that port

Index

A

Attack Surfaces
about 42, 43
Nmap to Map, leveraging 49-55
penetration test, stages 43, 44
small business, monitoring 55, 56
Attack Surfaces, challenge
home network, mapping 57
scan with hand-on, getting 56
Attack Surfaces, Nmap flags
-A 45
-iL 47
-open 48
-oX 47
-p 47, 48
--reason 48
-sU 48
-sV 44
-T 46
-v 46

B

Blue Team Detection, avoiding 125, 126

C

Client System
benefits 160, 161
communcating, results 160
key, considering 158-160
scans, types 155-157
Common Platform Enumeration (CPE)
about 63, 64
common vulnerabilities and exposures (CVEs) 64, 65
versioning techniques 64
CSRF 82

I

Intrusion Detection System (IDS) 124

K

kali-virtual-machines
reference link 26

L

lab environment
about 24, 25
securing 34, 35
Virtual box, Nmap installing 25-30

lab environment servers, setting up
  Linux 30, 31
  Windows 31-33
Large Enterprise Network
  about 90-92
  black box subnet discovery 92, 93
  mass, scanning 94, 95
  speed, optimizing 95-98
Large Enterprise Network, case study
  real world, pentesting 98, 99
  speed, scan optimizing 100
Large Enterprise Network, flags
  --defeat-icmp-ratelimit 97
  --defeat-rst-ratelimit 96
  --host-timeout 96
  --initial-rtt-timeout 95
  --max-retries 96
  --min-hostgroup 95
Legion
  analysis, scanning 107-110
  file configure, modifying 110-112
  zenmap, configuring 114
Legion Scanning, situations
  large scope 114
  medium scope 113
  small scope 113

N

Nmap
  about 2-9
  career, boosting 9-11
  legally, ethically using 12, 13
  penetration, testing 15
  purple, red teaming 16
  TCP 3
  vulnerability scanner 14
Nmap Flags, intermediate
  -6 68
  --exclude-ports 71
  -F 69
  --max-os-tries 70
  -Pn 69
  --script 67
  --script-help 67
  -sn 68
  --top-ports 69
  --version-all 70
  --version-intensity 70
  --version-light 70
Nmap Flags, usage
  -sC 142
  --script 141
  --script-args 142
Nmap Scan obfuscation, flags
  -D 123
  --data-length 122
  --discovery-ignore-rst 123
  exclude-host 122
  --exclude-port 122
  -f 121
  -Pn 123
  --randomize-hosts 122
Nmap Scan Parameter 120, 121
Nmap Scan Parameter, case study
  purple, teaming 126-128
  red, teaming 129-132
Nmap Scan Parameter, challenge
  complex scans, breaking 133
  lab detect, evading 132
Nmap Scripting Engine
  about 66
  directory, modifying 143-145
  exploring 71
  flawed protocols, inherently 77

locating 143
security, misconfiguring 75, 76
system, service determine 75
technical debt 78, 79
vulnerability, scanning 79-82
Nmap Scripting Engine, case study
external penetration, real world testing 83, 84
home network, scanning 84
system, fingerprinting 84
Nmap Scripting Engine, categories
Auth 138
Broadcast 138
brute 138, 139
default 139
discovery 139
DoS 139
Exploit 139
External 139
Fuzzing 139
intrusive 140
Malware 140
safe 140
version 140
Vuln 140
Nmap Scripting Engine, corporations
Broadcast-jenkins-discover.nse 73
Firewalk.nse 73
Http-wordpress-enum.nse 73
Ms-exchange-version.nse 72
Mysql-empty-password.nse 74
Smb-enum 73
Smb-os-discovery.nse 73
Smb-security-mode.nse 72
Smb-vuln 73
Vulners.nse 72
Nmap Scripting Engine, scripts
host 140
Postrule 141
Prerule 140
service 140
Nmap script, operations
script + [name of script] 142
--script "category" 141
-- script "keyword-*" 141
NSE Scripting 146, 147
NSE Scripting, challenges
concurrent scripts, scanning 148
GitHub post, creating 148
lab environment test, refining 148

R

Right Scan, identifying 154, 155

S

SchedulerSettings 111
StagedNmapSettings 112

T

TCP 3

Z

zenmap 26
zenmap, leveraging
analysis, scanning 104-107